THE NEW VENTURERS

THE NEW VENTURERS

Inside
the High-Stakes World
of Venture Capital

John W. Wilson

ADDISON-WESLEY PUBLISHING COMPANY

Reading, Massachusetts • Menlo Park, California
Don Mills, Ontario • Wokingham, England • Amsterdam
Sydney • Singapore • Tokyo • Mexico City • Bogotá
Santiago • San Juan

Library of Congress Cataloging in Publication Data

Wilson, John W., 1936–
The new venturers.

Includes bibliographies and index.
1. Venture capital—United States.   I. Title.
HG4963.W55   1985   332'.0415'0973   85-755
ISBN 0-201-09681-1

Cover design by Marshall Henrichs
Text design by Outside Designs
Set in 11 point Goudy Old Style by Compset, Inc.,
Beverly, MA

ISBN 0-201-09681-1

ABCDEFGHIJ-DO-865

For Sallyanne, Jonathan, and Amy

ACKNOWLEDGMENTS

Perhaps I have been a *Business Week* correspondent for too many years, but I must begin by thanking my employer and especially my former boss, Lew Young, for providing the opportunities that made this book possible. Lew had the good sense to move me to San Francisco just as the Silicon Valley phenomenon was taking shape, and he and Bob Henkel urged me to pay attention to struggling entrepreneurs and their backers at a time when our competitors seldom traveled south of Market Street. Lew's decision to send me to Germany did not seem so sensible at the time, but my exposure to Europe's efforts to become more entrepreneurial brought home the importance of the venture capital process. By allowing me to return to San Francisco with considerable editorial freedom, Lew and Steve Shepard gave me the chance to report on the outbreak of venture fever that made the book seem inevitable. Most of the research and writing was done during a leave of absence from the magazine, but in a very real sense this book originated at *Business Week,* and I am grateful for the opportunities my work there has brought me.

It was a former *Business Week* colleague, Mitchel Resnick, who first suggested this project. Ann Dilworth and Doe Coover of Addison-Wesley provided the encouragement I needed to get started, and Anne Eldridge was a constructive and demanding editor. In addition to canny legal advice, Brad Bunnin gave me a sense of confidence that the project made sense personally. Most important, the venture community opened its doors for hundreds of hours of interviews that became the core of the book. Venture capital is largely a private business and venture capitalists have a reputation for secrecy rivaling that of the Swiss bankers. The truth is that until recently few of us in the media or in academia have taken the trouble to inquire about the workings of this emerging profession. Almost without exception, the individuals and firms I asked for help were generous with their time and—as best as I could discover—forthcoming about their philosophies and strategies, their winners and their losers. I am grateful for their kindness and their assistance. Finally, none of this would have been possible without the support and tolerance of my remarkable family.

This book is based largely on personal interviews with venture capitalists, entrepreneurs, attorneys, academics, and consultants, most of whom are identified in the text. Where quotations or ideas have been drawn from books or periodicals, I have followed the customary practice of citing the sources.

John W. Wilson
Larkspur, December 1984

CONTENTS

THE NEW VENTURERS

1

BROKERS OF RISK

At eight o'clock on a Monday morning in mid-January 1983, Casey Powell presented himself at the desk of his supervisor and resigned from his job as general manager of microprocessor operations for Intel Corp. "You turkey," said Powell's boss, as if unwilling to believe he was serious even though Powell had flown from Portland, Oregon, to Santa Clara in California's Silicon Valley to make the announcement. Intel, inventor of the microprocessor, still dominated the market for this paragon of products, and still, therefore, was world champion—technology leader of the world's electronics giants. For a competitive, ambitious engineer/salesman in the age of the microchip, running microprocessor operations for Intel ranked right up there with managing the Yankees in their heyday. Powell even thought of Intel in baseball metaphors: "If you are the best third baseman in the league, you want to play on the team with the best players at every position."

But Powell was deadly serious about leaving after nine years with Intel's all-stars. Karl C. Powell, known from infancy as Casey, is a prime example of the entrepreneurial personality. Outwardly informal and easygoing, Powell displays his real nature when he climbs behind the wheel of his red Ferrari 308 GT4. Powell roams the freeways and backroads of Oregon very carefully—he was once a professional driver of 240 mph dragsters—but no one passes him. The radar detector on the dashboard is always on, and Powell takes every opportunity he is offered, and some he isn't, to get out in front. Powell brings the same competitive drive to his work, and it is a quality cherished by entrepreneurial companies like Intel. But it is not a quality that conforms easily to a corporate culture. Intel is proud of the "constructive confrontations" it encourages managers to employ, but Powell had suffered one too many. More important, he wanted to stay in Oregon and it was becoming clear that his future with Intel, if he had one, lay in California. He was serious. And he had more news: "There are others involved." "More than one or two?" "Yes." "You mean a lot of people, like six or seven?" "Probably more than that."

In fact, while Casey Powell was engaged in this cat-and-mouse conversation in California, a total of fifteen of his coworkers back at the Intel operation in Oregon and another in Santa Clara were also handing in letters of resignation. One was boyish Scott Gibson, another nine-year veteran, the general manager in charge of memory components. And there was Larry Wade, also a general manager but a recent arrival at Intel from Digital Equipment Corp., the country's second largest computer company. And Barbara Slaughter, a marketing manager. And Gary Fielland and Walt Mayberry, both engineering project leaders. Even Linda Farina, Powell's secretary. The list kept growing. It was the largest simultaneous defection anybody in the electronics business could remember—all the more remarkable because the defectors were leaving good jobs at one of the most successful companies in the country.

What was going on? No mystery there for anyone at Intel. Only one force could so dramatically strip away so many top people. Not a huge competitor. Not the wily Japanese. Only venture capital. Powell, Gibson, Wade, and the others were going to start a company of their own. All they needed was $5 million. And there was no doubt whatever that they could get it, they told each other that night as they pinned on their "I Made My Move" badges at a celebration in the Upper Level Pub, a shopping center bar handy to the Intel plant. "I don't think there was ever a fear that we wouldn't be able to raise the money," recalls Scott Gibson.

It was a dramatic and highly public birth of a new enterprise. More than 600,000 companies were incorporated in America in 1983 but even the *New York Times* reported at length on the arrival of Sequel (the name was later changed to Sequent) Computer Systems. Intel executives were outraged, although at first their reaction was muted. "We're sorry to see them go," a company spokesman told the *Times*. But three months later Intel's soft-spoken chairman, Gordon Moore, told his shareholders—in what was clearly a message to employees as well—that what Powell's group had done was "unmistakably unethical and wrong."

With the help of Portland-area boosters, eager to promote new industry in a region long dependent for jobs on now-declining stands of timber, Sequent became a going concern almost from its first day in business. A generous landlord deferred payments on the lease of a factory building for six months; a telephone supplier collected one dollar for the first year's use of the equipment; an office furniture company chipped in eighteen desks and thirty-six chairs; insurance brokers and accountants offered cut-rate deals.

Attracted by the publicity, by the size of the group, and by the Intel connection, the venture capitalists came swarming. At least fifty different investor groups made contact, although many of them went away again muttering when they heard the terms under which the Sequent group would consent to be financed. Their company should be valued at $15 million, said Powell, Gibson, and Wade, and the employees should retain two-thirds of the equity. That made it the most expensive venture capital deal anybody could remember, but in the end four nationally prominent venture firms and one local group swallowed hard and provided a total of $5.2 million on Sequent's terms. The deal went down, said Scott Gibson later, "like a tennis ball through a 40' hose."

Sequent's founders were looking for more than money from their venture investors. They chose Kleiner Perkins Caufield & Byers of San Francisco for the reputation of its partners as strategic thinkers; Venrock Associates of New York for its East Coast connections; Institutional Venture Partners of Menlo Park for the three decades of experience represented by its senior partner, Reid Dennis; Hambrecht & Quist of San Francisco for its expertise as an investment banker; Shaw Venture Partners of Portland for Ralph Shaw's local contacts.

Then began a breathless dash to build a product and a company. In March, when the business plan was completed, Sequent's founders had little more than a vague notion of the powerful computer for technical applications they hoped to sell. By the end of June, after three months of intense interaction between marketing managers and engineers, the rough specifications for a product that was codenamed Multix and eventually christened Balance spewed out of a computer printer. It was a concept that was disarmingly simple yet difficult enough to execute to discourage competition: take the hottest new microprocessor, essentially a superminicomputer on a chip, and combine several in what computer architects call a multiprocessor system. The project might take $20 million and considerable luck, because distributing a computer's workload to more than one processor is a formidable hardware and software design challenge. The method is used primarily in the largest mainframes. If it worked, Sequent could deliver mainframe performance at microcomputer prices. But others would be trying the same approach. They had to move fast.

The hardware designers took over. With the help of engineering workstations—personal computers that automate much of an engineer's pencil work—they started translating the specifications to detailed circuit designs for the chips that would play supporting roles to the powerful microprocessors. Powell played motivational games with his team. He told The Bicycle Story, about a boy who saved a nickel an hour for a year to buy a shiny new bike, to encourage them to set measurable goals. Before long someone had set up a big jar to hold the nickels, one for every engineering milestone. When the timetable slipped, Powell passed out buttons. Red ones, labeled PRIORITY, for key engineers. Green ones, reading HOW CAN I HELP?, for everyone else. With birthday and Christmas parties, campouts and a First Annual Sequent Inner Tube Float, with computer terminals in every employee's home and an entire vocabulary of homebrewed acronyms and buzzwords, Powell built a culture that encouraged loyalty and intense effort.

Finally, in October, orders went out to LSI Logic, a so-called "silicon foundry" that manufactures complex integrated circuits to order.

By December the first working components arrived and were eagerly popped into the GenRad tester—an enormously complex machine worth more than $300,000—to probe the 5,000 microdevices embedded in each chip. Disaster: a major defect rendered the chips useless. "We thought we were all going to die," recalls one engineer. It might take LSI Logic three months to re-do the chips, and Sequent didn't have three months. Powell and Gibson flew to California to plead their case with Wilfred J. Corrigan, the tough British-born entrepreneur who had founded LSI Logic only three years earlier with the help of some of Sequent's venture capitalists. The problem couldn't be Sequent's fault, they told Corrigan. Would he expedite things?

Corrigan agreed, and shortly after New Year's Day a fresh batch of chips arrived. Back to the GenRad, and this time—perfection. Now the engineering prototype of the computer could be completed and turned on. In mid-January the prototype ran a diagnostic program and was pronounced healthy. Powell celebrated at Sequent's first birthday party by keeping his promise to jump from a cake "in appropriate attire." He was dressed as Bozo the Clown (a bozo in computer lingo is a nontechnical person, a dumb user who doesn't understand the equipment) to salute the superiority and the achievement of the engineers. Sequent was on its way.

BROKERS OF RISK

The creation of Sequent was a unique event. The size of the founding group, the controversy attending the defection, and the value placed on the infant company set Sequent apart in the annals of modern entrepreneurship. Whether it could fulfill its early promise and take its place with Digital Equipment, Intel, Tandem, Apple, and a handful of others as an entrepreneurial superstar was unforeseeable as this book was written, and probably unlikely. That kind of success is truly uncommon. But Sequent had a good chance of becoming an important innovator, manufacturer, and employer before it was more than two years old. And it is that kind of opportunity that this book is really about. In some very significant ways Sequent is not so rare a bird at all. More than 1,000 fledgling companies received, like Sequent, significant private financing in 1983, perhaps 200 of them brand-new enterprises.[1] These are no mom-and-pop pizzerias or laundromats, no garage shops housing oddball inventors. They are, in many cases, organizations so well staffed, equipped, and financed as to rival divisions of the most important companies in America. They are developing products that press the limits of what is possible in computers, software, telecommunications, semiconductors, biomedicine, robotics, and the other technologies on which we are climbing toward the twenty-first century. Many of them will fail but more will survive, and a few will become major players in important world markets. They are the products of an incredible investment mechanism, the venture capital process, that is one of the least understood but most important business developments of the postwar era.

Venture capital is a uniquely American process. What has emerged here, primarily in only the past two decades, is a community of a few hundred professional investors whose specialty is to combine risk capital with entrepreneurial management and advanced technology to create new products, new companies, and new wealth. It is easy to take this for granted. After all, advances in science and technology after World War II have created an abundance of opportunities to be exploited. And changes in society have brought forward such brilliant entrepreneurs as Robert Noyce, the founder of Intel, and Steven Jobs of Apple. But the fact is that similar technological opportunities exist in every advanced country, and entrepreneurship is a talent that is found to some degree in every society. Occasionally those opportunities and talents come together to produce a Nixdorf Computer in Germany or a Sord Computer in Japan. But only in America, and only recently, has a vigorous process developed whereby highly sophisticated enterprises can be designed and manufactured—on what amounts to an assembly line of capitalism—to address new market needs and to commercialize the ideas that the new technologies are generating.

Venture capitalists play many roles in this process. They are intermediaries between the vast pool of private and institutional wealth that is the fuel for all economic activity and the most hazardous use for investment capital: the formation of new companies. Their ability to assess and manage enormous risks, and to wring from them exceptional returns, is a critical element in America's ability to mobilize its entrepreneurial talent. They are brokers of risk, agents of a new style of financial service that is crucial to our ability to transfer resources from fading industries and technologies to the goods and services that will dominate a restructured world economy in the next century. Venture capitalists are also gatekeepers, to use a term communications researchers sometimes apply to the role of the press. Editors select from a torrent of ideas and events a few that become, by their fiat, news. Similarly, venture capitalists choose from hundreds or thousands of proposals in the course of a year only a handful to receive the infusion of capital that will turn them into living enterprises. This is an awesome power—calling the turn on new products and industries and deciding who will be given the chance to pursue them—that is exercised by a few individuals who have little or no public visibility and are accountable only to the laws of economics.

At the less cosmic level of the individual investment, the venture capitalist can serve as the catalyst, organizational architect, and strategic designer of the new firm—or simply a minor figure in the background, writing checks and waiting for a payoff. He (a few women have entered the venture capital field recently, but it remains a bastion of male supremacy) may be a respected adviser and confidant for the harried entrepreneur. Or he may be a feared and distrusted outsider waiting in the wings to fire the management or sell the company to the highest bidder when things go wrong. In most cases, the role is somewhere in the middle of that range. The best venture capitalists are far more than checkbook investors, and the best entrepreneurs have too strong a vision of their enterprise to brook much interference in its planning and operations. Success in venture capital comes most often from a creative partnership in which the investor's lengthy and often painful experience in the company formation process is combined with the entrepreneur's management skills and detailed knowledge of a market or technology. But as many venture capitalists have expensively learned, companies are not built or operated from the boardroom. The venture capitalist can counsel and assist, but in the end it is the abilities of the entrepreneur that determine the outcome of the investment.

Venture capital began as a hobby or sideline of the rich, and a few wealthy individuals continue to play the game. So do many smaller investors—often entrepreneurs seeking to recycle their gains from the process—who make up a vast network of informal venture capital. In large measure, though, venture capital today is an institutionalized business, both in the sense that the money comes mostly from pension funds, endowments, trust funds, and corporations and that the investing is done largely by highly specialized professionals organized in sizable partnerships as well as by subsidiaries of banks and corporations. These groups have experienced phenomenal growth in the last few years. The venture capital pool—capital under management by professional venture capital firms—grew from $2.5 billion in the 1970s to more than $16 billion by the end of 1984, according to Venture Economics Inc., a consulting and publishing firm that tracks the venture industry. The pool gained more than $4 billion in new capital in 1983 and although the pace was beginning to slacken it apparently added another $4 billion in 1984. Private partnerships controlled nearly 70 percent of the money; banks, corporations, and government-chartered small business investment companies accounted for the rest. In turn, venture capitalists have increased their rate of investment in new companies sixfold from less than $500 million per year in the 1970s to $3 billion in 1984. Since 1978, this handful of risk investors has pumped more than $11 billion into as many as 5,000 companies.[2] Venture capital has, without doubt, sparked the greatest burst of entrepreneurial activity the world has ever seen.

The causes of this risk-financing explosion are varied and the subject of debate. An explanation favored by venture capital industry lobbyists is that the 1978 cut in the capital gains tax unleashed pent-up capital by raising the effective rate of return on venture investments, which typically pay off largely through capital gains. That is a beguiling argument, but it fails to explain why endowments and pension funds—which pay no taxes—began increasing their commitments to venture capital at about the same time. In part, pension funds were responding to an easing of federal restrictions on their activities and endowments to a growing assurance that venture investments could meet the "prudent man" guideline they must follow. Probably most important was the revival of the market for new securities issues which began in the late 1970s and bestowed significant returns on the venture capitalists who had stayed the course through the barren early years of the decade. As company after company went public and as offering prices climbed, venture capital portfolios began to show annual investment returns of 20 percent, 30 percent, and in some cases considerably more. Venture capitalists finally were able to demonstrate the validity of their approach and compete successfully in the marketplace of investment vehicles.

The venture capital process begins with the deal that organizes a new company and sets the terms under which the investment is made. A venture firm is measured by the quality of its deals, which in turn is a function of the quality of its deal flow. Proposals come to the venture capitalist in the form of business plans that describe, in fifteen to 100 pages or more, the product or service to be developed, the market to be served, the credentials of the founders, and the financing required. Some proposals are far-fetched, to say the least. Harry Rein, who heads General Electric's venture capital subsidiary, likes to quote from a letter he received from Georgia:

Gentlemen:

I am a minister of the Gospel who by the will of God has been called to start the Enterprise. The Enterprise is a series of businesses. The first will be a dry cleaners. The Lord has commanded that I go to a certain city in Georgia and dwell there. And there I will establish His church and laundry. Therefore I ask for $50,000. . . . I know the Lord will do the rest.

Not many venture proposals have divine backing, but it is usually the quality of the references that determines whether a proposal becomes a deal. Few experienced venture capitalists will back entrepreneurs who do not come recommended by other venturers, lawyers, accountants, or trustworthy contacts in industry. By the same token, the quality of a venture firm's deal flow reflects the quality of its contacts and especially its place in the venture capital pecking order. To spread the risk and the work, deals are often shared or syndicated among several firms; by immutable law of the venture world, those unable to offer good deals never share in the best deals of others.

Deciding which deals to support, and on what terms, is the crux of the venturers' task. Often, their decisions seem heavily influenced by hunches or blind intuition. With little to go on in the way of facts, venture capitalists must rely on opinions and estimates from consultants and industry sources and their own judgment of people and risk. But what appears to be a stab in the dark is usually a shrewd calculation based on long experience with entrepreneurs and the characteristics of successful—and unsuccessful—deals. Some winning venture capitalists claim to look almost exclusively at the backgrounds and personalities of the founders; others focus mostly on the technology involved and the market opportunity the venture addresses. Both approaches are usually blended in the furious few weeks of research—due diligence, in legal terms—that precede a venture decision. Venture capitalists being human, there is also an element of fashion that enters into the decision. After Genentech became the first startup company to clone a gene, almost every venture firm scrambled to invest in biotechnology; after Lotus Development struck it rich with its 1-2-3 software package early in 1983, personal computer software startups appeared in every portfolio. It was like interior decorating, grumbled one skeptical observer of the scene: everybody had to have one couch, two end tables, and a floor lamp.

Pricing a venture deal—setting a value for a company that typically has no assets, no products, no sales, and decidedly no profits—is an arcane process that can involve as much negotiation as calculation. Valuation is expressed in terms that all entrepreneurs can understand: How much money can they raise, and how much of their venture do they have to give up to get it? Sequent's $5 million for only a third of the equity was a remarkable achievement, even in the ebullient venture market that prevailed in early 1983. More typically, venture capitalists demand half the equity or more for a $5 million investment, placing the valuation of a major, Sequent-scale startup at $10 million or less. Assuming the company eventually is worth $500 million—unlikely but possible—the difference between a Sequent valuation and a standard valuation would be worth a not inconsiderable $100 million to the founders. Pricing is thus often the first point of disagreement between investors and entrepreneurs. In the absence of hard facts about the company-to-be, venture capitalists base their pricing decisions on assumptions about its future earning power and the value that public markets or potential merger partners will assign it. A more important factor, often, is the state of the market for venture deals. It is a shadowy, private market that gets little publicity. But like public markets that are reported in financial journals, the market for private deals moves through its own cycles that may have more impact on pricing than all the glowing forecasts an entrepreneur can muster.

Venture capitalists like to say they do not just *invest*, they *build* companies. Some of that idealism was tarnished during the go-go years of the late 1960s and again in the early 1980s, when the temptation to grab the fast returns offered by a booming market for new public offerings was overwhelming. But the best practitioners have a long-term view of their role. They think not in terms of preserving their capital or of maximizing short-term returns but in terms of creating value by developing profitable businesses that eventually can be taken public or acquired. They are equity investors, which means there is no mechanism for returning their investment except growth in the underlying value of the company. If something goes wrong—an almost inevitable development as inexperienced businessmen struggle to create a product and build an organization—the venturers cannot cover their mistake by selling the investment to others or by hoping for a miracle. They must act. They demand new strategies, they install new management, they even take the helm themselves in extreme situations. They are in for the long pull, and the pull is often strenuous. "I would be less than honest if I said I don't at times question why I keep pounding at this business," admits Burt McMurtry after fifteen years in venture capital. "When you get into trouble you might as well be a brand-new venture capitalist as an old experienced one because some of the problems you face don't get a whole lot easier."

At some point, the venture capitalist must make an exit. Long-term investor or not, he will only stay in business if he can realize returns that are substantially better than those available in more conventional investment vehicles. In as many as fifteen deals out of every 100, the exit decision will be made for him in bankruptcy court or at a distress auction of the company's assets. In as few as ten deals out of 100, the company's success will be so obvious that taking it public is only a matter of timing and method. For the seventy-five investments in between, the decision can be painful.

Whether they are successful or not, growing companies need capital. Do you find a merger partner? Sell to an industrial giant? Go public at a low valuation? During the mid-1970s, when the new-issues market was all but dead, merger or sale was often the only exit available even for enormously successful ventures. During the early 1980s even the marginal cases found a warm welcome in the public markets. In 1984 acquisition of venture-backed companies was back in vogue. Either way, the venture capitalist will have severed the investment link, although in the case of a public offering there are restrictions that limit his ability to dispose of his holdings immediately. But in many cases, in testimony to the value entrepreneurs derive from the relationship, he will stay on the board of directors long after the chips have been cashed in. James G. Treybig, the founder of Tandem Computers, still had four venture capitalists on his board of directors in 1984—seven years after Tandem became a public company. "I have a board that helps me," he explains. "The computer business is undergoing incredible change and venture capitalists understand these changes better than anybody."

The payoff from venture capital investing has been significant in many ways. Typically, the active general partners in a venture partnership share a 20 percent "carried interest" in the profits of every fund they manage. That practice has made many of them millionaires several times over, but the institutions and other limited partners who supply the investment capital usually have no objections. Returns to investors in the frenzied years since the mid-1970s have ranged as high as 50 percent per year or more, compounded, and even viewed over a longer time horizon, including cyclical dips as well as booms, annual returns of 20 percent have been reported. By contrast, Standard & Poor's 500 Stock Index showed a compound annual rate of return of 7.9 percent between 1968 and 1983. Some individual deals, of course, have produced far greater returns. Apple Computer, for example, was a 170-to-1 winner for Venrock Associates on the day it went public; Genentech provided a return of 164-to-1 for Kleiner Perkins Caufield & Byers at its offering price of $35 and more than twice that at its highest point; the acquisition of Scientific Data Systems by Xerox handed $60 million to Davis & Rock, which had invested less than $300,000; the sale of Qume to ITT gave Sutter Hill Ventures a seventyfold return on a $700,000 investment. It is the occasional superwinner, together with the more common 10-to-1 or 20-to-1 return, that allows a venture capitalist to tolerate the inevitable losers in his portfolio and turn heart-stopping risk into prudent investing.

Most important from a macroeconomic point of view, these returns have stimulated a significant flow of equity capital into the industries and technologies that are most important to productivity and international competitiveness. One review of venture investments in the early 1980s showed this breakdown:

computer-related, 30 to 40 percent;

communications, 10 percent;

other electronics, 12 to 14 percent;

medical-related, 7 to 8 percent;

genetic engineering, 4 percent;

industrial automation, 3 to 4 percent.[3]

Other investments went into energy, consumer products and services, and a variety of industrial innovations. Venture capital acts as an accelerator in these crucial industries, enabling spinoff and startup companies to leapfrog established players in price or performance or invention and force them to respond. It also encourages multiple attacks on crucial technical problems, an essential part of the development of new classes of products and the commercialization of new technology.

This amounts to an updated version of the classic role of the entrepreneur as enunciated more than seventy years ago by the great economist, Joseph Schumpeter. It was the entrepreneur, Schumpeter wrote, who presided over the process of "creative destruction" whereby one technological era was replaced with a new one. That has clearly been under way in the U.S. economy for at least the past decade as capital and talent have flowed from heavy industry to high technology and services. Other countries, where the venture capital process is less developed, have not matched the United States lead in these "postindustrial" industries.

What follows is an informal portrait of this nascent profession that is institutionalizing the risk-taking process that economic progress requires. For all their importance, little formal or even journalistic research has been undertaken on the methods and strategies of venture capitalists. For the most part, I have attempted to describe the world of the leading venture capitalists in their own words and the words of the entrepreneurs they back. The result, I hope, is a candid description of the people and the process that explains how venture capital works, why it is important, and the role it plays in the creation of new companies, new technologies, and new wealth.

NOTES

1. "Venture Capitalists Invest $2.8 Billion in 1983," *Venture Capital Journal*, May 1984, p. 7.
2. All figures are taken from Venture Economics Inc.
3. *Technology, Innovation, and Regional Economic Development.* Office of Technology Assessment, Washington, D.C., 1984, p. 44.

2

BEGINNINGS

Before World War II rearranged American society and produced a cornucopia of new technology to be commercialized, venture capital was more a rich man's whim than an industry. Enterprising lads, in the Horatio Alger tradition, could occasionally find a benefactor who recognized their worth and provided the wherewithal to launch a business. Pioneers in electric power, automobiles, and commercial aviation got their start that way. But it was a haphazard, undisciplined process incapable of coping with the burst of new ideas that came bubbling to the surface of the economy when the war ended. Moreover, the immensely wealthy individual capable of playing the patron's role was in short supply in an economic landscape increasingly dominated by giant corporations.

There was an urgent need for a new kind of financial service, one that could capitalize on the opportunities presented by accelerating changes in science and technology by organizing the process of finding, evaluating, and funding promising ideas. Three men stand out among those who began to put risk investment on a permanent institutional footing. Laurance S. Rockefeller and John Hay Whitney, heirs to great fortunes, were prominent among the prewar venture experimenters; Georges F. Doriot, a French-born Harvard Business School professor, taught unconventional ideas about entrepreneurship. Separately but almost simultaneously on their return from wartime service the three assembled organizations that laid out the conceptual framework for today's venture industry. Two steps remained to be accomplished. More capital than could be provided by a few individuals was required to meet the growing demands of new and expensive technologies. And a cadre of trained and experienced professionals was needed to invest and supervise that capital. Government stepped in to create the flawed but significant Small Business Investment Company program, which created hundreds of venture investors overnight, and later to reshape the tax system to stimulate equity investing. Finally, the institutions that control the bulk of America's financial assets began to perceive venture capital as a prudent and profitable vehicle for large-scale investment.

SETTING THE STAGE

Techniques for recycling wealth into high-risk endeavors have been evolving at least since the Middle Ages, when merchants, noblemen, or clergy commonly joined in partnerships to underwrite trading voyages and other commercial ventures. Modern banking developed in Florence during the thirteenth century and under the Medici became a driving force behind the changes that created the Renaissance. "Promissory notes," remarks one commentator on the era of Lorenzo the Magnificent, "created new cities, new states, new churches, new aristocracies and a new morality."[1] The conquest of Peru by Francisco Pizarro and Diego de Almagro, a pair of middle-aged adventurers, was financed through a partnership organized by a well-connected priest named Fernando de Luque, who raised 20,000 pesos for the venture.[2] Still, the Medici were lenders rather than investors, and the partnership vehicle was inadequate to fund the increasingly expensive and risky attempts to exploit the New World and develop new industries. By the sixteenth century the joint stock company, precursor of the modern corporation, had become a common device for pooling the capital required for such undertakings as Sir Francis Drake's voyage of 1577–1580, on which investors realized a profit of 4,600 percent after the Queen had taken her share of the treasure.[3] But the joint stock company fell into disrepute in England with the crash that followed the speculative episode known as the South Sea Company bubble in 1719–1720. The entrepreneurs who created the Industrial Revolution, for the most part, had to provide their own capital or seek help from their suppliers or customers.

The modern concept of the investment banker emerged in Europe during the latter half of the nineteenth century. Private banks were especially important in Germany, where financiers such as the Rothschilds, Bleichroeders, and Oppenheims played a vital role in backing railroads, mining ventures, and manufacturers and often were represented on the boards of directors of the new companies. In America much of the energy of the great financiers of the Gilded Age was directed to stock manipulations and business combinations, although investments in new ventures were not unheard of. The young Andrew Carnegie, who as an executive of the Pennsylvania Railroad began building his fortune by backing entrepreneurs in promising growth industries, usually confined his deals to companies doing business with the railroad.[4] Charles R. Flint, who helped start W. R. Grace & Co. at the age of twenty-one and who later assembled the company now known as International Business Machines, was best known as "Father of Trusts" for his zealous efforts to eliminate competition in rubber, electric lighting, chewing gum, and other industries.[5] John Pierpont Morgan, the greatest of the Wall Street bankers of his day, was first of all a reorganizer and consolidator of railroads and industrial companies and only occasionally an investor in new ideas. Only the persuasive tongue of Grosvenor Lowrey, a patent lawyer he respected, convinced Morgan that he should put a few dollars into the tinkerings of Thomas A. Edison and help launch the electrical revolution.[6]

For the most part, American entrepreneurs of the nineteenth and early twentieth centuries depended on friends, relatives, local merchants, and other sources of what we would now call informal venture capital. Cyrus Hall McCormick, the Virginian who invented the reaper and first demonstrated it in 1831, was finally able to start production in the Midwest sixteen years later when he persuaded William Ogden, a former mayor of Chicago, to put up $25,000 for a half-interest in a factory. Two Bostonians, Gardiner G. Hubbard and Thomas Sanders, were so impressed with the young Scot, Alexander Graham Bell, who was teaching the deaf in a local school, that they sent their children to him for help and agreed to finance his efforts to develop the telephone. It was copper baron Samuel L. Smith who backed Ransom Olds, retailer J. L. Hudson who financed Roy Chapin and Howard Coffin in their Hudson Motor Co., and coal dealer Alexander Y. Malcomson who organized Henry Ford's third and finally successful effort to get started as the auto industry began to emerge around the turn of the century. In the 1920s Juan Terry Trippe and John Hambleton turned to Cornelius Vanderbilt Whitney and William H. Vanderbilt for the cash that got Pan American Airways off the ground.[7] But by the 1930s a few individuals were beginning to pursue risk investing in a formal and disciplined way.

THE VIEW FROM ROOM 5600

Laurance Spelman Rockefeller, third of the five sons of John D. Rockefeller Jr., majored in philosophy at Princeton and was a modest, idealistic young man who had no desire to run the family enterprises. He gladly took up his father's causes—conservation and cancer research, primarily—but in business matters he went his own way. Laurance developed an abiding interest in science and technology that he expressed not just in fascination with aircraft, rockets, electronics, and other gadgetry but in a commitment to help entrepreneurs in these fields bring their ideas to fruition. As he later told a biographer: "What we want to do is the opposite of the old system of holding back capital until a field or an idea is proved completely safe. We are undertaking pioneering projects that with proper backing will encourage sound scientific and economic progress in new fields—fields that hold the promise of tremendous future development."[8]

Two of Laurance's prewar investments had proved the value of those precepts and the accuracy of his judgment of people. In 1938 he met Eddie Rickenbacker and agreed to back the World War I flying hero in his plan to resurrect Eastern Air Lines from North American Aviation, a discarded subsidiary of General Motors. Rickenbacker's flamboyant personality had alienated many bankers, but Laurance was impressed with Rickenbacker's energy and with the idea of building a low-overhead airline to serve the heavily traveled East Coast corridor. He invested $550,000, helping to give Rickenbacker the credibility he needed on Wall Street, and by 1946 Eastern was profitable and poised to become a major carrier. Laurance was also won over by James S. McDonnell Jr., an aircraft designer whose first company had failed in the 1929 crash. McDonnell showed Laurance the preliminary designs for a new military fighter and got an immediate pledge of $10,000 to start work. By 1941 Laurance and his brothers had invested $475,000 in McDonnell Aircraft Corp., and although the fighter contract eventually was canceled McDonnell Aircraft prospered during the war as a subcontractor and went on to become an important factor in the postwar aerospace industry.[9]

Laurance came back from service in the navy determined to formalize his high-risk investing. The conservative financial advisers in Room 5600 of the RCA Building in Rockefeller Center, the nerve center of the family's investment and philanthropic empire, were appalled. One writer observed: "Recognizing the philosophic and idealistic streak in the young man, they feared that Laurance was not temperamentally equipped to succeed in the fierce world of highly speculative investments."[10] But Laurance was not to be dissuaded, and he assembled his own team of advisers: Harper Woodward, a lawyer; Randolph Marston, a banker, and later Teddy Walkowicz, a former air force officer with contacts in the research establishment, and Peter Crisp, a young aviation buff. They began to carry out Laurance's plan to invest in science-based or socially-useful projects that had the potential for substantial growth and profit. Recalls Crisp, who joined the Rockefeller team in 1960: "Those early investments were made as a result of Laurance and his staff sitting down and figuring out trends and technologies that were moving, identifying people they knew when they were in the military service, and putting together companies to address various issues." Out of that process came Piasecki Helicopter, renamed Vertol, and now owned by Boeing; Reaction Motors, builder of the rocket engine that powered the Bell X-1 through the sound barrier, subsequently taken over by Thiokol; and Marquardt Aircraft, an early maker of ramjet engines.

Laurance's idealism occasionally overcame investment sense. He lost $500,000 on a grand scheme to employ Fiji Islanders to harvest the South Seas and another $250,000 on a prefabricated housing project proposed by an architect friend. Those experiences, Laurance said later, "taught me a lesson about going too far afield where my contacts with conditions and people weren't first-hand."[11] After that, Laurance stayed with aerospace-related ventures and then moved into the emerging nuclear and electronics industries. As the market for science-based stocks boomed in the late 1950s, Laurance's publicity-shy operation was dragged into the spotlight. Itek Corp., launched with

Rockefeller funding in 1957, became a leader of the new crop of glamour issues when its stock soared from $2 to $345 two years later. By 1961, *Barron's* reported, Laurance had sowed a total of $9 million and reaped profits of $40 million in fifteen years of venture investing.

The world became aware of Laurance's achievements—in their own way perhaps as significant for our era as his grandfather's had been for his—and of his common-sense rules for successful venturing. A key tenet was to make each of his investments "one leg of a three-legged stool," with the management and other knowledgeable investors also sharing in it.[12] In contrast to old John D.'s ruthless tactics, Laurance hoped to make clear that he was not seeking to control the enterprises he backed. On the other hand, wary of egocentric entrepreneurs, he would not give control to any one individual. Laurance never found it easy to drop a relationship. He remains one of the largest shareholders in Eastern, and his organization—now a limited partnership called Venrock Associates—still is committed to unusually long-term ties with the companies it backs.

"CALL IT VENTURE CAPITAL"

Jock Whitney was possibly the richest man in America after the Rockefellers. He was best known to the celebrity-watching public of the 1930s as a polo champion, a horse breeder, and a very big spender even by the larger-than-life standards of the Whitney family.[13] But Jock was also a shrewd judge of talent in many fields, and he began backing plays (*Life with Father*), films (*Gone with the Wind*)—and entrepreneurs. He had some successes, including Technicolor and Freeport Sulphur, along with several outright losers in his venture portfolio. But he was dissatisfied with his ability to consistently select the right investments and—just as important—to provide the support most new businesses require.

After the war, Whitney set aside $10 million to create an organization, J. H. Whitney & Co., that would institutionalize the process of risk investment. It was Whitney, in fact, according to his long-time associate Benno Schmidt, who coined the term "venture capital" as a generic name for this kind of investing. "We had a discussion at lunch one day," Schmidt recalls, "during which Jock said we needed a better way of describing our firm. We called ourselves a private investment firm but nobody knew what that meant." One of the partners offered "risk capital investment firm," and Schmidt suggested a refinement: "Maybe we can combine the risk element and the adventuresome element of this kind of investing by calling it a private venture capital investment firm." Said Whitney: "That's it."

Whether or not the Whitney firm was the first to use the name, it did pioneer the organizational arrangement that characterizes today's

venture capital industry. J. H. Whitney & Co. was set up as a partnership in which Schmidt and Whitney's other associates were able
to build up a significant financial interest. Because the partnership
format provides so much incentive, it has since become the preferred
organizational form in venture capital. But it was far from obvious at
the time that a partnership devoted exclusively to risk investing could
even pay the rent, let alone generate returns that would attract real
talent. The whole idea, Wall Street veterans told Whitney, was absurd. To which Whitney, according to Schmidt, replied: "Ten million
dollars is not all the money I have, so I can afford to take a gamble
and see whether or not this thing works."

Whitney was named Ambassador to the Court of St. James's in
1957 and later became engrossed in an ill-starred attempt to revive
the New York *Herald Tribune*, activities that took him away from the
venture business. Up to that time, however, Whitney took the lead
in evaluating many of the firm's investment opportunities. He had
little interest in either the financial or the technical aspects of the
companies. "The details of business interested him far less than the
human aspects of it," says Schmidt. "He loved the entrepreneurs and
their successes, not because of the financial rewards they brought him
but because of the creativity that went into them."

J. H. Whitney & Co.'s first investment paid off quickly. Kenneth
Spencer, who had operated a chemical plant for the government during the war years, wanted to buy the facility and start making fertilizer.
Whitney put up $1.25 million in the form of preferred stock and an-
other $250,000 for a third of the common shares in Spencer Chemi-
cal. So fast did the business take off that before a year was out Spencer
was able to redeem the preferred, and Whitney calculated that the
modest investment in the common already was worth more than the
$10 million with which he had started. Whitney made other
important bets on such companies as General Signal, Memorex, and
the television properties eventually pulled together as Corinthian
Broadcasting.

One early winner was Minute Maid, the first successful producer of
frozen orange juice, which grew out of an otherwise-unpromising investment Whitney had made before the war in Vacuum Foods, a company in Cambridge, Massachusetts that was attempting to perfect a
system of vacuum evaporation in food production. Minute Maid, a
Vacuum Foods spinoff that J. H. Whitney & Co. financed separately,
was working on an orange juice powder. But John Fox, Minute Maid's
president, asked Whitney for an additional $15,000 to test the con-
cept of producing a frozen concentrate instead. Schmidt recalls the
meeting at which Fox brought out one of the first cans of concentrate,
pried it open with a screw driver and a pair of pliers, then poured out
a glass for Whitney. "Jock picked it up, like he was tasting some fine

French wine, and he said, 'It tastes a little tinny to me.' But we all tasted it and we thought it tasted pretty good so we went ahead and put the additional money in and got Minute Maid started in the frozen food business."

THE BOSTON DREAM FACTORY

Jock Whitney and Laurance Rockefeller were not in venture capital primarily for the financial rewards. Rather, it seemed, they were conducting a kind of experiment to see if an industry could be created that would provide a place where entrepreneurs could get a hearing and an opportunity to start a business. A similarly high-minded motivation led to the founding, in 1946, of American Research & Development Corp. and to the decision of General Georges Doriot to become its president. ARD was a product of Boston's unique blend of financial power and intellectual excellence, a tradition of mutually supporting establishments that made the city the preeminent center of American technology. The instigators were leaders of those establishments—Merrill Griswold, chairman of the venerable Massachusetts Investors Trust; Ralph E. Flanders, president of the Federal Reserve Bank of Boston, and the physicist Karl T. Compton, president of Massachusetts Institute of Technology. Believing Boston should have an organized source of capital and support for its scientist-entrepreneurs, they had prevailed on the trust and other large institutions to pledge $2.5 million of a planned $5 million risk-capital pool. They recruited Doriot, then a reserve officer serving as deputy director of research and development on the War Department's general staff, as ARD's president.[14]

The idea was too far-fetched for most investors. ARD was unable to reach its $5 million goal and in fact barely raised the $3 million that had been set as a minimum. "It was nip and tuck whether we were going to make it," one early ARD employee recalled later. "ARD came close to scratching before it ever got off the ground."[15] But ARD did prove for the first time that it was possible to sell shares privately in a venture capital company, and it was later able to tap the public market for additional capital. Although it did not start reporting gains of any consequence until 1955, Doriot's "Dream Factory," as *Fortune* called it, went on to build its assets to a peak value of $555 million in 1969. More than 80 percent of ARD's assets, however, consisted of shares in one enormously successful venture—a computer company, started in a pre-Civil War woolen mill, called Digital Equipment Corp. Kenneth H. Olsen, the hard-driving engineer from MIT's Lincoln Laboratory who founded DEC in 1957, complained later that "half the staff at ARD voted against us" and that it took them three months to arrive at a decision to invest $70,000 for 78 percent of the company.[16] That was all the equity Olsen needed for eight years, and by the time Doriot distributed the DEC holding to his shareholders in 1972, in connection with ARD's acquisition by Textron Inc., it was worth $350 million.[17]

Aside from that one huge payoff, ARD's influence on the subsequent development of venture capital as an industry stemmed mainly from the example Doriot set of the investor as nurturing father-figure, a patient, helpful counselor willing to stay with his "children," as he often called them, through good times and bad. Doriot had been at the Harvard Business School, first as a student and then as a controversial but much-admired professor, since he arrived from France in 1921. His classes influenced many future venture capitalists, including Thomas J. Perkins, who recalls: "It was an approach to the way you deal with people, an understanding of how an engineer thinks, how a financial person thinks, how the president needs to think to make them interact as a team. There was no analysis, no numbers, it was all an attitude. Some of the students thought it was just nonsense. But when I think of Harvard, I think of him."

Doriot continued to teach while he ran ARD, and his philosophy spilled into his approach to venturing. A cardinal rule in evaluating an investment was to look first at the quality of the individuals involved, a precept to which most of today's leading venture capitalists at least pay lip service. What Doriot was looking for, more than mere genius, was resourcefulness. "A man comes in here and says he invented the pencil," he told Gene Bylinsky. "Okay. What I want to know is whether he can improve the pencil."[18] Doriot was contemptuous of the new breed of venture investors seeking only profit. "Our aim is to build up creative men and their companies, and capital gains are a reward, not a goal," he said on the eve of his retirement.[19] Charles P. Waite, a venture capitalist who worked for ARD in the early 1960s, recalls that Doriot stressed the long view: "Your job was to pick a good guy and a good business and help build the business. If it took five years or ten years or fifteen years that was fine. If you picked the right guy and the right business you'd be successful and you'd be rewarded."

At times Doriot was carried away with his enthusiasm for a bright entrepreneur and ended up backing a development with little hope of commercial success. And his reluctance to write off a struggling enterprise left ARD with considerable dead wood in its portfolio, by present standards. ARD's biggest failing, which eventually led to a corrosive loss of talent, was its inability to adequately compensate its principals. As employees of a publicly held investment company, Doriot's disciples could not share in the gains as their investments began to pay off. "We were involved in companies that were very successful," notes Waite, "and the people in those companies made a lot of money. But the associates at ARD, who helped that process, didn't make anything." Still, Doriot's view of the venture process as a dynamic, personal relationship between investors and entrepreneurs left an indelible imprint on the emerging risk capital industry as his apprentices departed to implement his teachings in their own firms.

GOVERNMENT TRIES ITS HAND

Venture capital might have remained the low-key, small-scale domain of the Rockefellers, Whitneys, and Doriots had it not been for Lyndon Johnson's passion for the presidency. The Commerce Department had been studying the idea of a government program to promote financing for small businesses since the 1930s, and Alabama Senator John Sparkman's Small Business Investment Act, first proposed in 1950, would have created "capital banks" to carry out that concept. But nothing happened until 1958, when Johnson, then Senate Majority Leader, seized on the latest version of Sparkman's bill as a vehicle to win small business support for his run at the Democratic presidential nomination in 1960. With Johnson twisting arms in the Senate and Speaker Sam Rayburn helping out in the House, the act creating a Small Business Investment Company program sailed through Congress and was signed into law by President Eisenhower in August 1958.[20]

Instead of the government-backed banks in Sparkman's original plan, the new SBICs were to be private investment companies with tax breaks and the power to leverage their resources by borrowing from the Small Business Administration. They were "a license to steal," said one critic.[21] In the surge of enthusiasm for entrepreneurial investing that accompanied Wall Street's over-the-counter stock binge in 1960, promoters began forming SBICs at a headlong pace. Some of the first ones, notably James Ling's Electro-Science Investors and Charles E. Salik's Electronics Capital Corp., quickly went public themselves and rode the early high-tech boom to impressive, if temporary, heights.[22] Others joined the rush, and by the end of 1961 more than 500 SBIC licenses had been issued. Banks hungry for new financial services to offer snapped up many of them, and the bankers contributed an element of stability to what otherwise was a freewheeling industry. But not all of the new players, by any means, engaged in the kind of new-business investing that Congress had envisioned. Real estate speculators and developers, eager to tap this new source of government money, may have accounted for as many as half of the early licenses. A few out-and-out crooks crept in through the SBA's superficial licensing controls, and there were many practitioners of not-quite-illegal "daisy chain" investing, in which SBICs loaned each other enough money to recover their private contributions to the business before they started risking the SBA money.[23]

Congress eventually gave SBA the power to clean up the worst abuses of the SBIC program, and the stock market collapse of the mid-1960s effectively cooled off the speculative excitement. The market break also set up many of the publicly held SBICs later in the decade for attacks by corporate raiders who noted that their share price had dropped below the value of the assets they held. The number of active SBICs peaked at 649 in 1964 and dropped to a nadir of 248 in 1973 before stabilizing recently at about 360. At one time the largest source of risk capital for small companies, SBICs now account for only about 25 percent of small-business investment activity.[24]

As a venture capital vehicle, SBICs proved to have a number of shortcomings. Because a leveraged SBIC must meet payments on the government loans that make up as much as three-quarters of its capital base, most of its investing also has to be in the form of debt or debt-like securities. That makes it next to impossible for an SBIC to back startup companies that may generate no cash right away. Additionally, SBA's lending authority is limited, currently to $35 million to a single SBIC, and SBA is further restricted by its dependence on the annual Washington budget ritual, in which the SBIC program is a favorite sacrificial victim. During the Nixon Administration SBA lending to SBICs dropped as low as $10 million one year. And the level was frozen at $160 million for three years recently, even though both houses of Congress had approved an increase to $250 million, because of squabbling over other provisions in the bills. Perhaps most demoralizing for operators of public SBICs has been the maze of regulations and paperwork caused by the often conflicting efforts of the Securities and Exchange Commission and the SBA to regulate the industry. SEC regulation of venture capital, says one industry veteran, "is almost the same as having football rules when the game is baseball and the officials have had all their experience in basketball."

Despite its flaws, the SBIC program fueled the creation of today's venture capital industry by drawing hundreds of new players into the field of risk investment and by funding some of the most important startups of the 1960s. One of the most successful of the SBIC pioneers was Frank G. Chambers, whose Continental Capital Corp. raised a total of $5.5 million and has distributed cash and securities worth almost $90 million since it started liquidating its assets in 1980. Chambers and his brother, Robert, had both been exposed to Doriot's message at Harvard in the 1930s, and after the war they got together in San Francisco to start a company, Magna Power Tools, with a design for a combination tool for home workshops they called the Shopsmith. Montgomery Ward bought all the Shopsmiths the little company could make and by 1958 the Chambers brothers were able to sell

out and look for other challenges. At a dinner party one night, a
friend asked Frank Chambers, "Why don't we start a bank?" Congress
had just passed the SBIC act, and Chambers replied: "That's no fun.
Let's start a venture capital company."

Continental Capital, the first SBIC in northern California, opened
for business in June 1959. Chambers was already part of the informal
luncheon-and-investment club that constituted San Francisco's venture capital community at the time, and he joined in a few small
investments. Seeking interesting deals, he backed a company making
a plastic key and tape recorder system to inform zoo visitors about the
animals they were viewing, forgetting that zoos can be visited 365 days
a year in California and only about 150 elsewhere in the country. The
company failed. Chambers decided to aim at bigger game. With $3
million from an underwriting, he started looking for high-technology
deals and found Dataproducts Corp., a new Southern California spinoff of Telex Inc. Dataproducts was already a public company, because
Telex had distributed its stock to Telex shareholders as part of the deal
spinning off its computer memory operation. But Dataproducts had no
money. President Erwin Tomash had planned a public offering, but
the market collapse of 1962 killed that idea. Tomash turned to the
SBICs—to Bank of America's Small Business Enterprise Corp., to
Greater Washington Industrial Investments of Washington, D.C., and
to Continental Capital—for the $1 million he needed to finance his
new company.[25] Dataproducts survived and succeeded (in printers,
rather than memories), and Chambers's $250,000 investment multi-
plied to at least $12 million.

Chambers went on to back such high-tech winners as ROLM,
American Microsystems Inc. and KLA Instruments. But he never felt
that he got much value from the SBIC connection. "You could borrow
money at what originally was a very favorable rate." Chambers explains, "but subsequent Congresses raised the rate to the point that
eventually it wasn't all that favorable." And he was fed up with the
government red tape that went with running a public company. In
1980 he closed Continental Capital Corp. and launched a $22 million
private partnership free of all ties to Washington. "It's a lot easier to
do it the way we're doing it now," he says.

Now that pension funds, endowments, and other institutions are
supplying the venture industry with more capital than it knows how
to invest, SBICs have been largely overshadowed by independent venture firms that prefer to operate without the restrictions of a government program. And unless the SBICs can free themselves of their dependence on congressional appropriations (a proposal to privatize the
whole lending program was introduced in 1984) they are not likely to
regain their former importance. But the SBICs still have a role to play
in funding minority enterprise, in regional economic development,

and in supporting a wide range of new-business opportunities outside the high-growth, high-tech arena favored by the big independent funds. By means of leverage SBICs can show impressive returns on investment in situations that other venture firms snub. And it is certainly possible that the SBICs will be called upon again, as they were in the dark days of the mid-1960s and the mid-1970s, to keep the venture business going during a cyclical shakeout. If the flow of private funds to venture capital freezes up again, declares Walter Stults, the SBIC industry's chief spokesman, "[we] may well preserve an investing function."

Government's most important role in the development of venture investing, it could be argued, is its ability to affect returns through the tax system. Capital gains have enjoyed preferential status under the federal tax code since 1921, but much of the preference was taken away by the Tax Reform acts of 1969 and 1976, which raised the effective maximum rate on capital gains from 25 percent to 49 percent. Partly by coincidence but partly no doubt because of the tax changes, the markets for venture capital and new public issues substantially dried up after 1969. Venture capitalists, still more a collection of individuals than an industry, put together one of the most impressive lobbying efforts Washington has ever seen to fight what seemed at the time an impossible battle to restore capital gains preferences against the strong opposition of the newly-installed Carter Administration.

True to their role as instigators, the venturers succeeded by enlisting to their cause the entrepreneurs they had backed and through them the American Electronics Association, a dynamic young trade association of 900 companies. Under the leadership of Edwin V. W. Zschau, an articulate entrepreneur who chaired the group's San Francisco area council, AEA threw itself into the campaign with a concrete proposal to halve the maximum tax on capital gains. Again, as had been the case with the SBIC effort, the lobbyists found a legislator who saw political gain in supporting their proposal. Rep. William A. Steiger, a Republican from Wisconsin who sat on the Ways and Means Committee, surprised Zschau by offering to introduce tax-cutting legislation even before he had heard Zschau's testimony before the committee. Steiger saw little chance that the attempt would succeed, but sponsoring it would "help him appease some of his conservative constituents who had been offended by his support of the OSHA (Occupational Safety and Health Administration) Act and other liberal-supported initiatives," according to one report on the lobbying effort.[26] But Steiger's Investment Incentive Act of 1978 passed both houses by large margins and was reluctantly signed into law by President Jimmy Carter. The stage was set for a resurgence of venture capital investment.

ENTER THE INSTITUTIONS

To become a significant fixture in the capital markets, any new form of investment must prove itself attractive not just to well-heeled individuals but to the banks, corporations, pension funds, endowments, and other institutions that now control most of America's financial assets. Almost by definition, an individual venture investment is enormously risky. Even the best-planned new business is about as likely to fail as to succeed, and even the smartest investors admit that it is almost impossible to predict the outcome of a single investment. By itself, such an investment would be rank speculation—and institutions theoretically or by law do not engage in speculation. But the institutions have seen that by selecting and nurturing a portfolio of new companies, a professional venture capitalist can not only live with risks that would discourage most investors but in fact achieve rates of return strikingly higher than other equity investment vehicles. It is equally impressive that few long-term players in professional venture capital have lost money.

Of course, those who leave the field during its down cycles can lose substantial sums. One of those cycles apparently began in 1984, as declining prices in the public market for new issues infected the pricing of private deals and as growing numbers of problem companies began to surface in even the best portfolios.[27] A revival of the new-issues market would set things right at least for a time, but history teaches that the venture capital business is highly cyclical. A shakeout of the weaker participants is almost inevitable. It happened in the late 1960s when many investment bankers who had entered the field as a sideline broke for the exits. It happened again in the mid-1970s as a number of banks and insurance companies followed suit. But history also teaches that those prepared to stay the course and support their portfolio companies through the bad times will be handsomely rewarded, and the institutions have acted on that lesson.

Because most venture firms are private partnerships, they commonly disclose their results only to their investors. But there is substantial evidence that venture investments over the long haul have generated annual rates of return of at least 20 percent. One study of 110 investments made by three leading venture groups between 1960 and 1968 found an 18.9 percent annualized rate of return through 1975.[28] More recently, General Electric Investment Corp.—the largest pension fund investor in venture capital partnerships—did a performance analysis on its investments over a 10- to 12-year period and found a compounded return of about 22 percent. Janet A. Hickey, the senior vice president in charge of private placements for GE Investment, explains that GE had no returns at all on its venture investments for the first few years: "You don't earn 20 percent a year in the venture business. You earn 100 percent in one year and nothing in the next."

Returns are high because most venture capital portfolios include enough big winners to more than offset the outright losers and the modest successes. The Huntsman and Hoban study of 110 investments found that one in six were total failures and only eleven produced annual rates of return of 50 percent or more. Eliminating those eleven deals dropped the overall return of the combined portfolio from almost 20 percent to a modest 3.9 percent.[29] Stanley Pratt, who as chairman of Venture Economics, Inc. serves as an informal scorekeeper for the industry, analyzed the performance of eight funds and found a similar pattern: 15 percent of the deals were written off completely, 25 percent lost money, 30 percent no more than doubled the investment and only a third of the remainder generated returns of 500 percent or better. That final group, constituting just 11 percent of the investments, produced more than half of the total returns for those funds, Pratt adds. In the early 1980s a number of funds were able to show early returns of 50 percent per year or more thanks to the strength of the new-issues market. But Pratt and others believe historic patterns will prevail and returns for the ten-year cycle that started in 1979 will come in at roughly the same 20 percent to 25 percent range that was normal from 1969 to 1979.

Venture capital first became attractive to most institutional investors in the late 1970s as evidence of these long-term returns began to surface. Hickey explains how GE was converted: "Two existing partnerships had been assigned to me when I was a portfolio manager and one of them went into liquidation in 1978. That tends to catch one's attention. It was one of the worst performing funds in the industry. It gave us from 1969 to 1978 a 9 percent compounded return. However in the same period the Standard & Poor's 500 gave you about a 4.5 percent return. So it wasn't the wonderful 20 percent a year that everybody wants but net of all expenses and the carried interest (of the general partners) it was still twice the rate of return in stocks. And in early 1979 a few funds started coming in, and they were [managed by] terrific people. Because the only ones who could come and ask you for money were those with a good record and had made it through the great crash. I began to talk more with the venture capitalists and we came to the decision that this was an attractive area for the pension funds to invest in because we are in the business of generating a real rate of return." GE started out with a $20 million authorization and raised it every year to a recent level of $250 million.

A crucial factor in the acceptability of venture investments for pension fund managers has been Washington's shifting interpretation of the 1974 Employee Retirement Income Security Act (ERISA), which was intended to crack down on the abuses of some union and multiemployer plans but initially seemed to restrict all pension funds to investing in blue-chip stocks and bonds. In 1978, the Department of Labor finally clarified ERISA in a way that allowed a fund to place a percentage of its assets in supposedly riskier investments that offered higher rates of return. Since then, although Labor has issued proposals for rules that could adversely affect venture investments, pension money has flooded into venture funds and accounts for almost a third of their resources. According to Venture Economics, pension funds more than quintupled their annual contributions to venture capital funds in the early 1980s, reaching more than $1 billion in 1983. And there seems little chance that ERISA will rock the boat. Robert Monks, who served as administrator of ERISA in 1984, reassured fund managers that "imaginative and new kinds of investment vehicles will not subject them to liability."[30]

Managers of endowments are not ruled by ERISA but they have had similar problems adapting venture investments to the "prudent man rule" that still guides their actions more than 150 years after it was first enunciated by Justice Samuel Putnam of Massachusetts:

All that can be required of a Trustee to invest is that he conduct himself faithfully and exercise a sound discretion. He is to observe how men of prudence, discretion, and intelligence manage their own affairs, not in regard to speculation, but in regard to permanent disposition of their funds, considering the probable income, as well as the probable safety of the capital to be invested.

Walter M. Cabot, president of Harvard Management Company Inc., which manages Harvard's $2.6 billion endowment and pension reserves, recalls consulting three different law firms before deciding in 1977 that venture capital could meet Justice Putnam's stringent standards. There were two basic standards he had to meet, Cabot concluded. "One was, what do other trustees do under like circumstances? So I called up thirty-three different endowments and asked if they ever messed around in venture capital. The other standard is, basically, have you done your homework? So I spent a lot of time talking to general partners trying to figure out who I could believe and trust." Between half and two thirds of the endowments he talked to were already making venture capital investments, Cabot found. And discussions with Tommy Davis, Peter Brooke, and other leading venturers produced a set of criteria for selecting funds. The most important? "Quality and credibility of the individuals." By early 1984 Harvard Management had invested or committed over $130 million to venture capital. "Harvard can afford a certain amount of illiquidity," Cabot explains. "Harvard's long-term investment objective and the long-term investment objective of venture capital give us a commonality of perspective."

By 1984, many institutional investors turned cautious as the venture capital cycle appeared to peak. Harvard Management began curtailing its new commitments, but Cabot retains an unflappable view of the field: "A lot of people have come into this with the idea that it's a free ride to heaven. We know it isn't going to be. I really believe there is going to be a shakeout and there will be a lot of companies that go under. It is certainly an area that is still developing and growing, and there will be problems. I believe in this business long-term, but there will be times when you should step back and kind of let the hurricane blow by you."

NOTES

1. Maurice Rowdon, *Lorenzo the Magnificent*. Henry Regnery Co., Chicago, 1974, p. 28.
2. Hubert Herring, *A History of Latin America*. Alfred A. Knopf, New York, 1963, p. 136.
3. Herbert Heaton, *Economic History of Europe*. Harper Brothers, New York, 1948, p. 361.
4. Harold C. Livesay, *Andrew Carnegie and the Rise of Big Business*. Little, Brown & Company, Boston and Toronto, 1975, pp. 45–58.
5. Charles R. Flint, *Memories of an Active Life*. G. P. Putnam's Sons, New York and London, 1923.
6. John Chamberlain, *The Enterprising Americans: A Business History of the United States*. Harper & Row, New York and Evanston, 1963, p. 185.
7. Ibid., pp. 188–241.
8. Joe Alex Morris, *Those Rockefeller Brothers*. Harper Brothers, New York, 1953, p. 169.
9. Laurance Rockefeller's prewar investments are recounted in Alvin Moscow, *The Rockefeller Inheritance*. Doubleday & Co., New York, 1977, pp. 179–181; in Peter Collier and David Horowitz, *The Rockefellers: an American Dynasty*. Holt, Rinehart & Winston, New York, 1976; and in Morris, *Those Rockefeller Brothers*, pp. 103–105.
10. Moscow, *The Rockefeller Inheritance*, p. 179.
11. Charles M. Macko, "Venture Capitalist," *Barron's*, August 14, 1961, p. 9.
12. Richard P. Cooke, "Laurance Rockefeller Finds Risky New Uses for Old Oil Millions," *The Wall Street Journal*, July 15, 1959, p. 1.
13. Edwin P. Hoyt, *The Whitneys*. Weybright and Talley, New York, 1976, pp. 241–244.
14. Gene Bylinsky, "General Doriot's Dream Factory," *Fortune*, August 1967, p. 104.

15. Joseph W. Powell, Jr. in remarks at the Second Annual Boston College Management Seminar on Venture Capital, May 1970.

16. Kenneth H. Olsen in remarks at the Second Annual Boston College Management Seminar on Venture Capital.

17. "A Risk Capitalist Bids a Golden Adieu," *Business Week*, January 22, 1972, p. 17.

18. Bylinsky, *Dream Factory*, p. 132.

19. Note 17.

20. Data gathered from an interview with Walter B. Stults, former staff director of the Senate Select Committee on Small Business, who is now president of the National Association of Small Business Investment Companies.

21. Phil David Fine, head of the Small Business Administration's Investment Division, quoted in Charles M. Noone and Stanley M. Rubel, *SBIC's: Pioneers in Organized Venture Capital*, Capital Publishing Co., Chicago, 1970, p. 46.

22. Ibid., pp. 41–43.

23. Stults interview.

24. "SBICs After 25 Years," *Venture Capital Journal*, October 1983, p. 6.

25. Dataproducts' financial history is recounted in a corporate publication, *Dataprintout*, Sept./Oct., 1979, pp. 10–13.

26. Robert Wolcott Johnson, "The Passage of the Investment Incentive Act of 1978: A Case Study of Business Influencing Public Policy" (Ph.D. diss., Harvard University, 1980), p. 324.

27. "It's the Morning After for Venture Capitalists," *Business Week*, September 24, 1984, p. 118.

28. Blaine Huntsman and James P. Hoban, Jr., "Investment in New Enterprise: Some Empirical Observations on Risk, Return, and Market Structure," *Financial Management*, Summer 1980, p. 44.

29. Ibid.

30. Fran Hawthorne, "How Bob Monks Plans to Shake up Pensionland," *Institutional Investor*, March 1984, p. 113.

3

VALLEY OF THE DEALS

Born in New York, nurtured in Boston, and almost smothered in Washington, venture capital did not really come of age until it moved to California and joined forces with the brash young technologists who were using bits of silicon to create an information revolution as profound as the industrial revolution a century earlier. The bucolic Santa Clara Valley was an unlikely place for a revolution, but it had two important attractions for the new breed of scientist-entrepreneur: nice weather and Stanford University. Frederick Terman, Stanford's legendary engineering dean, encouraged his best students to stay in the area, and the balmy weather persuaded some of them to take his advice. A small electronics industry began to coalesce around the university before World War II, and in the post-war years a venture capital community took root in San Francisco, thirty miles to the north. By the late 1960s the combination of technology and risk capital had snowballed into a phenomenon known around the world as Silicon Valley—a center of entrepreneurship so powerful that officials from Bonn to Tokyo would wonder how to emulate it.

EAST MEETS WEST

No name is more closely associated with the creation of what came to be known as Silicon Valley than that of Arthur Rock, a Wall Street investment banker who transplanted himself and his quiet passion for backing entrepreneurs to San Francisco in 1961. Ironically, because Rock is a withdrawn and taciturn man who never seeks publicity, he has become something of a media hero for the role he played in starting Fairchild Semiconductor and the fortune he accumulated with investments in Scientific Data Systems, Teledyne, Intel, and Apple Computer. Dressed by an imaginative artist in a suit of money, Rock even appeared on the cover of *Time*, the highest accolade American pop culture can bestow.[1]

Rock discovered the opportunities in high technology while serving his Wall Street apprenticeship at Hayden Stone & Co. He was a sober, diligent researcher whose work habits reflected his middle-class upbringing in Rochester, N.Y., where he had always had some kind of job—clerking in his father's candy store, selling magazines door to door, distributing newspapers. Except for a sporadic interest in politics he stayed focused on a business career through four years at Syracuse

University and two at the Harvard Business School. Rock started on Wall Street with Werthheim & Co., took a few months off to work for the Eisenhower-Nixon campaign in 1952, and then moved to Shields & Co., another investment banking firm, where he began to appreciate the potential in the new electronics companies then being formed. Three years later, he moved again to Hayden Stone, which he felt "was more open to those kinds of ideas."

One idea arrived in the spring of 1957 in the form of a letter to a customer's man, as Wall Street calls the sales people who deal with small investors. The letter was from Eugene Kleiner, an engineer who was the son of a Hayden Stone client, and it outlined an unusual proposition. Kleiner was one of several young employees of Shockley Semiconductor Laboratories who were not getting along with their boss. William Shockley had just won a Nobel Prize for his role in the invention of the transistor but he was having trouble managing the company he had started in Palo Alto two years before, to bring the new technology of solid-state electronics to market. Dissatisfied with Shockley's leadership, seven of his top scientists and engineers were ready to leave and were looking for a corporate sponsor to keep the group intact. But Kleiner was the only one in the group who had even the slightest idea who to approach. "It was really ridiculous," Kleiner says now. "We didn't have much of a plan. We kind of said, we work for a Nobel Prize winner but we don't think he's very good. We don't like him and he doesn't like us but we like each other."

The letter ended up on Rock's desk. He had already arranged the public financings for General Transistor, one of the first semiconductor companies, and was impressed at the speed with which a $50,000 initial investment had multiplied. Rock persuaded Alfred "Bud" Coyle, a Hayden Stone partner, that this new proposal was worth investigating. Rock and Coyle endured the 11-hour flight to San Francisco and spent the 4th of July weekend meeting with the defectors in a hotel room. Robert Noyce, a twenty-nine year old physicist who until then had not been part of the group but would later emerge as its leader, attended the meeting without any real hope that backing could be found to start a company. "Prior to that time that sort of thing had not crossed my mind," he recalls. "We thought maybe we could get somebody to hire us. We wanted to stay in California, but there wasn't anybody else here then that would hire a group to work in silicon. Silicon Valley didn't exist." But Coyle and Rock saw an opportunity to put a deal together. "I knew the semiconductor business was going to be something or other, I wasn't quite sure what," says Rock. "And I really liked the eight of them and thought they would accomplish something." Noyce's impression was that Coyle and Rock saw an opportunity to earn a fast commission, and that their enthusiasm in turn was infecting the group with startup fever.

THE FAIRCHILD CONNECTION

The defectors agreed to give Hayden Stone a few weeks to raise the money, and Rock had to start traveling. He talked to two dozen potential corporate backers and got a negative response from all of them. "They were all interested," he says, "but none of them could see how they could finance a company outside of their own business. Nobody had done it before, and they were concerned about how it would affect their employees." Finally Rock heard that Sherman Fairchild might be worth approaching. Fairchild, the immensely wealthy scion of a founder of IBM, controlled both Fairchild Camera & Instrument, a maker of aerial cameras and a hodgepodge of other products, and Fairchild Industries, an aircraft builder. Fairchild was an inventive and imaginative man willing to take a chance on new ideas. More to the point, Rock learned, Fairchild Camera was floundering around for new directions and had already done a study that pinpointed the emerging semiconductor industry. By September Noyce and Kleiner were in New York to negotiate a deal.

In their crude, 10-page business plan the Shockley deserters sketched a budget that suggested a need for $800,000. John Carter, Fairchild Camera's new president, offered them almost twice that—$1.5 million—in the form of a loan. In return, Fairchild received an option to buy the new company for $3 million, 20 percent of which would go to Hayden Stone and 10 percent to each of the founders, within three years. Today, both parties would find such a structure laughable. The founders would see themselves locked into a rigid payoff, no matter how successful they should be, and the investor would face owning a subsidiary run by restive employees instead of inspired entrepreneurs. In fact, the flaws in that agreement eventually resulted in an explosion of talent that helped create Silicon Valley. At the time, though, it was unheard of for scientists and engineers to share in the fruits of their discoveries to the degree that Fairchild was offering. And the prospect of that $3 million bonanza helped drive the youthful founders of Fairchild Semiconductor to overnight success. By 1959 sales were over $3 million and profits were running at 10 percent after taxes, and Carter—presumably eager to get those earnings on his books—chose to exercise the option a year early.

Under Noyce's leadership, first as director of research and development and later as general manager, Fairchild Semiconductor shot ahead in transistors and then in the manufacture of integrated circuits, which combine many electrical functions on a single chip. Fairchild was successful, Noyce believes, partly because it built a scientific base for its products rather than using trial-and-error methods that had characterized the industry until then. And it reinforced this edge by offering economic incentives to an unusually large number of technologists. "Up to that point," Noyce points out, "it was very rare to take research people and motivate them by commercial success. Research people wore white smocks and were locked up in the laboratory. Here the research people were out talking to the customers."

After the Fairchild deal, Rock maintained his West Coast contacts and on a trip to Los Angeles was introduced to Henry Singleton, then running a division of Litton Industries. Singleton struck him as "a guy you want to believe"—and when he called to say he was leaving Litton to form a new company, Rock agreed to help. In 1960 Hayden Stone arranged a private placement of shares in Teledyne Inc.—25 percent of the company for $1.8 million—that valued Singleton's infant conglomerate at more than $7 million. "There wasn't much of a business there," Rock says. "You had to have a lot of faith in Singleton in order to invest at that price." With Teledyne's market valuation now well over $3 billion, Rock's faith certainly seems well placed. But he was concerned about the prospects for the public market, which was nearing the peak of a great speculative boom in electronics stocks. "I used to write a report on scientific companies," Rock says, "and the average price/earnings ratio was 50 or 60. I just didn't think that could continue." It was time to leave Wall Street, he decided.

"BACK THE RIGHT PEOPLE"

Rock's experiences with new California companies had convinced him there was an important venture capital opportunity opening up in the West. "The fact that we could do Fairchild and Teledyne from the East Coast indicated to me that there weren't enough people out here to do whatever there was to do," he recalls. Aside from Frank Chambers's SBIC and a few individual investors, the only venture investment group of any consequence in California at the time was Draper, Gaither & Anderson of Palo Alto, which was proving curiously ineffective at investing the $6 million it had raised from the Rockefeller clan and other blue-ribbon investors. DG&A had been formed by some of the biggest names on the West Coast. William H. Draper, Jr. was a former Dillon, Read & Co. vice president who became a roving ambassador in Europe after World War II; Rowan Gaither was a founder of Rand Corp.; Frederick L. Anderson was a retired air force general.[2] But the general partners were obviously too important to actually get involved in the day-to-day effort of finding and screening deals. This was left to a crew of young associates, some of whom a contemporary describes as "wild men," who never managed to find enough good investments to offset the inevitable losers. By the mid-1960s DG&A was out of business.

Thomas J. Davis, known universally as Tommy, was also eager to play the California venture game. Trained as a lawyer and though the gentlest of souls, Davis had spent World War II as an OSS operative in the jungles of Southeast Asia. After the war, his quest for adventure led him to San Francisco and to a vice presidency at Kern County Land Co., a cash-rich oil and cattle empire that needed modernizing. Davis decided that Kern County Land was going to have to deploy its cash into new businesses or become a target for corporate raiders. Knowing nothing at all about the new technologies that he thought held promise, he dropped in on Terman for advice. Soon he was flying around the country with Stanford experts in tow, discovering the new world of high technology. He even took night courses in electronics, in hopes that learning how to hook up a voltmeter would help him understand what his new pals were talking about. Terman introduced him to Dean Watkins, a young professor who wanted to start a company making traveling wave tubes, used to generate high-frequency electromagnetic radiation, and Davis was able to talk Kern County Land into backing him. Watkins-Johnson Co. was immediately successful, but all that Davis got for his trouble was a pat on the back. And although he kept suggesting investments, Kern County Land never made another one. "I had pictured outdoing Litton Industries," Davis recalls, "but I began to realize this was just not compatible with the kind of people they were. They were light-years from being able to understand this sort of thing."

Rock and Davis had been trading information for some time. If Davis wanted to know something you could find out on Wall Street he would call up Rock, and Rock added Davis to his California network. The two talked occasionally about starting their own firm, and finally in 1961 Rock insisted on a decision. "Are we going to do this or not?" he demanded, and Davis replied, "We're going to do it, aren't we?" They raised $3.5 million, all from individuals—including Singleton and several of the Fairchild Semiconductor founders—and opened an office in San Francisco. In terms of personality, they could hardly be more different. Davis is open and friendly with a talent for conversation; Rock is silent and brooding, a keen listener who rarely offers more than a sentence or two of reaction. But they worked well together. Davis puts it this way: "It's a pleasure to deal with a guy whose mind is as clear as Art's is and doesn't get distracted by a lot of irrelevancies. I think we were a pretty good team. When we were interviewing these fellows, I would do most of the talking and Art could watch them react to the questions I was asking. Then he would come in with a question when he wanted to. But he's very laconic."

The two of them agreed on the fundamentals of venture investing, however. First and foremost, they tried to back outstanding people—superior managers of high-technology ventures—without worrying too much about the details of product and marketing strategy. "I believe so strongly in people," says Rock, "that I think talking to the individuals is much more important than finding out too much about what they want to do." Rock disagrees with investors who put great weight on the technical breakthrough or the market opportunity in evaluating deals. "It takes good people not only to run a company but to figure out what will be dynamic and grow," he points out. Davis once summed up their philosophy in a speech, modestly titled "How to Pick a Winner," in which he stated The Principle as, simply, "Back the right people." Who are the right people? Davis listed six characteristics: Integrity, motivation, market orientation, technical capability, accounting ability, and leadership. The most important, he said, was motivation. "A man is entitled to set his own goals," he said, "but when I go to the race track, I try to pick the horse that wants to run."[3]

Shortly before they set up shop, Davis gave an interview in which he declared, as emphatically as possible, "You're not going to catch me trying to fight IBM in the computer business." But on the day he moved into their Montgomery Street office—Rock was still in New York—Davis got a call from a Los Angeles consultant who had come across a group headed by a mathematician named Max Palevsky. "The most exciting proposition you ever saw, Tommy." Davis, seated on the floor in the absence of furniture, began to get emotional. "My voice shot up in the treble clef," he recalls, "and finally I said, 'wait a minute, what's this guy going to do?'" "He's going to start a computer company." Davis toppled over in mock dismay, but he agreed to meet with Palevsky. After a 13-hour meeting, in which Palevsky outlined his plan for Scientific Data Systems (SDS), Davis was convinced. He called Rock, who was packing for San Francisco, and relayed the idea. "There was a silence at the other end," Davis says, "and finally, 'Jesus, I've gone into partnership with an idiot.'" But Rock agreed to stop in Los Angeles on his way, and Palevsky won him over as well.

Palevsky had designed a small computer for a company called Packard Bell, but Packard Bell got into deep financial trouble and Palevsky started looking for capital to go off on his own. At the time, most computers were bulky boxes of vacuum tubes designed to sit in air-conditioned isolation and plod through bookkeeping tasks. Palevsky proposed to use the new solid-state technology to produce a compact computer that could deal with real-world problems. What made SDS attractive to Davis and Rock, besides Palevsky's driving ambition, was that the concept steered well clear of IBM's stronghold of business computing. "They were interested in tracking satellites, running refineries, boring engine blocks," Davis explains. "I said it would be years and years before there would be any conflict with IBM, and Art agreed."

Altogether, Palevsky gave up about 80 percent of his company for investments that totaled less than $1 million. Davis urged Rock to sit on the SDS board, feeling that Palevsky might not bear down hard enough on some aspects of running the business and that of the two of them Rock would be best at keeping him focused. Rock later became chairman, and SDS turned into the fastest-growing computer company of the 1960s. By 1968, SDS was twice the size of Digital Equipment with sales of $100 million and Xerox Corp. acquired it for stock worth just short of $1 billion. Ironically, Xerox then proceeded to push its new subsidiary into direct competition with IBM, where it managed to lose $100 million in five years and finally went out of business. The payoff to Davis & Rock was $60 million—a 233-fold return on a $257,000 investment.

Davis & Rock made other venture investments, and although none achieved anything like the success of SDS the firm became a model for later groups. For one thing, Davis & Rock was the first successful venture partnership in which the general partners received a substantial—20 percent—carried interest in the profits. They were true partners, agreed from the beginning that they would make no investment unless both were strongly in favor of it. They did their own research but they also made extensive use of limited partners such as Singleton of Teledyne and Kleiner of Fairchild, who agreed to help out in evaluating investments. "I know I did four or five companies a year for them," Kleiner recalls, "and I imagine the others did the same." Perhaps most important, they were both interested in the process of building companies, not just in financial transactions. Rock relished playing father-confessor to his stable of entrepreneurs: "I had one guy who used to come to my house once a week and he would actually lie down on the couch and start talking. I don't think he realized what he was doing, but in a way I think I play the role of corporate psychologist."

"THE BEST GUY IN THE BUSINESS"

The partnership between Davis and Rock was set up to run for seven years, and after their fund was distributed in 1968 they could both afford to relax for a time. Their 20 percent share in the profits came to at least $16 million. But Rock was not idle. In the late 1960s the timebomb at the core of Fairchild Camera's relationship with its semiconductor subsidiary finally exploded. The free spirits at Fairchild Semiconductor were chafing under Carter's autocratic, long-distance command, and even loyal Bob Noyce winced when a Fairchild director responded to a suggestion of giving someone incentive pay: "Isn't the fact that we're not going to fire him tomorrow morning incentive enough?" One by one, and often in groups, the scientists and engineers who had built Fairchild Semiconductor began to dismantle it. Charles Sporck, Fairchild's cigar-chomping manufacturing genius, took over at National Semiconductor Corp., a moribund company

that investor Peter Sprague was attempting to rescue, and quickly recruited Donald Valentine, Fairchild's brilliant marketing director.
Jean Hoerni, one of the original eight founders, prevailed on Rock to
help finance Intersil Inc. The flamboyant salesman, W. J. "Jerry"
Sanders III, found backing for his Advanced Micro Devices Inc. at a
Los Angeles money-management organization. And the coup de grace
to the original Fairchild team was administered by Noyce and Gordon
Moore, the last of the founders still on the premises, when they
walked out in 1968 to organize Intel Corp.

Once again, they turned to Arthur Rock. Noyce had had no significant contacts with Rock since the early Fairchild days, but he considered him the most successful venture capitalist around. "When you
want to get something done," Noyce says, "you get the best guy in the
business." Noyce called Rock before leaving Fairchild, just to test the
water: "If I wanted to start a company, could you find me some
money?" "Sure," Rock replied without reflection, and when Noyce
gave the go-ahead a few weeks later it took just days to assemble $2.5
million. Rock's partnership with Davis had already ended but he put
$300,000 of his own money into the deal. Palevsky of SDS came up
with another $300,000, Houston investor Fayez Sarofim, a classmate
of Rock's at Harvard, contributed $200,000, and Hayden Stone pro-
vided $100,000. Noyce and Moore may not have needed much help.
They had personally put up a combined $500,000 before the $2.5
million was raised and had guaranteed $1.5 million worth of equip-
ment. Their six Fairchild co-founders chipped in a total of $500,000.
Noyce served on a board of directors with Charles B. Smith of
Laurance Rockefeller's organization, and that contact brought in
$300,000. "It's conceivable I could have raised the money," says
Noyce, "but I had no idea how to go about it."

For Rock, backing Noyce and Moore was an obvious move even
though Trude Taylor, a manufacturer of ferrite core computer memories and an investor in Davis & Rock, tried to convince him that there
would never be a big market for the semiconductor memory devices
Intel proposed to make. Eventually, of course, the semiconductor
memories pioneered by Intel would almost completely supplant core
technology and even Taylor's Electronic Memories & Magnetics
would attempt to make them. Rock couldn't know that, but he knew
Noyce and Moore and considered them outstanding individuals.
Moore, head of research at Fairchild, was strong on long-range technology planning. Noyce was a great motivator of people and an important inventor in his own right. It was a combination that couldn't
miss, and Intel emerged during the 1970s as the country's leading
technology-based growth company. Rock served as chairman of the
board, consulting on financial moves and corporate strategies, until
1975, and his holdings of stock in the company by that time were

worth some $25 million. He played a key role in the private and public financings which ensured that Intel never was squeezed for money. "Art says relatively little," Noyce says, "but his advice on when to go to the [financial] market has always been superb."

Rock's assurance sometimes plays a crucial role in stabilizing events at the fast-moving companies he backs. Frederick R. Adler, a leading New York venture capitalist who joined the board of Intersil just as Rock was leaving it, recalls that Rock was one of the few people the brilliant but mercurial Hoerni, Intersil's founder, would listen to. "When Hoerni used to flip out," Adler says, "Arthur would take him on a hike and unflip him." Don Valentine, the former Fairchild marketeer who now is a top venture capitalist, calls Rock's style supportive. "If management appears to be faltering in their conviction," Valentine says, "Arthur's approach is to supply them with some more conviction."

For Max Palevsky, Rock's great contribution to the success of SDS was an implacable will. "At the beginning it really required a very steady hand on the helm because we were out there in uncharted waters," Palevsky says. "What Arthur brings to companies is a will that won't conceive of not winning. People tend to think of high technology as the sort of place where intelligence and technical brilliance wins. That is true, partially. But the other side of it is just having the drive and the motivation that won't give up. That is a certain attitude toward one's life and one's work that has nothing to do with intelligence. Arthur doesn't want to know what the facts are, Arthur just wants to know what the bottom line is." Rock is famous in high technology circles for his nagging references to prices, which he nearly always considers too low. Says a former Intel manager: "He never said much at staff meetings when I was there, aside from asking on numerous occasions why I didn't raise the prices." Palevsky recalls that the first SDS machine, which cost $18,000 to build, carried a pricetag of $100,000, partly because of Rock's urgings. "And we couldn't build them fast enough."

Neither of the funds that Rock and Tommy Davis established separately in 1969 were able to recapture the glory of the past. The funds, after all, were set up when the market was at a cyclical peak and liquidated near its bottom. Rock and a new partner, C. Richard Kramlich, operating out of the old Davis & Rock office on Montgomery Street, raised $10 million, invested some $6.5 million of it, and eventually distributed $30 million. But the partnership dissolved in acrimony, Rock returned to personal investing, and Kramlich joined forces with an East Coast mutual fund organization to launch a transcontinental venture firm. Davis started the Mayfield Fund with Wallace F. Davis (no relation, they had to keep reminding people), raised $3.8 million and eventually returned stock worth a modest

$13 million by 1983. But the two Davises hit it off, learned from their mistakes, and ultimately built an influential, top-tier venture partnership.

It could be said of Arthur Rock that there has been an element of luck in his successes. Certainly there was serendipity in Eugene Kleiner's inspiration to direct his plea for help to Hayden Stone; in Tommy Davis's ability to set aside a prejudice against computer investments, and in Bob Noyce's decision to seek outside help in financing his second startup. Rock's $57,000 investment in Apple Computer—worth $14 million when Apple went public three years later—was apparently a last-minute inspiration, as Venrock Associates was wrapping up the initial financing, based in part on a presentation Apple's founders made at an Intel staff meeting. Rock has never been one to beat the bushes for investment opportunities in the aggressive manner of modern venture funds. But he is gifted at recognizing an opportunity and always prepared to seize it, and his drive to succeed carries over to the entrepreneurs he backs. "Arthur's not lucky," says Don Valentine, "he's very good. In my opinion, nobody is even close to Arthur as an individual investor."

There is a double irony in Rock's recent celebrity because he is not at all representative of the modern style of venture capital. In an era of large firms making dozens of investments in the course of a year, Rock plays a lone hand from the same cramped office in San Franciso's financial center that he first occupied more than two decades ago. There is not even a sign on the door. Investing for himself and a few friends, he may do only two or three deals in a year. When I visited him late in 1983, he was active in only five investments. And where the major venture funds today are staffing up with high-powered technology aces and rely heavily on expert consultants to buttress their own research, a technically unsophisticated Arthur Rock continues to make up his mind mainly on the basis of conversation and his own intuitive reading of the abilities and prospects of the entrepreneurs who seek his help. Rock himself wonders occasionally if his approach is outdated. "The deals are so complicated and the technology is so sophisticated," he told me, "maybe you do need an engineering background. I'm not a disbeliever in that approach—but I'm still not convinced."

THE INVESTOR AS ENTREPRENEUR

When San Francisco's venture capital community began moving south in the 1970s, one firm was already there and wondering why the others had waited so long. Paul M. Wythes, the senior partner in Sutter Hill Ventures, recalls taunting his city-based colleagues: "You're having lunch with investment bankers while we're getting together with a guy at Hewlett-Packard who wants to start a company." Wythes and his partner William H. Draper III had been working together in Palo Alto since the mid-1960s and they had developed an approach to venturing that would strongly influence the West Coast style that evolved through the 1970s.

Both Wythes and Draper had business experience—Wythes in electronics, Draper in steel—instead of the usual financial background. They were fascinated with the process of starting companies, and they preferred to invest their limited capital in a few raw startups where they could be useful rather than climb aboard later rounds of financing for companies that were well established. Often they acted more like founders than investors. "Draper had all kinds of ideas," recalls one entrepreneur who was backed by Sutter Hill. "He would go to a pay phone between flights to call us with an idea."

This was something new—the investor acting as an entrepreneur and seeking a return from effort and ideas as well as from capital—but the payoff was limited at first. Draper had worked with his father at Draper, Gaither & Anderson, the West Coast's first attempt at organized venture capital, and then had joined Franklin "Pitch" Johnson in an early SBIC. Deals were few and far between—it was hard to earn enough to pay his own salary, Draper found—and he moved in with Sutter Hill, then mainly a real estate operation, to share expenses. Sutter Hill's founder Frank J. Lodato had taken out an SBIC license in a diversification move, and Wythes soon persuaded Draper to join forces in building up Sutter Hill's venture side. They made a formidable team. Draper, a charismatic, ever-optimistic dealmaker, was counterbalanced by the conservative Wythes, who took a methodical approach to everything he did. David L. Anderson, who joined the firm in 1971, recalls being struck by the contrasting styles of the senior partners: "I could see immediately that Paul would come at it by looking at the numbers, doing some real analytical work right on his feet, while Bill had a much more intuitive sense. Occasionally they might frustrate themselves, but together they worked very well."

Sutter Hill launched some important companies in the 1960s: Kasper Instruments, a semiconductor equipment maker now part of Eaton Corp.; Diablo Systems, the pioneer in "daisy wheel" printers for word processors, now owned by Xerox; and Xidex, which became the world leader in microfilm for storing computerized records. But Wythes and Draper were frustrated by the secondary positions they had to take in the increasingly costly deals that came along in the late 1960s. Electronics was becoming a high-stakes game, and Sutter Hill lacked the chips to stay at the table.

The financing of Measurex Corp. in 1968 was the final straw. Sutter Hill had provided founder David A. Bossen with an office to work up his business plan and pledged $250,000 toward starting his company to make computerized controls for papermaking and other process industries. But Bossen needed $1.3 million, and it was not until New York-based Bessemer Securities came through with a commitment of $600,000 that the package could be wrapped up. The company went on to become a huge winner, but Wythes was bitter: "We put the whole deal together, helped Dave write the business plan, spent all the time and energy to help raise the money. Then they walked in and took the big chunk."

The answer was obviously to bring in more capital. But raising money privately, as other firms were beginning to do, would create problems for Sutter Hill, which already had about seventy local stockholders and could not take on too many more without coming under the stringent reporting requirements of the 1940 Act governing investment companies. The problem was solved in 1970 by selling the firm to Genstar, a Canadian real estate conglomerate looking for a U.S. toehold. Genstar, now headquartered in San Francisco, did not make the mistake of viewing venture capital as a "window" on technology or a source of acquisitions—blunders that have misled any number of would-be corporate venturers. The Sutter Hill partners were given a 20 percent share in the profits, and they were left strictly alone. They did well. Sutter Hill provided startup financing for Qume, Apollo Computer, Activision, and Priam—all companies that went on to achieve sales of $100 million or more—and by 1983 had pyramided a $10 million stake into more than $500 million.

Sutter Hill used its new clout to take positions that gave it more say in the structure and strategy of the ventures it backed. Never again, the partners said, would they allow an entrepreneur to end up with voting control, as had happened with a company making dollar bill changers. The founder had started out saying all the right things, how he wanted to build it up and take it public, then had decided he liked running his own show. Sutter Hill lacked the votes to change his mind or force him out. The company landed in bankruptcy court and Sutter Hill had to write off the investment. "I wouldn't go into a deal where one individual owns majority control," Wythes says now. "I don't mind if there is a third party who with that one person owns control and your job is to convince the third party that a change ought to be made. But when you're dealing with one guy and he says for whatever reason he's going to be a proprietor instead of an entrepreneur, there's nothing you can do."

In the case of Xidex, Sutter Hill was able to rescue a disintegrating situation by recruiting a strong leader in Lester L. Colbert, a top executive of Reichhold Chemical who was a Princeton classmate of Wythes. With Qume, Sutter Hill proved the value of taking an active part in shaping a management team from the start. Qume Corp., which quickly dominated the noncaptive market for daisy wheel printers, was started in 1973 and acquired by International Telephone & Telegraph Corp. for $155 million only five years later. Sutter Hill contributed $700,000 of the $2.5 million Qume raised privately and came away with more than $50 million in ITT stock. Wythes and Draper earned their payoff by putting together the management team that drove Qume to overnight success and then by holding firm when sales were slow to take off and the fledgling company was hit with a $20 million lawsuit.

Qume was the brainchild of David Lee, a Chinese-born mechanical engineer who had developed the first commercially successful daisy wheel printer at Diablo, a company which Sutter Hill had helped finance in 1969 and then sold to Xerox. Lee disliked the Xerox bureaucracy. "Every time we had a meeting there would be twenty people there, each saying what the machine should be," he later told a reporter. "I didn't know who my boss was."[4] Lee's response was to drop in on Wythes, who jumped at the chance to back him in a new venture. But there was one proviso: "Dave, you need a business manager to be your partner and we're going to call him the president and chief executive."

The perfect candidate turned up a few months after Sutter Hill and J. H. Whitney of New York advanced the money to allow Lee to start work on a new daisy wheel design. Sutter Hill had worked with Whitney before in launching Lexitron Corp., which turned into a cliffhanger of a deal after an inexperienced management team missed its cost goals badly in designing an early word processor. Sutter Hill insisted on proven leadership in starting Qume. In fact, Lee got only half of the startup money at first, with the rest contingent on hiring a professional manager.

At about this time, Robert E. Schroeder was looking for alternatives to his $90,000-a-year job running a group of diversified subsidiaries for Cummins Engine Co. in Indiana. Wythes heard about Schroeder from G. Leonard Baker, a young Cummins manager he had been trying to hire (Baker joined Sutter Hill a few months later), and Schroeder, then thirty-five, agreed to take a $60,000 pay cut to join Qume. He and Lee started with the same $30,000 salary and the same package of stock that together represented a one third share in the company. "I could have asked for more," Schroeder says, "but I felt there would be a lot of stresses and strains between the professional manager and the technical genius. If we were in the same position financially, our interests would coincide."

Schroeder and Lee, as Wythes remarks, "made mad music together for the next five years." But the venture investors had to sit through some discordant notes, including a lawsuit in which Xerox alleged patent infringement and theft of trade secrets, that arrived the day before the third and final round of financing was to close. Things had not gone well. The second round of $1.1 million was to have been the last injection of venture capital, but a recession intervened and the company was in danger of running out of money. This had happened before, and Whitney had come through with a bank contact willing to advance enough money to tide Qume over until the second round. Schroeder tried the same trick again, but came up $750,000 short. By now, Whitney and Sutter Hill had assembled a supporting team of nearby venture firms—but would the suit frighten them off? The answer, after eight days of marathon sessions between investors and management: Not at all. The financing closed at the original price, and Qume never looked back.

Sutter Hill's cast of characters has changed over the years, but its style still reflects the original blend of conservatism and daring that was reflected in such deals as Activision, the producer of entertainment programs for home computers and video games. James H. Levy, Activision's founder, still marvels that Draper was eager to back the company in 1979, even though it was unlike anything Sutter Hill had ever done. In fact, he recalls, it took only about two hours to convince Draper that the concept was sound. But it took another ten weeks to answer all the questions raised by the other Sutter Hill partners and to produce a bankable business plan. "It was a very strange sort of beast to them," Levy concludes. But a profitable one. As Sutter Hill structured the investment, a mere $100,000 in outside equity purchased 60 percent of the company, a price equivalent to ½¢ a share on stock that went public at $12 and remained a big winner although it had plunged below $2 late in 1984.

Draper, whose fascination with politics had once lured him into a disastrous run for a Congressional seat (against Paul N. McCloskey and Shirley Temple Black), eventually went off to Washington to serve as chairman of the Export-Import Bank for the Reagan Administration. Dave Anderson, an outgoing, enthusiastic sort with MIT and Harvard Business School credentials, continues Draper's boosterism approach to dealmaking. But Len Baker, studious and reserved, reinforces Wythes's role as devil's advocate, and only a few proposals get through Sutter Hill's fine screen of analysis. Out of 569 written business proposals in 1983, Sutter Hill financed eleven. Says Wythes: "We don't measure our success by how much money we put out."

By going into deals early, when the prices are lowest, Sutter Hill can afford to ride without panic through the trauma most startups encounter in their early years. In fact, Sutter Hill may hold the record for the longest wait for a payoff from a venture investment—eighteen years. Dionex Corp. began in 1964 as a maker of esoteric instruments—Wythes joked it could sell one to every Nobel Prize winner—and it managed to survive without ever threatening to be really successful. But after a series of mergers, divestitures, and management changes, the company emerged as a leader in a hot new technology called ion chromatography and went public in 1982. Most venture capitalists would long since have written Dionex off as a member of the "living dead." But with only $300,000 invested, Sutter Hill ultimately realized a 30 percent annual rate of return. Looking about him at the big, high-priced deals being put together in the 1980s, Wythes likes to keep the Dionex example fresh in his mind. "The concept now is to put in some money in 1980 and take it public at fifty-five times our price in 1983 and aren't we smart," he says with a grimace. "Those days are going. There are going to be some more 18-year rates of return that will have to be realized, and I hope they will be good ones."

THINKING SMALL

Another prototype for the new West Coast style of venturing was the partnership organized in 1969 by Burton J. McMurtry and Jack Melchor. Both had been engineering managers at Sylvania's electronic warfare operation in Mountain View, and Melchor had gone on to start two successful companies and to dabble in venture capital with his winnings. One of Melchor's startups, HP Associates, was a joint venture with Hewlett-Packard Co. that was ultimately swallowed up by his partner, and he had ended up running another HP division. But Melchor is a fierce individualist, motivated by what he calls the number one human drive—for freedom of action—and it was a natural move to turn his venture capital hobby into a full-time business. McMurtry, who had discovered at Sylvania that he enjoyed starting projects more than he did running them, was willing to join him. And the money was at hand. Melchor had been in touch with the attorney representing Saudi Arabian tycoon Adnan Khashoggi, who was building a multinational business empire. Khashoggi wanted to hazard a few of his millions in venture capital, and that was enough to put the Palo Alto Investment Company in business.

Melchor and McMurtry invested only $3.2 million in sixteen deals over the next four years, but they proved that a strategy of putting modest amounts into startup situations could pay off for those who recognized the right opportunities. The advice they got from others in the business, McCurtry recalls, was to do "mezzanine" investing—financing established companies that were about to go public. "But we could see that the mezzanine thing had crested," he says. "We believed you could make a lot of money by financing new companies that wouldn't necessarily be huge but would be profitable, productive companies." If all the securities in Palo Alto Investment had been held until 1982 they would have been worth over $100 million.

Much of that gain came from a deal that to other investors at the

time looked singularly unpromising. Four Rice and Stanford class-
mates, engineers with no experience in the computer industry and the
oldest only thirty-two, were trying to set up a computer company.
They called it ROLM for Richeson, Oshman, Loewenstern, and Maxfield—names that otherwise did not seem destined for immortality.
M. Kenneth Oshman, who is still chief executive of what became one
of the most successful new companies in America, with sales of over
$600 million in 1984 when it was acquired by IBM, recalls approach-
ing Arthur Rock for funding and getting a careful explanation of the
group's shortcomings. "He said, 'You've got Oshman as president, he's
never managed anything except a few technicians; Walter Loewenstern is heading your digital research and he has never had anything
to do with digital electronics; Bob Maxfield is head of engineering and
he has never designed a computer nor even been on a team that designed computers; and Gene Richeson, your marketing vice president,
has never been in marketing or sales.' So he found it difficult to invest
and of course did not." Rock's response was typical, if better articulated than most, of the chilly reception Oshman was getting in the
venture community. Then he called Jack Melchor.

Even Melchor, who loved to gamble on bright young engineers,
boggled at this group. Not only were they inexperienced, but the business plan they showed him indicated they were planning to pursue
three different products. "You guys are crazy as hell," Melchor told
them. "What you should do is focus on one thing and make that happen. Now go decide which one it should be." Actually, Oshman insists, the group had already decided to specialize in "ruggedized" minicomputers for the military market but had not had a chance to put
the strategy in writing. Once that was cleared up, Melchor agreed to
match the ante put up by each founder with $15,000 of his own
money—Palo Alto Investment was not yet organized—and to guarantee a line of credit. Melchor never did explain to Oshman why he
agreed to invest, although an endorsement from McMurtry, who knew
some of the group at Sylvania, certainly helped. "It wasn't so much
that he thought the military market was good, bad, or indifferent,"
Oshman speculates. "Jack invests in people he thinks might make it."

Nine months later, with Palo Alto Investment in business, Melchor
was in a position to help ROLM raise some serious money. But time
was running out because the company's initial $75,000 of capital and
more than $100,000 in bank borrowings had been soaked up in the
development of its first product. And once again Oshman was getting
fishy looks from investors. He recalls a meeting at which principals of
two venture firms bargained him down from $14 to $12 per share,
shook hands and promised that they would have approvals from their
investment committees within a week. "Two weeks later they called
and said they were sorry but they weren't going to do it." At that

point, with ROLM near bankruptcy, Melchor stepped in and put the
deal together with a display of machismo: "I called all these guys who
were screwing around with it and said I'm going to my ranch (in Morgan Hill, south of San Jose) for the weekend and if I don't hear from
you by Monday it'll be done. I was prepared to do it all, between Palo
Alto Investment and myself, but finally several of them came back
in." The deal was done at $8, which in current terms, after splits,
means the investors paid 16¢ per share for stock that went as high as
$80, and for which IBM agreed to pay $70 in its offer to buy the
company.

Melchor's approach to full-time venturing reflected the success he
had enjoyed as leader of an informal investment and drinking club at
Hewlett-Packard. A dozen or so executives put about $5,000 apiece
into the pot, then gathered once a month to discuss deals. HP was a
magnet for people with new ideas in electronics, and HP people knew
how to judge talent. So the Page Mill Group, as it came to be called
after HP's headquarters address, profited hugely on modest early-stage
investments in such companies as Biomation, Kasper Instruments,
and Anderson-Jacobson. At Palo Alto Investment, Melchor continued to seek the low-capitalization deals, solid companies with no exaggerated goals, rather than expensive long shots trying to take on
IBM. "I have never been a proponent that the first product has to be
a multimillion-dollar type of market," he says. "What I want the first
product to do is provide a viable base from which to move." ROLM
became an outstanding practitioner of that strategy by using its base
in military computers to jump into digital telephone equipment just
in time to ride to glory on the deregulation wave that swept over the
telecommunications industry in the late 1970s.

Despite the success of Palo Alto Investment, Melchor disliked the
day-to-day drudgery of running a large fund. Strong-willed and im-
patient of detail work, Melchor impressed George Polos, an entrepreneur who worked for him briefly in the early 1980s, as "a seat-of-the-
pants manager who doesn't do much homework. He makes good
decisions but you wonder how he gets his information." In 1973 Melchor told McMurtry he wanted to be "less engaged" and returned to
private investing, doing occasional deals for an expanded Page Mill
Group—it now included such Silicon Valley luminaries as Noyce of
Intel and C. Lester Hogan of Fairchild—and for his own account. His
return to active venturing with a $12 million fund in 1980 produced
some modest winners and one spectacular failure in Osborne Computer Corp., which collapsed into bankruptcy after racing to a sales
level of $100 million in three years. As a specialist in low-capitaliza-
tion "seed" investments, Melchor has opted out of the new-era venture business with its enormous funds, multiple-partner firms, and
multimillion-dollar syndicated financings. "I don't even feel comfort-

able going into those big deals," he says. But his little deals have a way of turning into big opportunities for other investors, and his willingness to back untested talent and unpretentious ideas is a valued resource for Silicon Valley entrepreneurs.

NOTES

1. "Making a Mint Overnight," *Time*, January 23, 1984, p. 44.
2. "Blue-Ribbon Venture Capital," *Business Week*, October 29, 1960, p. 65.
3. Thomas J. Davis Jr., "How to Pick a Winner in the Electronics Industry," address to the Western Electronic Manufacturers Association, Palo Alto, September 15, 1966.
4. "Why Qume Shot Ahead in Electronic Printers," *Business Week*, June 13, 1977, p. 42J.

4

THE SAN FRANCISCO MAFIA

The venture capital community that grew up in San Francisco in the 1960s was a closeknit fraternity. The handful of serious investors who backed entrepreneurs was known as The Group or The Boys Club, amused references to the ties many of them had to private wealth as well as their clannishness. One noontime each month they would troop up Nob Hill to the University Club for a meeting of the Western Association of Venture Capitalists, ideas and gossip flowing with the martinis. Deals were put together over lunch at Jack's or Sam's, venerable Financial District restaurants where the sole was dependable and the sourdough fresh. "We'd get together and listen to the entrepreneur's story," recalls Reid Dennis, a charter member of The Group. "Sometimes we would poll the table and get $100,000 committed over coffee, and we had others we could call so that in a week or two we'd have a $300,000 financing put together."

During the 1970s The Group moved its center of gravity thirty miles south to Sand Hill Road, a four-lane barrier between the Stanford University campus and the pleasant suburb of Menlo Park. Now it is geographically as well as financially part of Silicon Valley, the citadel of entrepreneurship it helped build. And it is the most powerful venture capital enclave in the country, capable of raising in 1982–83 over $1 billion—a quarter of all the funds committed to private venture capital groups in that two-year period.[1] In 1983 seven venture firms based in Northern California controlled megafunds—pools of capital over $100 million—and twenty-three groups invested a total of almost $500 million in more than 750 transactions.[2] But the clubby, comradely spirit of the early days on Montgomery Street persists.

There are two dozen venture capital firms in residence today at 3000 Sand Hill, a sloping sixteen-acre site facing the fog-capped Santa Cruz Mountains where owner-developer Thomas W. Ford has sprawled four clusters of comfortable offices around a rustic restaurant. Table hopping is encouraged and frequently results in deals. One entrepreneur, former Atari executive Roger H. Badertscher, was able to put together a $4 million financing for his new home computer company in a month of trudging between conference rooms at 3000 Sand Hill.[3]

Here and at other low-rise office developments in nearby Palo Alto, Los Altos, and Mountain View, deals can be discussed in low-key comfort, supplicants calmed with views of brown-and-green hills. It is a

49

lifestyle that combines California casualness with Ivy League exclusiv-
ity, a tight little island of brainy, high-energy individuals, almost all
of them white males with engineering and business degrees from top
universities. They are lavishly rewarded. Salaries run from $80,000 to
$150,000, and bonuses can push a year's compensation to $200,000
or more. On top of that, those who share in the partnership interest
of at least 20 percent of the profits can count on a significant additional payoff whenever the firm distributes some stock in one of its
portfolio companies. One young partner told me in wonderment:
"There are a lot of 1040s from venture capitalists in my class of well
over $1 million in one year."

Business relationships evolve into close personal ties between partnerships. The older partners invite each other to dinner parties, the
younger generation organizes raft trips and barbecues to size each other
up. And it is often these connections that determine who is invited
into deals, who not. Don Valentine, a leader of the Sand Hill Road
community, explains: "You work with guys who, first, you like and,
second, whose dependability you understand. Our companies go
through very fragile periods and we want partners in each company
whose behavior we can predict."

At first the Californians had to rely on outside help to swing the
bigger deals. But their growing financial power made it less and less
necessary to look east for capital. In contrast to the Measurex deal,
Bessemer and Oak Investment Partners, the only East Coast funds in
the initial financing for Badertscher's Mindset Corp., took just 30
percent of the deal this time. The Group provided all of a $4.5 million
startup financing for Linear Technology and two-thirds of the $7.7
million raised in 1984 by Sierra Semiconductor. East Coast venturers
began referring to the "San Francisco Mafia" as a closed club that
keeps the best deals to itself. "I've had people call up and berate me
for not letting New York into deals," says Wallace F. Davis, a founder
of the Mayfield Fund. "They should have set up shop out here fifteen
years ago." Bessemer and several others have done just that, but the
bias in favor of working with fellow Group members persists.

Of course, not every venture firm in the San Francisco area is part
of The Group. There is a hierarchy among venture capitalists, compounded from such ingredients as a firm's longevity, its past successes,
its deal flow, and the personal ties built up over the years, that determines who works with whom, who sees the best deals and who has
the most leverage in setting prices. No one firm or individual is at the
top of every list, and the lists change constantly as winners and losers
emerge from old funds, as partners come and go and—infrequently—
change firms, and as new partnerships are formed. By the early 1980s
there was a common denominator among the groups at the top of most
lists in the Sand Hill Road neighborhood: They were dominated by
partners recruited from the ranks of industry, and their approach to

the business of venture investing reflected that background. They were, they said, "pro-active," implying that others were mere passive investors. True to their training in product development groups and marketing teams at fast-moving electronics companies, the new venturers refused to sit waiting for deals to materialize. Rather, they went after them with a broad network of industry contacts, often starting with their own analysis of industry trends. They supervised the writing of business plans. They matched people with ideas, recruited managers and engineers, provided contacts with lawyers, product designers, accountants, real estate agents, and public relations counselors. As directors of the ventures they backed, they rode herd not just on financial performance but on engineering progress and marketing strategies. In their own minds they were not just investors but corporate architects who measured their achievements as much in terms of organizational growth or market penetration or technical excellence as return on investment.

WINNING THROUGH DISCORD

With Jack Melchor in quasi-retirement, Burt McMurtry started looking for a new partner and new investors. He found both in Reid W. Dennis, a jowly, ruddy-complexioned native San Franciscan who ran a big mutual fund organization for Fireman's Fund Insurance. Dennis had been involved in venture capital virtually from the day he went to work as a securities analyst in 1952, perhaps urged on by the example of his grandfather, who had declined when a friend offered to sell him half of his struggling business for $12,000. The friend's name, Dennis swears, was Harvey Firestone. Dennis talked his way into a private placement for Ampex Corp., then a floundering newcomer, using $15,000 in family money to buy a holding later worth close to $1 million. He became a stalwart of The Group that met occasionally to do deals over lunch. He also persuaded Fireman's Fund to begin doing some venture investing but found it stifling to operate in an institutional setting. So he had decided to set up his own venture fund, and American Express, which had acquired Fireman's Fund, was willing to back him with $5 million. But he needed partners and another $15 million.

Dennis and McMurtry recruited two other partners—one departed early on—and set out late in 1973 to raise money for the fund they called Institutional Venture Associates just as the entire securities industry was sinking into deep recession. They talked to thirty insurance companies, assuming that Dennis's connections would pay off, but generated little enthusiasm. One problem, Dennis felt, was that many of the money managers they talked to had already invested in the enormous $81 million venture fund raised in Chicago four years earlier by Edgar F. Heizer, Jr. Heizer would eventually do well on his big stake in Amdahl Corp. but at the time Amdahl was struggling and the investors were nervous. After six months of traveling, the IVA partners finally settled for $14 million from five insurance companies and the Ford Foundation, which with the American Express contribution gave them a third of all the money raised for venture capital that year.

They were an ill-assorted group. Dennis was a breezy optimist who made investment decisions on the spur of the moment, and he was used to getting his way. Burgess Jamieson, a recruit from another venture group, was reserved where Dennis was outgoing and cautious where Dennis was eager. McMurtry, something of a blend of the other two personalities, took a methodical approach to the business of investing that reflected his engineering background, but he was capable of working up enthusiasm that spilled out in a disarming smile. Inevitably, there was conflict. The partnership nearly tore itself apart in 1975 when Dennis developed an infatuation for a little company called Collagen Corp., which consisted of a research project aimed at developing a treatment for burns and scars. The partners agreed to put in an initial $150,000 to fund the work, but no progress was reported after a few months and Jamieson and McMurtry voted to shut it down. "We weren't going to get sucked in," McMurtry says. Dennis, who by now had become acting president of Collagen, pleaded for continuing support. "I think there's still room for gut feel in venture capital," Dennis told his partners, "and I feel Collagen is something we should do." McMurtry finally backed him, "because you want to do it, not because I think we should do it." IVA ended up pouring $2.25 million into Collagen and managed to achieve a fivefold return when the company finally went public in 1981. "He just dragged us into this thing and it took phenomenal amounts of his time," says McMurtry, "but it ultimately became something successful in the IVA portfolio and Reid deserves all the credit."

Despite the friction, IVA went on to record one of the best track records of the 1970s. Its portfolio was worth $90 million by the end of 1979 and over $200 million by 1983, thanks in large measure to follow-on investments McMurtry arranged in ROLM and Triad Systems, his two big winners in Palo Alto Investment. But the biggest payoff—$55 million in distributed stock—came from a $1.7 million investment in NBI Inc. of Boulder, Colo. NBI, a maker of word processing equipment which had sales of over $175 million in 1984, now is seen as a model of how the top venture capitalists can add value to a startup situation. But things were so dark at one point that McMurtry scribbled a note to himself during a particularly gloomy NBI board meeting: "Write off $1 million (the amount IVA had invested at that point) against R (meaning ROLM) profits. Shut it down or start over?" He was not despairing, only reminding himself that there was no point in worrying about his million dollars. "A mistake a lot of venture investors make," he says, "is they get into a situation like that and start ranting and raving at the management or they disappear from the scene and won't return calls. They've suddenly become frightened that they've lost their money."

McMurtry very nearly rejected NBI before he had looked at it. Thomas Kavanagh, a founder of Storage Technology Corp., had taken over the struggling little computer company and needed substantial backing for his attempt to push it into the office automation field. He knew Dennis, who was a director of STC, but his call to IVA was bounced to McMurtry. Recalls Kavanagh: "Burt gets on the phone and in the first thirty seconds proceeds to tell me that it was nice of me to call but probably wasted effort because IVA had just looked at a company called Vydec and while they hadn't done the investment it obviously was going to be the last word processing company that was going to make it." But McMurtry was impressed by Kavanagh's pitch on his strategy to seek the most difficult—and profitable—office applications. He and Dennis flew to Boulder and promised to invest providing Kavanagh could find a star-quality marketing vice president. That was fine with Kavanagh, and he promptly enlisted IVA to aid in the search. McMurtry turned up a promising candidate in Mark Stevenson, then national sales manager for Xerox's word processing operation in Texas. And when Stevenson turned down NBI's offer at first, McMurtry and Kavanagh flew to Dallas on Thanksgiving weekend to change his mind. Says a grateful Kavanagh: "It was a classical example of how a venture guy can assist a startup company in helping to attract the kind of talent you have to have."

NBI succeeded, McMurtry believes, largely because of the strength of its management. "The major lesson to me out of NBI," he says, "is to get involved only with teams of top-flight people." IVA turned down an investment in Atari because McMurtry thought it was running "open-loop"—engineering argot for a lack of control. What McMurtry liked about the venture capital business, he discovered, was the chance to work closely with talented managers in building an enterprise. He found the end of a relationship, even a successful public offering that substantially increased his wealth, to be oddly depressing. It was anticlimactic in the sense that that particular game was over. As the IVA fund began wrapping up in 1979, McMurtry decided to form a new partnership, one that would reflect his style of participative investing—a "partnership of peers," he called it. Dennis agreed to the separation. "We weren't enjoying it as much as we should have," he explains.

DIVIDING TO MULTIPLY

Out of IVA's breakup came two important new firms, neighbors in the 3000 Sand Hill Road complex but worlds apart in style. Dennis's Institutional Venture Partners raised $22 million and scored immediately by putting $500,000 into Seagate Technology, a maker of disk drives for personal computers. Dennis distributed $55 million in Seagate stock to his investors three years later. But it was David F. Marquardt, a brilliant young engineer recently hired by IVA, who had persuaded Dennis to do the Seagate deal. And Marquardt decided, shortly before the firm divided, to go with McMurtry and his $24 million Technology Venture Investors fund instead of staying with Dennis. McMurtry had already brought in James J. Bochnowski, a venture capitalist turned high-tech manager, and the addition of Marquardt and later Pete Thomas from Intel, James A. Katzman from Tandem Computers, and Robert C. Cagle from the Boston Consulting Group gave him a team of partners who could play the startup game with as much fervor as he did.

McMurtry believes that only a peer partnership, where even the most senior partner has just one vote and no veto, can attract the best talent to venture capital. "In most venture groups somebody with my seniority would be able to invest on his own," he says. "But I wanted to get guys who I perceived were very very good, and the way you find world class guys is to bring them in on a peer basis." TVI operates on the assumption that venture investing has changed radically in the last few years, in part because the pace of change in entrepreneurial organizations has accelerated. Marquardt, a serious student of his industry, puts it this way: "Product life cycles are so short and the markets are getting so competitive that companies are looking for more than financial guidance. They want to get investors involved who are able to help them with strategy issues, with recruiting, with a whole range of things. I really view our role as more applied business policy than straight financial guidance."

Money alone was certainly not what won TVI a chance to put $1 million into Microsoft Corp., an early leader in microcomputer software. The company, which had been co-founded in 1975 by William H. Gates, then a Harvard sophomore, was generating more cash than it could use when Marquardt heard in the fall of 1980 that Gates was interested in lining up his first outside investor. "They absolutely didn't need our money," Marquardt recalls, "but they wanted outside counsel and I was the first venture capitalist they had talked to who understood their business." Marquardt, who had been a computer hobbyist for years, spoke Gates's language well enough to win a place on the Microsoft board of directors, an honor that sometimes involves 2 a.m. debates on subtleties of computer design.

Bochnowski's background—he left venture capital for four years to become chief operating officer and then president of disk drive maker Shugart Associates—assures that TVI at least hears about every new company formation in the overcrowded field of computer peripheral equipment. With a shakeout inevitable, Bochnowski says, "the key is to pick areas where we can be one of the top three." TVI tries to do that not by second-guessing the direction of technology but by applying McMurtry's philosophy: management is all-important. "It's people in the industry who have the best ideas of where the opportunities are," Bochnowski explains. To make sure they are backing top people, the TVI partners will often do a dozen or more reference checks on each individual, trying not to be overly influenced by their personal reactions. Says Bochnowski: "Personal chemistry is not a totally reliable guide. We have to talk to people who've been with them through good times and bad."

In contrast to McMurtry's partnership of peers, Dennis at first ran IVP as his personal fiefdom. This was partly because John K. Poitras, the only associate remaining when Marquardt decamped, had only modest experience in venture capital. Mary Jane Elmore, who joined IVP from Intel two years later, was an investment novice. Dennis felt he had to exert strong leadership until his new partners were up to speed. "In terms of making investment decisions," he says, "the most important single thing is to judge the people and it takes a long time to develop the frame of reference to do that." Just as important, perhaps, was the reliance Dennis placed on his own intuition. In one case, early in 1981, he and Poitras met with Wilf Corrigan, the former chief executive of Fairchild, then trying to raise $6 million for his new venture in chipmaking. They agreed they should do the deal. "John wanted to wait and make a couple of calls on Monday," Dennis recalls, "but I had a hunch that the deal would come together so rapidly that we'd have a much bigger position if we committed on Friday." IVP did commit $1 million immediately and although its position was cut back later to $700,000 ended up as the second largest investor in LSI Logic, a holding valued at $22 million at the end of 1983.

Dennis still believes in his hunches, but he has been working on making IVP more of a true partnership. In the case of Sequent, all three IVP partners were in on a fast-paced maneuver that got them into an important deal at the cost of some hurt feelings in The Group. Elmore had known the Sequent team at Intel and started calling them as soon as she heard they had left. A deal was already in the works, it seemed, but as a courtesy to a former colleague Sequent invited Elmore to drop in. The IVP partners piled into Dennis's Cessna turboprop (he is an instrument-rated pilot) and flew to Oregon. They were impressed by the enthusiasm—even arrogance, Dennis thought—of the Sequent team and learned that the price being discussed by other venture firms was a problem. "They had what I saw as unrealistic thoughts about the valuation of the company," Dennis says, "but there are a number of ways to value these things and there was a substantial reserve for future employees."

The partners excused themselves for a brief meeting in a warehouse behind Sequent's rented building, then marched back in to make an offer that was too good to refuse, one that valued the company at $15 million instead of the $10 million that would be standard for a computer startup. IVP was in the deal and TVI, which had been talking to Sequent but decided the price was now too steep, was out. "No hard feelings," says Bochnowski. "We just feel we have to impose discipline on ourselves." But a partner in another firm that stayed in the deal is critical: "That is probably the most egregious example of overzealous competition that I can cite in recent times."

"A PARTNERSHIP
TWENTY-FOUR HOURS A DAY"

Mayfield Fund grew out of a dream Wally Davis had nurtured of repaying Stanford University, his alma mater, for the contributions its engineering department was making to the high-tech industries, in which he had made a modest fortune. Wally had graduated in aeronautical engineering just before World War II and gone right into the advanced aircraft work going on at nearby Moffett Field. He ended up working for NASA and when the Sputnik era arrived was able to get backing from Laurance Rockefeller and from Itek Corp., one of Rockefeller's most successful early investments, to start his own company, Vidya Inc., doing contract research for the new ballistic missile program. Within a few years Vidya had been merged into Itek and Wally was commuting to Boston as Itek's director of research and development. The obvious thing would have been to move to Boston, but Wally preferred California. And he had a plan for a venture fund that would be closely tied to the academic community at Stanford, with the university taking a cut of the profits. When a mutual friend introduced the two Davises, Tommy thought it sounded like a good idea.

Stanford's trustees thought it was a terrible idea, likely to cause conflicts of interest, and ruled out a formal tie. Undaunted, the Davises raised their fund from individuals willing to donate 15 percent of their returns to Stanford, and they lined up several engineering professors to help evaluate deals in return for a share in the carried interest of the partnership. The payoff from this arrangement was slender. Few of the professors knew or cared enough about the business world to be of much use as advisers, and the largesse to Stanford was hardly large enough to dispel the trustees' qualms. The whole concept was greatly toned down in the next fund that the Davises raised, and eventually it was scrapped altogether. But the ties to Stanford still are obvious in Mayfield's choice of partners—all but Tommy Davis have at least one Stanford degree—and in the number of deals it builds around Stanford entrepreneurs. What truly sets Mayfield apart, though, is an earnest and low-key approach to the business that reflects the self-effacing personality and idealism of Tommy Davis. "If I could emulate anybody in this business," remarks a young partner in another firm, "it would be Tommy Davis. He is everything you want to be and none of the things you don't want to be."

Mayfield's partners make up an eclectic group, ranging in age from early seventies (Tommy Davis) to early thirties (Michael J. Levinthal) and in background from management consulting (Norman A. Fogelsong, who spent two years at McKinsey & Co., and Glenn M. Mueller, who ran his own consulting firm) to observing baboons (A. Grant Heidrich III, who worked with Jane Goodall while pursuing a biology degree). With the departure of Wally Davis, who moved down the hall to start a new firm, only F. Gibson Myers Jr., a onetime Hewlett-Packard manager, fits the new stereotype of the venturer as experienced high-tech operator. But they all fit the Tommy Davis model—energetic, likable, incredibly loquacious. Facility in communication is a requirement for employment in most venture capital firms today, but Mayfield carries it to an extreme of continuous discourse. Mueller has even installed telephones in both his car and his boat so as never to be out of touch. And Fogelsong employs something like total recall. Ask him anything, Tommy Davis says delightedly, "and pretty soon he comes out with the Encyclopedia Britannica." The Mayfield partners meet religiously every Monday morning to hash over deals, and they are more likely than most other firms to get together off the job. "It's a partnership twenty-four hours a day," says Levinthal.

Mayfield often backs companies in the early stages of development and has added 1,500 square feet of offices for entrepreneurs trying to "incubate" their ventures. But its size has led it to concentrate more and more on large projects, leading Wally Davis to raise his own fund to do the "seed" investments he enjoys. "When you have sixty companies," he declares, "you are really a portfolio manager and you can't pay very much attention to any one of them." What Mayfield looks for in an investment is a complete management team with a clear strategy, and it is usually willing to wait until a venture has met these criteria. This strategy does not guarantee a trouble-free investment, however. Mayfield turned down David Lam, a onetime Hewlett-Packard researcher, when he sought funding in 1980 for a company to develop exotic etching equipment for semiconductor manufacturing. "He came out of the labs and said he wanted to be president," explains Fogelsong. "We decided he didn't have the management experience that would be necessary." Lam went ahead with $1 million in backing from other sources, and within a year had produced a prototype on schedule, an impressive enough performance to persuade Mayfield to join in a $1.5 million followup financing. But a few months later Lam Research was out of money and Fogelsong had to jump into a crash effort with other investors to come up with another $1.5 million in "bridge" money to keep things going until a new chief executive could be recruited to turn the situation around. Mayfield realized a $3 million profit on its $838,000 investment when Lam Research went public in 1984.

For Mayfield's partners, the real test of a venture capitalist's worth comes when an entrepreneur needs advice or support or sterner measures. Again, it is Tommy Davis whose example they hope to follow. Jimmy Treybig, the founder of Tandem Computers Inc., recalls a session with Davis shortly after Tandem had shipped the first of the fault-tolerant computers that would ultimately make it one of the fastest-growing companies of the 1970s: "We shipped our first one in June and then in July we got no more orders. Tommy called me up and said why didn't I come down and have lunch. He spent a whole hour telling me how he had lived and survived as a guerrilla in World War II, which basically was to be careful, to conserve your energy. He was trying to tell me to be reasonable, not let my confidence be destroyed even though we were not going to get orders like we thought we would. So I wrote down on a napkin the orders we were going to get, and somehow I was right, in the next three weeks we got all of them. That was luck, but the point was that Tommy was willing to still stick with us." Because it can build this kind of trust, Mayfield frequently is called in first when things go sour at a portfolio company. As often as not, the problems require a management change. So Mayfield spends more time on hiring problems than most venture capital firms and even added a "recruiting partner" who specializes in filling management jobs at the portfolio companies. Says Tommy Davis: "We're taking a chance with him to see if this enhances our ability to find the kind of people our companies need."

Startup investments in Applied Biosystems, Businessland, Equatorial Communications, LSI Logic and other significant winners have given Mayfield one of the better rates of return in the venture business, but the decisions have often been made almost instinctively. For a while, Gib Myers and the newer partners tried nudging Mayfield toward a more rigorous decision making process, one based on regular strategic planning sessions and a search for strong positions in basic technology. In the end, the group found it impossible to be that formal, and Davis points to several successful investments that were based more on feel than conviction. One was Equatorial Communications Co., which proposed to build low-cost earth stations for receiving transmissions of data via satellite. This was in the mid-1970s, before deregulation of the telecommunications industry made it obvious there would be any kind of open market for such equipment. And the plan was to put the power of a 12′ antenna in a dish only three feet across. Davis thought the whole idea was absurd, but he was intrigued enough to put up a few thousand dollars to start work on the concept. The development work went well, Mayfield added $1.2 million, and the investment was worth $20 million when Equatorial went public. "I think a lot of people don't use intuition the way I do," Davis told me. "Venture capital is so uniquely an industry of human beings that all you can do is to try to hazard which way the odds are pointing. All I do is to tap some sort of data base that's been built up over years and years of sweating it out in this business. When I get a warm feeling about something, maybe it's because it has a relationship to this company or that person. What else is there when the facts are not comprehensible?"

At an age when most men have discarded their sense of wonder, Tommy Davis still is capable of an almost childlike delight in the new ideas that cross his desk. He recalls vividly the day he learned that genetic engineering was possible. "Gib and I were sitting around and he told me that Bob Swanson (the founder of Genentech Inc.) had got hold of a professor who had spliced a gene. He started talking about something else, but I couldn't listen to him. I was thinking, my God, think of altering one of nature's most fundamental processes. The world is different, it can never be the same." One of the joys of venture capital is the ability to do something useful when a great notion comes along. Davis and Myers went off to see Swanson and ended up putting $225,000 into Genentech. A similar thrill of discovery hit Davis when Mayfield funded a group of Stanford chemical engineers—including one who had financed his work on a doctorate by performing in a rock band—that was trying to shake the world with a new generation of catalysts. "When we meet with those fellows it's just marvelous," Davis exults. "We hug each other and dance around. I don't know if we're going to make any money out of this, but if it works we'll have done a wonderful thing. Made a lot of money, but that's not all of it. We'll have improved the production of fuel by great amounts, making less profligate use of materials. We've got a couple of things like that, so exciting to me that I can hardly stand it."

THE STRATEGIST

When Donald T. Valentine moved to Sand Hill Road late in 1972, he brought along the reputation and the network of contacts that befitted a certified hero of the chip wars. First he had crafted the marketing strategies and organized the sales forces that helped make Fairchild Semiconductor a winner in the early 1960s. Then he had duplicated that performance at National Semiconductor, a failed company that venture capital and a new management team had rescued and pushed to prominence. Everybody in the valley knew Don Valentine, and if Valentine didn't know them, he usually knew somebody who did. Valentine had looked for loyalty in building his marketing organizations, and as a venture capitalist he played his old networks for leads and intelligence. What was most remarkable about Valentine's approach to venturing, however, was his ability to formulate an investment strategy based on carefully articulated views of market opportunities and technology trends and then to stay with his plan. Says one admirer of Valentine's discipline: "If his strategy said he could only put 30 percent of his resources into, say, instrumentation but enough came through that he could put in 60 percent, he would put in 30. Not 31, 30."

Strategy, for Valentine, started with the assumption that a company serving a market where demand is high would be a better investment than a company forced to pioneer a product for which there was no market. To him, the market outlook was a far more important element of the investment decision than, for example, the quality of the management team. Valentine explains: "We isolate risks into four categories. There are people risks, market risks, product development risks, and finance risks. We will not invest in a company unless we understand and are comfortable with three of those risks. And the risk that I'm least willing to take is the market risk."

Valentine's aggressive networking and strategic insight made him the first venture capitalist to see the investment potential in Atari and Apple Computer, arguably the two most important high-tech startups of the 1970s. His returns on both deals were relatively modest—fourfold in a year on a $600,000 investment in Atari and thirtyfold in three years on $200,000 in Apple. But the subsequent growth of the companies lent credence to Valentine's strategic approach to venture investing. His first $7 million fund compounded at an annual rate of 51 percent between its initial investments in 1974 and its termination six years later. The second fund was three times larger and grew even faster—a 71 percent annual rate between April of 1979 and October of 1983—as a result of timely investments in companies making computer peripheral equipment. (Valentine figures returns conservatively, using the value of securities on the day they were distributed to his investors and ignoring subsequent appreciation.) A third fund launched late in 1981 with $44 million targeted communications, semiconductors, and medical electronics. By 1984 Valentine's Sequoia Capital partnership had raised over $150 million in four funds, the latest $90 million solicited largely from institutions contacted by telephone.

The philosophy that informs Valentine's investment decisions grew out of his days as a semiconductor marketing tactician. Fairchild was pioneering the use of integrated circuits by makers of electronic equipment, from computers to missile guidance systems, and Valentine as head of marketing soon found that demand was outstripping the ability of his engineers to develop new designs. "We had to have a way of analyzing the customer before we committed our limited resources to custom circuits," Valentine recalls. "I had a view into a lot of successful companies." The components of success, he decided, were product differentiation, a fast-growing market, a team of dedicated people, and money. "If you had all four you had a good company." At National, Valentine joined a team of ex-Fairchild managers in building a major company with limited resources and learned how to overcome deficiencies in the last category. "Lack of money is a terrific discipline," he says. "One of the things we try to impose on the companies we invest in is to insist that the amount of money they get focuses them into a very narrow channel. We don't want them moving off whatever they've decided to do."

Valentine's solution to the marketing problems created by National's cash shortage was a classic. Instead of following the traditional industry approach of selling perhaps 15 percent of his volume through independent distributors, Valentine upped the percentage to 40. "Because guess what?" chortles Marshall Cox, an old semiconductor hand who is now a distributor and part of Valentine's network. "He got to use the distributor's bucks. So he saved on having to expand the sales force, passed a sixty-day receivable on to the distributor and insisted that the distributor pay National in thirty days. And the distributors loved it and absolutely drove National up the scale."

Valentine started investing privately while he was at Fairchild and continued the practice at National. And because he was often pressed into service to make presentations on products, markets, and applications for the analysts and portfolio managers who followed the companies' stock, Valentine got to know R. Michael Shanahan of Capital Research & Management, now known as the Capital Group, a big money management organization based in Los Angeles. Shanahan had organized a rewarding investment in the startup of Advanced Micro Devices Inc. in 1968, and that had led Capital to think about backing a professionally managed venture fund. Shanahan approached Valentine: Would Don be willing to start investing fulltime if Capital started him off with $1 million? Valentine agreed, although it took him six months to raise another $6 million. In a sense, Valentine felt, it was the perfect time to be raising money. Only a few firms could raise any money at all, he reasoned, and therefore those who could raise money were in a position to do better deals at more favorable prices than when money was freely available. "Now I can raise $90 million on the telephone," he mused in early 1984. "The fact that it is easier for us to raise money indicates it is also easier for other people and therefore the commodity is less valuable."

A compact, athletic man with an Ivy League look and an ironic turn of phrase, Valentine delights in argument, particularly when he

can turn his acid humor on business shibboleths and traditions that
he has declared outworn. What he lacks in warmth, say acquaintances, he makes up in loyalty to those he works with and an ability
to bring out the best in people. A key element in Valentine's network
at first was the army of semiconductor salesmen who had worked for
him at Fairchild and National. They were constantly running across
new ventures, Valentine knew, and he made them a proposition: You
find the companies that look attractive, and if I invest I'll get you
shares at my price. Valentine eventually formalized that arrangement
by setting up a "side fund" for perhaps three dozen business acquaintances and entrepreneurs. The fund is invested in parallel with Sequoia's major funds, raised from institutions, but the investors pay no
fees and Valentine and his partners collect no carried interest. "They
pay us with one thing," Valentine says. "With help. Part of our staffing
is a phantom staffing of these independent people."

As he brought in partners, Valentine sought people he knew well
but who had networks of their own. Gordon Russell and Pierre R.
Lamond had both been at Fairchild, Russell moving on to head the
medical instruments operation at Syntex Corp., Lamond going to National and then to brief stints as president of two smaller companies.
Walter F. Baumgartner, a finance specialist, came from Bank of America's venture group. Valentine insists that the firm "isn't an environment where you have structure, where you can give people orders or
assignments." But Sequoia's partners do divide the flow of deals fairly
rigorously. Russell acts as point man on medical equipment, Lamond
on manufacturing-related technologies, Baumgartner on computer
memories, although all do deals in every area. Valentine at first had
the most visible deals, the big winners in computers, consumer products, or semiconductors, but in recent years the others have produced
a fair share of successes as well.

It was a Fairchild salesman who brought Atari to Valentine's attention in 1974. The company had been started two years earlier by Nolan K. Bushnell, a six-foot-four free spirit who had worked his way
through engineering school by managing games at an amusement
park. Bushnell wanted to use computer technology to create games,
and after an initial flop called *Computer Space* he had come up with
Pong, a kind of table tennis played on a TV screen. For a while, people
were dropping quarters into *Pong* consoles in bars and bus terminals
across the country as if hypnotized. But interest in *Pong* faded as fast
as it had grown, and by 1974 Atari was deeply in debt and losing
money. Nevertheless, Valentine was interested. Bushnell, he thought,
was "off the wall," but he discovered that Bushnell had an associate,
Joseph F. Keenan, who was a fine manager—a "brilliant hardhead,"
Bushnell called him. Keenan was off running Kee Games, a company
set up to handle distribution of Atari games, and Valentine suggested

merging the two companies to bring Keenan's skills to bear on Atari's problems. With that change accomplished, Valentine was willing to organize the financing for Atari's recovery strategy—a move into the home market.

Valentine had been doing a lot of thinking about the potential markets for video games and had decided—wrongly, it turned out—that the coin-operated game business would never be large enough to support a major company. What intrigued him about Atari was Bushnell's plans for a home game system, which fit into a conviction he had that the focus of electronic entertainment was shifting to the home. Valentine had no doubt at all that the market for home video games would be a large one. "People were pouring hundreds of thousands of quarters into arcade games," he points out. "The only question was, what would people pay to do this at home? At a low price per game player and a low price per game, I didn't perceive that there was much demand risk at all." By the summer of 1975, Valentine had found two investors willing to match the $600,000 he was putting into Atari— Mayfield Fund, which occupied a neighboring office, and Time Inc., which was beginning to dabble in venture capital—and by the end of the year he had snared another $300,000 from Fidelity Venture Associates of Boston. But the $2.1 million capital infusion was far from enough. Instead of the 50,000 home versions of *Pong* it expected to sell, Atari shipped over 200,000 in the first year and still failed to keep up with orders. With estimates of demand running into the millions, Atari was critically short of the working capital needed to build up its production and inventory capacity overnight.

The company had to be sold, Valentine decided. There had been some talk of taking it public, a course favored by Bushnell, but the need was for $50 million to $100 million—too much for the shaky mid-1970s market for initial public offerings to provide. It fell to Valentine and Keenan to persuade Bushnell to sell out, a process that had to be repeated two or three times. "It was his first company, like a child, and he didn't want to give it up," Valentine explains. Bushnell eventually came around and agreed to contacting three potential merger partners in the entertainment business—Walt Disney Productions, MCA, and Warner Communications—that had pockets deep enough to fund Atari's growth. Only Warner chairman Steven J. Ross expressed interest, and by September 1976 he had agreed to pay $28 million for Atari. Bushnell netted $15 million on the deal, the venture people quadrupled their money in only a year, and Warner started off on a wild ride that created a $2-billion-a-year enterprise and a new industry that lured an entire generation of Americans into intimate contact with computer technology. The fact that Atari, after a prolonged period of Warner mismanagement, also produced one of the biggest annual losses ($536 million in 1983) ever suffered by an American company in no way belittles Bushnell's accomplishment or Valentine's foresight in backing him.

Valentine got one other reward from his investment in Atari—an acquaintance with a brash kid named Steven Jobs, who worked for Atari and who showed up from time to time at Bushnell's parties. Early in 1977 Jobs came to see Valentine. He and a friend named Stephen Wozniak, an engineer at Hewlett-Packard, had designed a low-cost computer they thought would sell to the growing legion of computer hobbyists created by the microprocessor revolution. They had raised $1,200 by selling a used Volkswagen and a programmable calculator, but demand was so brisk for the kit of parts they called the Apple that Jobs and Wozniak felt they needed outside capital. Again, Valentine had a strategic concept that called for investing in personal computers. Not only did they fit his idea about the importance of home entertainment, but they rounded out a plan to back computers that could be sold to first-time users. IBM had pretty much locked up the established computer users, he figured, but the microprocessor was making possible a new generation of low-priced computers that could be sold to computer neophytes—small companies and individuals. Sequoia had already bought public shares in Microdata, which made low-cost minicomputers, and joined a second-round investment in CADO Systems, which was targeting its microcomputers at small-business customers. Apple was a chance to get on the last rung of that ladder, a truly personal computer.

But Valentine was reluctant to invest in two very junior engineers—Jobs then was only twenty-one and Wozniak twenty-six—and he suggested they bring in somebody who knew how to organize a business. He gave them three names, including that of A. C. "Mike" Markkula, a marketing whiz Valentine had hired at Fairchild and who had gone on to join Intel in its early days. Markkula now was semi-retired, consulting and doing some investing, but he was intrigued with the Apple concept and agreed to help. The rest is microcomputer history. But Valentine's doubts apparently cost him dearly. It was Venrock Associates, not Valentine, that ended up as lead investor in Apple. And although Valentine did commit $200,000 to the $500,000 first round financing and went on the board of directors, he sold out his position for $6 million in a subsequent private offering rather than waiting for Apple's successful public offering. Valentine's explanation: "When the world badly wants what we have and is willing to pay us twenty or thirty times what we paid for it, our inclination is to let them take it."

After the Apple investment had closed out Valentine's first-time-user strategy in computers, he moved on to deals involving the peripheral equipment new computer owners would have to acquire, including printers (Printronix), disk drives (Tandon and Priam) and magnetic media (Dysan). Altogether, he estimates, Sequoia sank $7 million into a dozen computer-related deals over five years and distributed securities worth more than $120 million. But Valentine's strategic focus also kept him out of opportunities that less disciplined, or more venturesome, investors turned into profits. Deliberately, he says, Sequoia stayed away from the dozens of biotechnology startups that lured more than $90 million a year in venture capital at the peak of the craze in the early 1980s. By mid-1983, according to one estimate, nineteen of these companies had a combined public market value of $2.5 billion.[4] Yet Valentine lays out a typically logical argument to defend his decision not to invest:

The position we took on biotechnology was as follows: There is no market; there are very few identified problems that are resolvable with this kind of technology, and the people currently managing these projects are research people. We probably looked at forty companies that had no management, no market identification, no product application, but were clearly interested in doing research. Terrific, but we're not in the research business. So we said to our clients, we're going to make zero investments in bioengineering. And we forecast this scenario: There will be fifty or sixty companies financed, none of them will have any sales or earn any money for three or four years of their lives, and at some point all these companies are going to collapse and the venture community is going to lose a lot of money. We were 90 percent right. Where we were embarrassingly wrong, it never occurred to us that the public would buy these companies and finance them, that you could raise money publicly for companies that had infinite losses and little damn prospect of sales.

A critical element in Valentine's market-focused strategy is timing. "If we get to a particular party late, we won't play," is his motto—and he cites the example of personal computer software. Sequoia didn't invest in VisiCorp, the leader in financial spread sheets, or in MicroPro, which markets the most successful word processing program, so it has no spread sheet or word processing investments. If he can't be early, Valentine wants nothing to do with the brutal competition in low-cost programs, where he sees too many players and too little profit, and his bets in the software area run to sophisticated products such as programming tools and relational data base management systems for large computers. An exception is a company called Electronic Arts that was launched in 1982 in the spare offices that Valentine maintains for incubating startups. Electronic Arts sells inexpensive programs, but Valentine decided its strategy of concentrating on entertainment- and education-related products for home use set it apart from the dozens of other software startups funded at what he called a "suicidal" pace. "Far too many identical companies are being financed," he grumbles. "The industry doesn't need them and users don't need them and they are going to go away."

Valentine's strongly stated opinions, which make him the reigning iconoclast of Sand Hill Road, stir the most controversy when he discusses the relative importance of management talent and market opportunity in weighing investment decisions. The conventional wisdom, often articulated by Arthur Rock and others, is along the lines of "I'd rather have A people and a B idea than B people and an A idea." The problem with that approach, in Valentine's view, is that it is seldom clear who the A people are. "You usually find out who they are three years later when the company has either crashed or is successful." In a panel discussion, Valentine once used Apple as an example of a company founded by "modest individuals, from any business perspective," that succeeded "well beyond any legitimate expectations of the skill factors of the people involved."[5] If there is no way of knowing in advance who can successfully start and run a new company, Valentine argues, the best way to screen deals is to use the market as a guide. "I am happy to back the best people," he says. "But I would rather be in a position of making judgments on markets than judgments on people," he says. "If it means I have to have B people and an A market, I'll take them every time."

Burt McMurtry, for one, takes exception to that line of thinking: "There are a number of things that Don has financed and made good money at that we probably could never have convinced ourselves to do because the management strength wasn't there." And Tommy Davis is eloquent on the philosophy that shaped his approach to venturing: "My notion was that the whole thing depended on absolutely superb human beings. It was not the gadget that was important, it was the people. And you appraised the chance of success basically on the capabilities of the human being." To which Valentine responds: "People you can change, but you can't change a market. When the demand part of the equation is not there, it is tough to launch a company." Clearly, this debate will never have an unchallenged winner. Both sides can point to winning investments that seem to vindicate their point of view, and both can point to losers or missed opportunities that flowed from the other's. But Don Valentine has demonstrated that a conceptual, market-driven strategy can pay off in venture investing as well as in an industrial setting.

NOTES

1. "Capital Transfusion 1983," *Venture Capital Journal*, January 1984, p. 6.
2. Jon Levine, "3000 Sand Hill Road," *Venture*, December 1983, p. 74.
3. "The Venture Capital 100," *Venture*, June 1984, p. 60.

4. Estimate of dollar investments in genetic engineering is taken from *Venture Capital Journal*, June 1983, p. 8. Market valuation from Office of Technology Assessment, *Commercial Biotechnology: An International Analysis*. Government Printing Office, Washington D.C., 1984, p. 282.

5. "Heel Marks at the Edge of the Cliff," *The Stanford Magazine*, Fall 1982, p. 16.

5

THE NEW
ENTREPRENEURS

The first venture capital team to take up residence at 3000 Sand Hill Road in 1972 seemed an oddly matched pair. Eugene Kleiner, sober and practical, balanced his old-world formality with a kindly nature and a genuine love for the dust and grease of a machine shop. Thomas J. Perkins, driving and restless, was a charismatic corporate gamesman with a gambler's nerve. They were both entrepreneurs, however, and they had the same activist approach to venturing. They managed to invest only $7 million in five years, and their first deals were disasters—seven out of seventeen were written off or marked far below cost. But two of the remaining ten were huge winners, and Kleiner & Perkins eventually distributed securities that in mid-1984 were worth $218 million. For a summary of this portfolio, see Table 1.

The startling success of their first fund allowed Kleiner and Perkins to raise a second of $15 million, a third of $55 million, and finally, in late 1982, a fourth of $150 million—a megafund that at the time was the largest pool of venture capital ever assembled by a private firm. By late 1984 the firm's total investment of $133 million had pyramided to some $600 million, and the companies it helped start had achieved a market value of nearly $5 billion. New partners—two up-and-comers from other firms in The Group, then two aggressive semiconductor samurai from Intel, later a senior executive from Apple Computer—made them "the best collection of venture capitalists in one office," one admirer claimed.

Kleiner Perkins Caufield & Byers, or just Kleiner Perkins, as the firm now is known, even though Eugene Kleiner is not active in the most recent funds, is in many ways the archetype of the West Coast approach to venturing. Although quantitative comparisons with other partnerships are complicated by differences in starting and ending points and thus not very meaningful, it is certain that few funds outperformed that first Kleiner & Perkins fund, which compounded at an annual rate of 51 percent over eight difficult years. But this group has a reputation, even a mystique, that goes beyond rate of return calculations.

What Eugene Kleiner and Tom Perkins did was to push to its logical conclusion the new style of participatory, value-added investment. Like their Sand Hill Road colleagues, they joined eagerly in designing and building the companies they backed, sometimes writing or re-writing the business plan to make it fit their notions of what was tech-

69

TABLE 1
Kleiner & Perkins Portfolio Summary

Venture	Year of Initial Investment	Cost of Investment	Value at June 30, 1984[*]
Advanced Recreation Equipment Corp. (recreational equipment)	1973	$ 229,200	$ 0
Antekna Inc. (electronic training systems)	1973	275,000	150,000
Antex Industries (light-emitting diodes)	1973	200,000	2,529
Applied Materials Inc. (semiconductor processing equipment)	1973	317,658	589,000
Dynastor Inc. (computer disk drives)	1973	497,405	2,713,540[**]
Novacor Medical Corp. (implantable medical products)	1973	219,058	3,369,836
Office Communications Inc. (word processing systems)	1973	429,748	94,453
Qume Corp. (computer printers)	1974	246,762	5,662,748[***]
Speech Technology Corp. (computerized speech products)	1974	41,353	0
American Athletic Shoe Corp. (athletic shoe repair and manufacture)	1975	418,782	0
Cetus Corp. (biomedical products)	1975	500,100	641,795
Tandem Computers Inc. (nonstop computers)	1975	1,450,001	152,204,847
Amdahl Corp. (mainframe computers)	1976	92,500	607,148
Genentech Inc. (biomedical products)	1976	200,005	47,289,150

TABLE 1 (Continued)

Venture	Year of Initial Investment	Cost of Investment	Value at June 30, 1984*
Collagen Corp. (medical products)	1977	655,211	2,370,913
Enviro Development Co. (waste treatment systems)	1977	953,495	0
Andros Analyzers Inc. (gas analysis equipment)	1980	279,059	2,677,010
Total		$7,005,337	$218,372,969

*Includes proceeds from sales, market value of distributed investments, and fair value of investments held by the partnership.
**Merged with Cipher Data Products Inc.
***Acquired by International Telephone & Telegraph Inc.

nically feasible or where the market was headed. But Kleiner and Perkins went a step farther. They hired associates and partners as entrepreneurial as they were, and turned them loose to start companies of their own. Three of these "incubations," as internally started ventures came to be called, were superhits. Tandem Computers Inc., Genentech Inc., and Hybritech Inc. all were the first companies in their respective fields, and all inspired waves of emulation by other venture capitalists.

"They acted as entrepreneurs," says San Francisco investment banker Sanford (Sandy) Robertson, who introduced Perkins to Kleiner and helped them raise money. "That is what really sets them apart." Venture capital neophytes L. J. Sevin and Benjamin M. Rosen delivered the ultimate accolade when they asked Kleiner Perkins for tutelage after raising their first venture fund in 1981. The collaboration resulted in the funding of Compaq Computer Corp. and Lotus Development Corp., two of the biggest venture winners of the early 1980s. "At the time, we viewed them as tops in the business," Sevin told me three years later, "and we haven't changed that opinion."

What has evolved at Kleiner Perkins is not just a successful venture capital firm but a collection of high-powered entrepreneurs who are perfectly capable of starting and running their own companies. They operate much like corporate officers working with a manager charged with bringing a new product to market. If the strategy is wrong, they suggest changes. If the product isn't selling, they go into the field and talk to customers. If the management is weak, they blow the whistle.

Other California firms, and increasingly East Coast firms as well, do all these things now. But at Kleiner Perkins, admits a partner in another top California firm, the level of expertise and of energy is unusually high. "The feedback we get from entrepreneurs," he says, "is that they can go to Kleiner Perkins and get more insight into a technology than we have here." But there is a flip side to this. "These people have very strong personalities. Some entrepreneurs like that and some don't."

"HOW CAN WE MISS?"

Tom Perkins is one of those people who can make a big move—invest a million dollars, quit a job, challenge a boss—without a second thought for the consequences of being wrong. Others might call it egoism or recklessness. Perkins, who dissects his own motivations as readily as he does a prospective investment, calls it a kind of blindness to certain aspects of reality. "I just say, 'How can we miss?,'" Perkins explains. "I hope it isn't megalomania, but I just think it will happen."

We are talking in his glass-walled office on the thirty-fifth floor of the San Francisco highrise to which, always willing to buck a trend, Perkins transplanted most of the firm a few years back. Now in his fifties, Perkins still has an almost boyish manner, a casual confidence that together with his actor's looks and unruly mop of dark hair barely flecked with gray gives him more the air of a yachtsman than a financier. He is that as well, although his days of skippering races in San Francisco Bay are behind him now. He talks animatedly about the art of restoring classic motorcars and proudly autographs a copy of the lavishly illustrated, expensively printed book he has just written about his collection of supercharged sports cars. Improbable question, but: What if you fail? "It doesn't always work out," he admits. "But if you proceed that way, you simply view the problem as a detour on the ultimate route."

Growing up in White Plains, N.Y., Perkins was a science-struck kid always tinkering with Tesla coils and ham radio equipment. He started no lemonade stands, didn't care to operate the radio gear he put together. But the "how can we miss?" confidence was there early. Encouraged by a high school physics teacher, he applied to Massachusetts Institute of Technology, probably the most competitive school for would-be physicists—and only to MIT. "If I can't get in," he thought, "the hell with it. I'll be a radio technician." He did get in, even won a scholarship, but he found the work difficult. Realizing he would be a mediocre physicist, never a great one, he switched from physics to engineering. But two years of working as an engineer was enough, and Perkins enrolled at the Harvard Business School in the fall of 1955, still searching for a role in life.

At Harvard, Perkins fell under the spell of Georges Doriot. The general's classes emphasized understanding the people who make up organizations, helping them interact as a team, and taking entrepreneurial risks. Perkins soaked it up and impressed Doriot as well—he was offered a job at ARD. But Perkins had found another mentor in David Packard, co-founder of what then was a $20-million upstart of a company in California making electronic test instruments. Perkins decided to approach Packard at a trade show in New York. Again: "How could he refuse me?" And again, the Perkins magic worked although the company had no apparent need for an ambitious MBA. He spent the first six months in the machine shop running a lathe and mill until they figured out what to do with him.

What they gave him was the dirty work—situations where something needed changing and Perkins was the designated changer. Hewlett-Packard at the time employed no company salesmen and Perkins was to help bring the independent sales representatives to heel. It was challenging but eventually frustrating. Within five years he had made two more impulsive moves. He left Hewlett-Packard for a consulting job, then bounced into a promising new company called Optics Technology, headed by a Sikh scientist—the father of fiber optics—named Narinder Kapani. But he and Kapani disagreed on virtually every issue, profits were elusive, and the company went through several rounds of venture capital without demonstrating much progress. Perkins finally demanded a showdown with the directors. "It's Kapani or Perkins," he told them—then had to leave when, incredibly, they elected to stay with Kapani. (Optics Technology disappeared into bankruptcy two years later, but not before a successful public offering made the directors' decision look smart.)

Perkins agreed to return to Hewlett-Packard in 1966, but he had one condition. He wanted to spend nights and weekends starting a company of his own to commercialize his idea for a laser that would be cheap to build and simple to operate. Looking back, Perkins realizes that the probability of failure in this venture was "horrendous." At the time, though, it was the most natural thing in the world to tell his wife "We're not going to buy the house, we'll put our savings into this and we'll get it back in a year or so." Of course the laser did work and the new company, University Laboratories, became profitable and eventually was merged into Spectra-Physics Inc., a leader in laser technology. And Gerd Perkins did get her house—on a hilltop in exclusive Belvedere, north of San Francisco, where Tom was remote from the passions of Silicon Valley and close to the bay and his classic wooden yawl.

At Hewlett-Packard, meanwhile, Perkins had been charged with getting the company into the computer business. HP had already developed a minicomputer under the direction of Jack Melchor, another future venture capitalist. But Melchor was leaving and the computer wasn't selling, and Perkins once again was cast in the role of squeaky wheel. "Everything had to be changed," he says, "and that led to a lot of conflict and turmoil." There was one battle after another—over funds for the operation, over creating a separate computer sales force, even over the question of discounts for the so-called original equipment manufacturers or OEM's who resold HP's computers in their own products. The showdown with Dave Packard over discounts was legendary. Packard opposed any kind of discounting in the company's instrument business and saw no reason for changing his philosophy to accommodate the practices of the upstart minicomputer industry. Perkins laid out all his arguments, and Packard pounded the table. "I just want it understood," he thundered, "that we will not do this. Figure out some other way to do it. And that is the end of this meeting." Packard stalked out. Bill Hewlett turned to Perkins and asked, "Well, what are you going to do now?" Replied Perkins: "He's wrong. I've just got a bigger job of persuading to do."

Perkins ultimately won that battle—no minicomputer maker could thrive without strong OEM customers—and Hewlett-Packard went on to challenge Digital Equipment for leadership in small computers. "He was the driving force to get HP into minicomputers," says an HP manager of that era, "and he was the person who recognized that the real opportunity lay in business computing." But an expensive effort to develop the hardware and software that would be needed to move into business applications—IBM's stronghold—almost came a cropper. The powerful HP 3000 was to be HP's entry in the battle, but when it was announced in late 1971 it was unable to live up to its advance billing. The 3000 had to be removed from the market while engineers raced to redesign it, and Perkins's star waned.

Packard had accepted a call to Washington, and Hewlett asked Perkins to move into a corporate planning assignment. He had been complaining for years about the way the company allocated resources, and this was a chance to put some of his ideas into practice. In particular, Perkins had recently developed one of his feverish enthusiasms for the management theories propounded by the Boston Consulting Group, which emphasized the importance of market share in product planning. Products that had a chance of dominating their markets should be nourished, those that were falling behind should be milked as "cash cows" or sent to slaughter.

The ensuing reorganization of Hewlett-Packard reflected that approach, at least in part, and word spread through the company that investing for market dominance was the way to get ahead. Perkins insists that this was never his intention, that his ideas were misapplied. But Packard returned to Palo Alto in 1972 and hit the roof. To him, Hewlett-Packard was successful because it was able to get top prices for high-quality products. Siphoning off cash by cutting prices or expanding advertising in pursuit of market share, he argued, would erode the company's pursuit of product excellence. Months later, at a meeting of HP managers, Packard was still making his view unmistakably clear: "Anyone can build market share; if you set your price low enough you can have the whole damn market. But I'll tell you it won't get you anywhere around here."[1]

Perkins's days at Hewlett-Packard were numbered. "It was clear I could stay there, keep the office and the symbols, but I just wouldn't be doing that exciting work anymore," he recalls. There was the prospect of getting another division to run. "But I said I think I'll just go into venture capital." Despite their differences, Perkins came away with profound respect for both Packard and Hewlett and made them role models in his approach to venture capital. Says Perkins: "They were tremendous risk-takers. Packard put them in the medical business, and nobody but Hewlett had anything to do with the handheld calculator. The point of it is, the president has to be the entrepreneur. No matter how big the corporation is, there is no substitute for that."

"HIS MOTIVES ARE PURE"

Eugene Kleiner, too, was interested in engineering but it was not in the cards that he would apply to MIT. The family had fled Vienna in 1939 when Eugene was fifteen, and money was short while his father struggled to reestablish the shoe manufacturing business he had left in Austria. Instead of finishing high school, the boy served an apprenticeship and went to work as a tool and die maker. By 1942 he was a shop foreman, turning out aircraft parts until the Army claimed him. And when, thanks to the GI Bill, Kleiner was able to start engineering school it was at Brooklyn Polytechnic Institute and in mechanical engineering.

Even after he had picked up an advanced degree at New York University, Kleiner always loved an opportunity to take off his coat and tie and actually make things. With his Viennese accent and courtly manner, Kleiner today seems more an old-country gentleman than a high-tech greasemonkey. But he still relishes the chance to work with new companies in their earliest stages, lending credibility and influence as well as sweat. "Gene's ego doesn't get in the way of things," says one of his partners. "His basic decency comes through and he is able to persuade people to do things because they are convinced his motives are pure."

At Western Electric, the production arm for the Bell System, Kleiner started as a manufacturing engineer for such things as switchboards and relays, and he was getting ahead. But scientists at Bell Laboratories had already invented the transistor, the miniature device that ultimately would make most electromechanical telephone equipment obsolete, and the leader of that research team, William Shockley, was planning to start a company that would focus on the new technology. Shockley struck up an acquaintance with Kleiner. He needed somebody with a manufacturing background to round out the team of scientists he was assembling. Would Kleiner join them? Kleiner had to think hard about that. He liked Shockley and the new field of transistors was fascinating. But ambitious engineers just didn't leave the Bell System, and this one had a wife and child to consider. Finally—and not until he had finished out the semester of a night school mechanical engineering class he was teaching—Kleiner put his family in the car and drove out to California.

The scene at Shockley Semiconductor Laboratory when Kleiner arrived in June 1955 was disheartening. Shockley had leased a tiny cinder-block building near the new Sears, Roebuck store in Mountain View, completely unsuitable in Kleiner's view for the kind of work that was to be done. But Kleiner took off his coat and tie and set about creating a semiconductor production line for the scientists—Noyce, Moore, Hoerni, and the rest—who would endeavor to invent an industry. It was heady stuff, but the challenge wore thin as Shockley's overbearing manner and uncertain leadership began to exhaust even Kleiner's loyalty. "It affected the physicists more than it affected me," Kleiner says now. "He knew less about my work than he knew about the physicists' work. But when you hire creative people you can't tell them minute to minute what they should be doing and how they should be doing it." The outcome was a palace revolt and the formation of Fairchild Semiconductor.

Again, Kleiner had to create a manufacturing plant from scratch. The new company had to invent or build much of the equipment it needed, and Kleiner moved around the company starting up departments, hiring his successor, and moving on to the next problem. By 1963 Fairchild Semiconductor was a ringing success, an industry leader and no longer a startup. Three of the eight founders were leaving to help Singleton's Teledyne get established in semiconductors, and Kleiner began to wonder: Could I do this on my own? Remembering the problems he had keeping students awake in his night school classes, Kleiner began tinkering with an idea for a teaching machine—a diabolical gadget that would allow teachers to elicit responses every few minutes from students who would be forced to prove they were awake enough to press a button. Not a big idea, but one that Kleiner could largely finance himself. His company, called Edex, grew to sales of $4 million in just two years and was acquired for $3 million in stock by Raytheon, then trying to enter the education market. Kleiner stayed on for two more years, "but they didn't offer me the presidency of Raytheon so I didn't see any reason why I should stay." He decided to go into venture capital.

Kleiner had more than a slight acquaintance with the field through Arthur Rock and Tommy Davis, who had invited all eight of the Fairchild partners to invest in their partnership. He and the other three eventual defectors put in between $50,000 and $100,000 each and became part of a network of well-placed limited partners who helped Rock and Davis evaluate deals. Kleiner's career as an independent venture capitalist got off to a good start when Noyce and Moore offered their old partners a chance to invest in Intel in 1968, and he can remember only one significant failure—a company called Cybercom that "spent money on schedule but did not progress on schedule." Kleiner liked rolling up his sleeves and working with entrepreneurs, but he missed the camaraderie of the early days at Shockley and Fairchild and Edex. "I didn't have anybody to discuss things with," he says. "I was lonely."

THE DO-IT-YOURSELFERS

Enter Sandy Robertson, founder of a fast-growing investment banking firm on San Francisco's Montgomery Street. Robertson, so energetic that one acquaintance calls him "the best two investment bankers I know," had been talking to Perkins about raising a fund but money was tight, especially for venture capital, and nothing came of it. Then, in April 1972, Robertson ran into a friend who had been trying for eighteen months to put a $6 million venture fund together—and had just succeeded. Robertson called Perkins and told him, "I think it's time to do your fund." That was Perkins's cue for his exit from Hewlett-Packard. But before he could make a move, Robertson called back. He had just heard from Kleiner, a recent investor in Robertson's firm. Kleiner had been approached by the Hillman family of Pittsburgh to manage a $4 million venture fund, and could Robertson raise a matching $4 million for him? Robertson could but he had a better idea: "You should meet Tom Perkins, you guys would be terrific together."

They were not so terrific at first. The $4 million proved harder to raise than Robertson had expected, even though he could sell both Kleiner and Perkins as experienced entrepreneurs and proven managers who could "go make it happen." Venture capital was still reeling from the blow it had received in the demise of the bull market of the late 1960s and the increase in capital gains taxes, and a mere $62 million was raised by all private funds that year.[2] By December Kleiner and Perkins had talked to some twenty-five prospects and secured only three sizable investments—$1 million from Rockefeller University and $800,000 each from two insurance companies. The rest was scraped together from various trusts and individuals, and the general partners each threw in $150,000. "It was like pulling teeth," Robertson remembers. And once ensconced in their Sand Hill Road offices, Kleiner and Perkins discovered the corollary to a shortage of venture capital—a shortage of entrepreneurs.

Their charter was to invest in new technology companies, but they beat the bushes for two years without finding anything exciting. They ended up doing some deals that bordered on the ludicrous—a combination snowmobile/motorcycle that died in the first energy crisis, a tennis shoe retreading business that misjudged a leap into manufacturing, a maker of light-emitting-diode displays that sold for $1.50 per digit when the investment was made and 30¢ per digit two weeks later. One gadget that almost worked taught them a valuable lesson in timing. They had put $500,000 into a Denver company called Dynastor Inc., which was trying to develop a flexible or "floppy" disk memory in which the recording head moved rapidly on a cushion of air to achieve very high data rates. There was a chance, Kleiner and Perkins thought, that this approach could become the industry standard for floppy disks, a market that was on the verge of real importance.

The problem was that "it kept almost working," as Perkins recalls— never quite failing completely but never really succeeding, either. When the founding president quit in despair, and a second president didn't work out, Perkins and fellow Silicon Valley investor Pitch Johnson took turns flying to Denver to keep the company alive. Finally, amazingly, the product worked and worked beautifully—but it was too late. Perkins: "By the time we could deliver it there was another standard. Nobody cared. We ended up with a high priced, niche market while everybody else was way down the learning curve." Dynastor ultimately was merged into another company, allowing the venture investors to make money, but the experience left its mark. "We still make mistakes," Perkins says, "but we get out of them quicker. We don't drag it out, just get it over with because they absorb so much time."

Late in 1974 Perkins confided to Robertson over lunch: "Well, no one is walking in with deals so we're going to create one. We want to do a minicomputer company." Robertson grimaced. "God, Tom, the world needs another minicomputer company like a hole in the head." But this would be different, Perkins promised. Early on, he and Kleiner had hired two young Hewlett-Packard managers to help out in the firm—John C. Loustanou, a serious-minded financial expert, and James G. Treybig, known as Jimmy, a curly-haired marketeer with an infectious grin. Treybig, who grew up in Houston "where you start playing poker at the age of six," shared Perkins's ability to plunge eagerly into the unknown. He developed a great enthusiasm for the ill-fated snowmobile/motorcycle, even went out and signed up dealers to test reaction to it. But he was thinking all the time about starting a company of his own.

One of Treybig's ideas involved a fail-safe computer. At Hewlett-Packard, he had seen that some customers were willing to pay handsomely for the extra software and hardware it took to tie together two computers so that one could back up the other in case of a failure. If you could get the cost down, Treybig reasoned, a lot of people would rather have a computer that didn't fail than one that did. The idea was just beginning to take shape when another deal involving a fault-tolerant computer suddenly materialized.

A Southern California company called Delphi wanted backing for an automated telephone answering service built around a nonstop computer. The Kleiner & Perkins crew was intrigued. How would the Delphi people like to split their concept into two companies, a hardware maker and a service provider, and let Treybig do the hardware end? Thanks but no thanks, was the response from Los Angeles. But Treybig was running with the idea now that Delphi had demonstrated that a fail-safe computer could be built, and he was sure that by designing one for data rather than voice processing he could steer clear of Delphi's proprietary architecture. Kleiner had reservations and Perkins was worried about getting slapped with a lawsuit, a move that might have stopped a new enterprise in its tracks. But Treybig by this time was going to start the company with or without the firm's help, and the partners caved in. They agreed to put up $1 million for 40 percent of what became Tandem Computers, an investment worth $12.5 million when Tandem went public three years later and $150 million if the stock had been held until 1984.

With Treybig and Loustanou spinning out to start Tandem, Kleiner and Perkins again were looking for help, and again they brought in a would-be entrepreneur. Robert A. Swanson, then in his mid-twenties, was a cheerful, cherub-faced whiz kid with degrees in chemistry and management from MIT who had gone West as a venture capitalist for Citibank. An offer to go to Hong Kong as a real banker forced Swanson to think about his future and he went to Kleiner and Perkins—coinvestors and fellow sufferers on a problem deal —to ask advice. "I wanted to get in and run something," Swanson recalls, "and they said why don't you join us for a year and maybe you can find the right thing to do."

Swanson worked on a few deals, but it was not until the end of that year—1975—that he ran across his big idea. Kleiner and Perkins had picked up a stake in a new company called Cetus Corp., which was trying to perfect a process for mutating and screening microorganisms, and Swanson went to the company one day for a luncheon at which there was talk about the potential for using recombinant DNA to move genes from one organism to another. Swanson was fascinated by the concept of genetic engineering and harped on it continually to Kleiner and Perkins, who saw precious little evidence that anything like a commercial product was going to emerge anytime soon. Finally Perkins suggested, "Why don't you go to work for Cetus and set up their department?" That was fine with Swanson but not with the management of Cetus. "They said I'd be the perfect guy to help them do this but that it wasn't going to happen for a while," Swanson recalls. Perkins remembers the response a bit differently: "They said they were not interested and certainly not with Swanson."

At this point, Kleiner and Perkins made a $100 million mistake. Rather than bankrolling Swanson immediately to start a company in genetic engineering, they allowed him to quit the partnership and start working on the idea alone. "In hindsight we should have said 'Okay, Bob,' and paid him $10,000 a month to come up with a business plan," Perkins admits. "But we didn't realize the technology was far enough along, and really it wasn't. In a sense we were right, but he was obviously more correct than we were."

They did give Swanson a desk and a telephone and he started calling scientists, asking "Why is it going to take so many years for this thing to develop?" No one was encouraging until he happened to call Herbert Boyer, a young biochemist at the University of California in San Francisco, who together with Dr. Stanley Cohen of Stanford had done the first successful gene splicing experiments two years earlier. Boyer considered Swanson's question and told him, "I think we can do something. I can spare you ten minutes Friday afternoon." The ten minutes stretched to four hours and several beers at a tavern near Boyer's lab as the two discussed the possibility of engineering a microorganism to produce a useful product. What emerged, said *The Wall Street Journal* a few years later, was "probably the most exciting partnership in recent years between entrepreneur and scientist."[3] Genentech Inc., as they decided to call the company, would be the first to use genetic engineering to produce a human protein—the brain hormone somatostatin—and both entrepreneur and scientist would become paper multimillionaires in one of the hottest public offerings ever.

Swanson and Boyer were able to convince Kleiner and Perkins that an experiment to test their theories could at least be run. But they were still skeptical enough to keep the initial investment to $100,000, and Swanson was a shrewd enough negotiator to keep the venture firm's initial share of the company to 25 percent. "He knew all my tricks," muses Perkins. That $100,000 was enough to finance the company for nine months, while Swanson and Boyer lined up university scientists to start the research. In February 1977 they raised another $850,000, including another $100,000 from Kleiner & Perkins, and late that summer the scientists announced they had created microorganisms that manufactured somatostatin. The venturers' $200,000 investment, after Genentech went public in 1980 and its stock hit $89, was at one point worth $83 million.

THE SECOND GENERATION

The winners were coming home, deal flow was picking up, and investors were warming up to venture capital again. It was time to expand the firm, and Kleiner and Perkins looked first to the new generation of venturers being groomed by their Menlo Park colleagues. Brook H. Byers had impressed them in the most intimate way possible—he had put $10,000 of his own (borrowed) money on the line when no one outside the firm was willing to invest in Tandem. Byers, a ham radio buff who had worked his way through Georgia Tech as an engineer for the Federal Communications Commission and then picked up an MBA at Stanford, apprenticed himself to Pitch Johnson in 1972. Johnson had one strict rule. To learn the real meaning of risk, Byers had to invest personally in every deal he recommended. Byers had no money, but Johnson guaranteed a line of credit for him at a local bank. It was the principle that counted.

Normally Byers would put a thousand dollars or so into the pot. But when Tandem came along in 1975 and he started doing background checks on Treybig and Loustanou and research on nonstop computers, it looked better than any deal he had seen yet. It felt right. So he put in $10,000 of the bank's money and lobbied Johnson to invest and go on Tandem's board. Even today, Byers counts that as the best investment he ever made. Not only did he get better than a 100-to-1 return but he mightily impressed Kleiner and Perkins. "We showed it to everybody—and nobody would invest," Perkins says. "But we convinced Brook and we got to know him in the process." Two years later, they brought Byers into the firm.

It wasn't long before Byers found an idea of his own to incubate, sparked by a call from Dr. Ivor Royston, a young medical researcher in San Diego who was a friend of a friend. Royston was working on a new technique for producing highly-specific antibodies—the body's defending molecules—by cloning the white blood cells that produce them. Byers was interested enough to ask for details, although research was just beginning. Royston wrote him a six-page letter describing the technology and its scientific implications, including the prospect that because of their purity and uniformity the new "monoclonal antibodies" would eventually displace those produced conventionally from the blood of human or animal donors for diagnosing and treating disease. That was the point that rang bells. "What struck me," Byers recalls, "was the analogy to Intel, which replaced ferrite core computer memories with silicon. When you change a fundamental raw material, whatever that material is used in is going to be enhanced."

Byers began calling the research directors of major pharmaceutical companies to ask if they thought the technology was ready to commercialize. They told him exactly what he was hoping to hear: the idea was probably valid, but it was not anything they were planning to do right away. Trained as an electronics engineer, Byers had to bone up fast on biology. Then he asked Perkins to fly to San Diego with him to meet Royston. The "how can we miss?" fever began building as they peered into microscopes and tried to watch cells fusing and throwing off antibodies. They rode back to the airport with Royston and his lab assistant, Howard Birndorf, who were still expounding on the future of monoclonals. In the airport coffee shop they kept talking over iced tea and finally grinned at each other. "We want to do this, don't we?" The next minute Royston had accepted an offer of $300,000 for 60 percent of the company, and Hybritech Inc. was in business.

While Royston and Birndorf set up an experiment aimed at proving the technology, Byers started commuting. As acting president, he was getting deeply involved in building a company, and he was enough of an idealist to believe that Hybritech was going to make a significant contribution to society. This might be his true calling. But the travel was wearing, and Byers was shaken when one day he missed his usual Monday morning flight and it went down with no survivors. Deciding, finally, to stay in venture capital, Byers looked for a replacement and hit two birds with one stone by recruiting the founder of a rival monoclonal startup. "We killed a competitor and got a president at the same time," Byers boasted. Kleiner Perkins ended up investing a total of $1.7 million in Hybritech, a stake worth $28 million when the company went public in 1981.

Frank J. Caufield, who joined the firm in 1978, had turned down the Tandem deal. But Kleiner and Perkins could hardly hold that against him after the mutual agonies they had undergone with an early word processing startup called Office Communications Inc. Caufield was a general's son and a West Point graduate who decided four years of soldiering was enough and went off to business school. A budding career as a management consultant brought him to California, where he was recruited to manage a venture capital fund set up by Paul M. Cook, the founder of Raychem Corp. Caufield eventually steered the $5 million Oak Grove Ventures fund to a 40 percent annual return. But his first investment was in OCI, which quickly ran into serious problems with the printer it was developing. "It worked nicely when I took the head of Raychem's word processing department to look at it," Caufield recalls, "but I think it never worked well again." Eventually Caufield was able to sell the company to Savin Business Machines Corp., after negotiations he describes as "like being massaged with sandpaper mittens," recovering something for the investors and gaining respect from Kleiner, who served with him on the OCI board and "liked the way he handled himself."

Caufield became an advocate for deals that broke with the Kleiner Perkins tradition of backing mainly electronics. After those early tennis shoe and snowmobile investments had flopped, Kleiner and Perkins were determined to stay with risks they understood. But Byers and Caufield fell in love with a raw startup called Home Health Care of America, which proposed to provide care such as intravenous feeding to patients at home. Perkins protested that no market existed for this service, but Caufield suggested investing just $250,000 at first to fund a pilot program, and Kleiner and Perkins agreed to go along. "The idea was to limit our exposure in case demand was not there," Caufield explains, "and they showed they could get the revenues they needed to cover their costs." Home Health Care went public three years later and when the stock quickly tripled became Kleiner Perkins's second (after Tandem) most successful investment in dollar terms.

For a time, Caufield appeared to have another big winner in the making with Imagic Inc., an investment he supported because of the potential for explosive growth in video games. This was another deal where all the risk was in the market, and it had another strike against it—put together in 1981, a good two years after Activision had pioneered the idea of developing game software for the players made by Atari and Mattel, it was late. Still, Caufield was impressed with Imagic's management, and when the company produced sales of $50 million in its first year all the partners were saying "we've done it again." But in the fall of 1982, as Imagic was shipping game cartridges at a $75 million annual rate and getting ready to offer its stock to the public, the game business collapsed. By 1984 Imagic had lost the $15 million it had raised in equity financing ($2 million of it from Kleiner Perkins) and was still in significant danger. "The perils of the consumer marketplace certainly came into sharper focus for us," says Caufield in a characteristic display of wry understatement.

CLONING A NEW BREED

L. John Doerr took a family tradition of entrepreneurship from St. Louis to engineering school at Rice University in Houston, and what could be more natural than to collect a few other computernik friends and start a software company. The business did well—still exists, in fact—and after business school at Harvard Doerr thought he would jump right into venture capital. But it was 1975 and none of the established firms needed help. Byers, still learning the trade himself, suggested that Doerr would do well to work for a good growth company for a while, and Doerr decided on Intel, where the microcomputer was just being offered to a wary world. Doerr poured his limitless nervous energy into becoming the company's best salesman of microcomputer systems, a background he would find useful in venture capital. "We're selling all the time," he says. "We're recruiting, finding deals, promoting our companies. We're selling a dream." Intel advanced him rapidly, but he still thought of himself as an entrepreneur. When Byers called five years later, he was ready to move—provided the firm agreed to back him if he decided to start a company.

As had happened with Byers and Hybritech, Doerr's chance came out of the blue. He attended a conference at California Institute of Technology on VLSI—very large scale integration, the new frontier of semiconductor technology—and ran into Carver Mead, a Caltech guru in the field. Mead's response to the venture capitalist's standard question, "What's new?" was evasive. He had something in the lab, he told Doerr, but it was premature to talk about it. Why didn't Doerr come back in six months or a year? Nothing could have been better calculated to keep Doerr hanging around. Within three weeks he had discovered the concept—a novel approach for using the power of computers to help design complex integrated circuits—and invited Mead to lunch with him and Perkins in San Francisco. Perkins, already impressed with Mead's reputation, agreed on the spot to advance him $100,000 to get the ball rolling—and also agreed to let Doerr spend half his time putting the company together.

By mid-1983, two years after that decision, Silicon Compilers Inc. was a going concern, delivering incredibly complex chips to Digital Equipment and other customers. But Doerr, after a lot of soul searching, had handed the presidency off to an executive he recruited from Intel and returned full-time to venture capital. "What it came down to," he explains, "was I thought Phil Kaufman (the new chief executive) could do a better job than I could of running that company. Plus, my partners were putting a lot of pressure on to get me back here."

The firm already had cloned, in a sense, another Doerr. James P. Lally was Doerr's boss at Intel, where he had specialized in launching new operations, and he had also known Perkins at Hewlett-Packard. When the two of them invited him to dinner one night, they were easily able to convince him that their brand of venture capital was more like the corporate startup role he was used to than a remote financial relationship. The pitch came at the right time, because Intel had just asked Lally to move to Phoenix and he had decided not to go. Like Doerr, Lally is slim, blond, and intense, although somewhat calmer and less likely to take the intellectual leaps that sometimes leave Doerr's interlocutors gasping. The two come at venture capital in the same hard-driving way, involving themselves deeply in the strategies and hiring decisions of their ventures even to the point of calling on customers with Intel-honed earnestness.

In 1984 Kleiner Perkins brought aboard E. Floyd Kvamme, who might be described as the prototype for the Doerr-Lally model of venture capitalist. Kvamme, pronounced Kwah-mee, was a marketing ace with a far bigger Silicon Valley reputation than the others. He was one of the Fairchild marketeers who joined Don Valentine in the rebuilding of National Semiconductor in the late 1960s, rose to general manager of the semiconductor operation there, then ended up at Apple Computer in the early 1980s as executive vice president in charge of sales. But the Apple job was less exciting after a reorganization, and when Kleiner Perkins offered to make him a full partner in their big new fund, he resigned the next day. "A guy like Floyd is a venture capitalist and doesn't know it," says Perkins in explaining the partners' willingness to make room for Kvamme. "Fixing problems is what we do, and Floyd will be very good at that."

FOLLOWING PERKINS'S LAW

Kleiner Perkins's high-tech connection guarantees a steady flow of investment opportunities. The key to getting in on the best deals now, with so much competition on the prowl, is to hear about them first, and that implies being part of the informal information network over which Silicon Valley gossip travels. Lally was a natural contact when Casey Powell and the Sequent 16 decided to leave Intel and start a computer company. And Doerr got word of Electronic Arts while founder William M. (Trip) Hawkins still was writing a business plan in Don Valentine's office, thanks to calls from friends at Apple. (Doerr and Byers then proceeded to talk their way into the Electronic Arts deal. "They were such hustlers," says Hawkins, "that I was very impressed with them personally.") Other ideas came from entrepreneurs in the Kleiner Perkins portfolio. Treybig found one opportunity across his back fence in Los Altos Hills, the horsey suburb that is to Silicon Valley what Scarsdale is to New York. Treybig's neighbor, Albert L. Horley, had assembled a prototype satellite receiver in his garage, and Treybig couldn't resist bringing over a team of Tandem experts to try it out. The upshot: Kleiner Perkins ended up helping Horley raise more than $30 million to launch Vitalink Communications Corp.

Kleiner Perkins's secret to picking good venture deals is no secret at all. The formula is stated in various ways, and Perkins puts it in one sentence: "If you have good people, proprietary technology, and a high growth market sector, you'll win every time." Like most simple rules, this one is extremely difficult to follow. Every venture firm has its own guidelines and procedures for weighing the relative merits of people, technology, and market opportunity in a prospective deal, usually relying heavily on outside experts and endless rounds of background checking. Kleiner Perkins does some of that but often decides on the basis of instinct or gut reaction to the people in a deal. The partners' opinions are formed through intensive, bantering sessions with the entrepreneurs at which they probe for weak points in strategy or character. Casey Powell of Sequent, for example, was taken aback when during an early discussion Caufield demanded to know why Powell and his team should be valued at $5 million. "I know what my $5 million is worth," he challenged. (As the deal finally was struck, Powell's group was worth more like $10 million.) The point of such sessions is partly to determine how deeply the entrepreneurs believe in themselves and their ideas. "If they say, 'maybe you're right,'" Perkins explains, "that's not the kind of people you'll risk your money with."

Perkins has strong notions about the qualities he is looking for in an entrepreneur. The stereotype of the lonely, driven genius who can't get along in a big company is all wrong, he says. "We have better luck with people who get along well with others. They may not be happy in a large firm but they do well there." The biggest challenge an entrepreneur faces, Perkins believes, is recruiting, motivating, and teaching other employees. A new company rises or falls on the quality and morale of its first employees and cannot tolerate the 20 percent annual turnover rates many established high-technology companies suffer. The model that Perkins often holds up is Tandem, still growing rapidly with little turnover a decade after the first investment, and famous around the world for its weekly beer busts where executives and workers mingle. The highest accolade an entrepreneur can win after a session with Kleiner Perkins is to be called a "Treybig type," sometimes implying mainly that this is someone Perkins and the others get along with. "If we are not going to enjoy working with him," says Perkins, "we may not invest."

Working toward a decision, the partners sometimes get into table-pounding shouting matches as advocates of an investment debate a point with someone playing devil's advocate. Often it is Byers, perhaps the quickest study of the partners, who makes the case for an esoteric idea. "Brook is like a laser beam in focusing on a new technology," Doerr says. "Tom is great at asking what the risks are, and Brook is best at answering those questions." Caufield, the least technical of the partners, may force the mercurial Doerr to slow down when the buzz words are flying too fast. The idea is to get to consensus, a process made increasingly difficult as the firm has grown. "Our style is for everyone to be enthusiastic about an investment before we make it," Doerr says, "but sometimes we'll figuratively drag one of the partners along." Or as Caufield puts it, "so they're surly but not quite mutinous."

When Kleiner Perkins turns down an investment, it may be because the deal involves too little technical risk. Perkins likes to state this philosophy in engineerese as Perkins's Law: "Market risk is inversely proportional to technical risk." In other words, if a product is easy to develop the market for it will be crowded. The best investment—and Tandem, Genentech, and Hybritech all fall into the category—is one in which the product looks so difficult that no one else even attempts it until you have shown it can be done. Tandem, as late as 1983, still held 98 percent of the market for fault-tolerant computers.[4] Ignoring Perkins's Law can be dangerous. As the firm learned with its investment in Imagic, market risks are sometimes deadly. But rigid adherence to the Law has also caused the partners some painful misses. They rejected Apple Computer, along with a score or more other microcomputer startups of the 1970s, in the conviction that the technical risk was so low that a free-for-all in the market was guaranteed. "We were obviously wrong to turn down Apple," Doerr argues, "but right to turn down the other twenty."

Kleiner Perkins also has an axiom for dealing with troubled investments. It is Kleiner's Second Law: "There is a time when panic is the appropriate response." What the partners mean by panic is a higher level of involvement, usually triggered by the failure of a portfolio company to meet its goals. Lally's response to problems at a startup called Northwest Instrument Systems Inc. was typical. Customers were happy with the company's low-priced oscilloscopes, which plug into personal computers, but sales were growing only 15 percent per quarter instead of the 50 percent rate that Kleiner Perkins hoped to see. In several lengthy sessions with President Jonathan D. Birck, Lally questioned Northwest's strategy of selling its products through independent sales representatives. "The problem they ran into with the sales reps," Lally says, "was that they wouldn't invest the time required to sell a $995 product. We thought the next product would solve the problem because it had a selling price of $5,000 or $6,000, but lo and behold we were still sitting in the same position."

With Lally prodding, the company came up with a new approach. It began to stress products aimed at digital engineers—designers and troubleshooters who need instruments that show the streams of zeros and ones that tell what is going on inside a computer. By finding other manufacturers to incorporate Northwest Instrument's products in their equipment, and by putting his own salesmen in the field to work with the recalcitrant reps, Birck was able to raise monthly sales from $150,000 to $500,000 in just sixty days. But Birck paid a heavy price for Lally's forceful assistance. His own expertise lay in the analog world of oscilloscopes, not the digital domain that now was Northwest

Instrument's focus, and he lacked the broad management background required by the new marketing strategy. By mid-1984 he was out of the company he had founded, asked to resign by Lally and the other directors. "I have no complaints against Jim," Birck says. "He has a role to play and he performs it well." But he adds: "He is very assertive, and he can tend to jerk a young company around."

This kind of intimacy, necessary as it may be to participate successfully in early-stage deals, consumes huge amounts of a venture capitalist's most precious resource—his time. And as Kleiner Perkins stepped up its investment pace to some $30 million per year, the partners have been stretched thin. Other firms have solved the problem of size by adding ranks of junior people and moving toward a corporate-style vertical organization, in which individual partners carry what amounts to a blank check to make their own investments. Kleiner Perkins refuses to move that way, for fear of losing the advantages of peer review. Says Byers: "There would be nobody saying, as my partners say, 'I respect you but I don't know where in the hell you think that could be a success.'"

Instead, Kleiner Perkins has forged a series of alliances with new funds that specialize in "seed" deals, investments in little more than an idea, with the expectation that it will get first crack at the most promising startups they generate. Doerr expects such relationships eventually to account for perhaps 5 percent of the companies in which Kleiner Perkins makes investments. But the partners have no intention of abandoning their own tradition of incubating ventures. Extra space in new offices the firm occupied in late 1983 was quickly filled by would-be entrepreneurs scribbling away at business plans. One of them, after all, could be planning the next Genentech—and Kleiner Perkins does not intend to let this one get away.

NOTES

1. "Hewlett-Packard: Where Slower Growth Is Smarter Management," *Business Week*, June 9, 1975, p. 50.
2. "Government-Industry Cooperation Can Enhance the Venture Capital Process," General Accounting Office, Washington, D.C., 1982, p. 37.
3. Kathryn Christensen, "Gene Splicers Develop a Product: New Breed of Scientist-Tycoons," *The Wall Street Journal*, November 24, 1980, p. 1.
4. "Computers That Don't Fail: A Risky Race to Catch Tandem," *Business Week*, May 14, 1984, p. 156D.

6

A NEW OLD SCHOOL

A visitor to Room 5600, which really is an entire floor of the RCA Building in midtown Manhattan, is struck by an almost tangible aura of permanence. Here, overlooking the twenty-two acres of "city within the city" that constitute Rockefeller Center, are the offices from which the worldwide interests and investments of the Rockefeller family have been guided for five decades. The curving hallways, the displays of art and artifacts, the solid wood and heavy cloth in place of the veneers and plastics of common office furnishings—all encourage the conviction that this place is here to stay. Whatever becomes of the legendary Rockefeller grit in subsequent generations, wrote "Adam Smith" in a worshipful profile of the five sons of John D. Jr., "Room 5600 continues, serene as a dreadnought on a flat sea; it will last the life of the Republic."[1]

Hyperbole aside, the twenty-two members of the fourth generation are probably too diverse a group to allow a single family office to control their financial destiny forever.[2] And immortal or not, Room 5600 is not immune to change. Laurance Rockefeller, having helped to create a flourishing venture capital industry, now spends most of his time on unfinished battles to preserve the environment and advance the cause of cancer research. The investment organization he fathered has grown up, and as a partnership called Venrock Associates emerged a knowledgable, aggressive backer of new companies in fields as diverse as biotechnology, artificial intelligence and microcomputers. An even greater transformation has come to J. H. Whitney & Co., headquartered in another Rockefeller Center spire. Since Jock Whitney's death in 1982 released long-standing emotional restraints on seeking outside investors, the firm he started has raised enough new capital and added enough new partners in California, Massachusetts, and New York to invest at a pace of $40 million a year across the country.

In Boston, also, the venture community has outgrown its Establishment roots and adopted styles and strategies that reflect the faster pace at which the game is played and the higher stakes at risk. Like Venrock and J. H. Whitney, Greylock Management and TA Associates of Boston now strongly resemble the San Francisco Mafia firms they often invest with. Like their West Coast counterparts, they have brought in technologists who scour the trade press and circulate at conventions in search of early-stage deals. But the East Coast firms retain a long-term outlook and an almost compulsive concern for their reputation that reflect patrician origins.

"WE'RE NOT IN ANY HURRY"

Don E. Ackerman's first assignment upon joining J. H. Whitney in 1967 involved a troubled wood products company in West Virginia. The company was beyond saving, and Whitney's investment was not to be recovered. Another investor might have walked away. But Benno Schmidt, by now J. H. Whitney's managing partner, charged Ackerman with protecting the holders of tax-exempt bonds secured by a plant the company was operating. Whitney assumed the lease, and Ackerman worked out a deal to have another company take over the plant until the bonds were paid off. "It was a real eye-opener," Ackerman says. "I had never been involved with anyone who was prepared to pay that price to protect their name."

A few years later, when Memorex Corp. hit the skids, Whitney volunteered again to help salvage a situation where it apparently had nothing to lose. Whitney had backed the computer memory giant during its startup days in the early 1960s, made a substantial profit, and was all but out of the investment a decade later when bankruptcy loomed. But the company's bankers asked Schmidt to reclaim Whitney's seat on the board and take a hand. He and Ackerman persuaded Robert Wilson to accept the Memorex turnaround assignment, then persuaded the banks to accept Wilson's ambitious compensation demands and to refinance the company by converting senior debt to preferred stock. Why bother? "Because it needed to be done," says Ackerman—an explanation that might be decoded as "noblesse oblige."

J. H. Whitney was all but inactive as an investor through most of the 1970s. For one thing, Ackerman points out, the combination of federal and state capital gains taxes exceeded 50 percent at the time. "We felt it was safer to ride our existing funds than liquidate, pay taxes, and seek high-risk situations." Furthermore, Whitney's first priority was to shore up the liquidity of its existing investments, some of which needed all the help they could get. One money-eater was Lexitron, the pioneer in word processing that Ackerman and Bill Draper of Sutter Hill had stumbled across simultaneously. Lexitron was a problem deal from the very beginning. The original management team broke up a few days after the initial $600,000 investment went in, and the developers of the first product missed their cost goals so badly that it had to be priced 50 percent higher than planned. "That made it a very tough sell and gave us very low marketing productivity," Ackerman recalls. Lexitron struggled along for several years, soaking up $9 million in equity including $3.3 million from a public offering, but never quite achieved real success and finally was sold to Raytheon. True to form, Whitney stayed with it to the end but Ackerman could find no support for a final round of venture financing that might have preserved the company's independence.

Investments in Qume, Storage Technology, Applicon, and other high-technology winners began paying off for Whitney in the late 1970s, and the new fund raised after Jock Whitney's death in 1982— evidently a large one, although the size is undisclosed—has made it a much more aggressive dealmaker. By 1984 there were eight Whitney partners, including three at 3000 Sand Hill in Menlo Park and one who spends most of his time in Boston. Most come from an operating background. Russell E. Planitzer in Boston was a vice president of Prime Computer; David T. Morgenthaler II in California headed corporate development for Amdahl. "We look for people you would look for if you were going to recruit a chief executive officer for a company," Ackerman says. No longer tied down to Rockefeller Center, the present Whitney partners operate independently and get together only for periodic cross-checking on future directions. They take a pragmatic approach to the venture business. Rather than try to develop an overarching strategy that targets technologies and markets for investment, Whitney's partners prefer to pick opportunities as they arise and use them to understand new industries from the inside. "Ours is a business in which you shouldn't constrain yourself with preconceived notions," Ackerman says. "Every deal that comes in you should look at and say, 'I hadn't thought about that.'"

Occasionally, Whitney will use the leveraged buyout technique to get into an industry in a hurry. Leveraged buyouts, in which a combination of debt and equity financing is used to spin off part of a company or take a public company private, normally aren't interesting to venture capital firms because the equity return is often limited. But Whitney finds that by picking buyout candidates in growth industries and applying venture-honed techniques of restaffing and repositioning them, it can make the technique pay off. Ackerman explains: "The buyouts we've done have tended to have some flaws in them. So the same skills we bring to a venture we can bring to a buyout. You do all the things you do to build value in a venture company but you shorten the cycle by three to five years." In the case of Genigraphics, Whitney and Welsh, Carson, Anderson & Stowe, another New York venture firm, put up $2 million in equity and $18 million in borrowings to buy a leaderless division of General Electric making equipment to produce slides for business presentations. Ackerman and Bruce K. Anderson shared the chief executive's job for a time, while Charles G. Moore of Welsh Carson became acting vice president of engineering. As they put seasoned new managers in place, the venturers pulled back, each firm ending up with 40 percent of the equity in a company that was headed for sales of $75 million. "It's a quick way to get a major company going," comments Ackerman.

The partners are still guided by many of Whitney's precepts, as laid down in a mellifluous Texas drawl by Managing Partner Benno Schmidt. Whitney looks hardest at two vital elements in assessing a business plan, according to Schmidt: the caliber of the people and the soundness of the idea as the basis for an important company. "We want a guy who looks like he is capable of running a business and who has surrounded himself with a team that is capable of running a business," Schmidt says. "And the second sine qua non for us is the belief that this is a business concept with potential for very substantial growth. You live in this game not so much on your batting average as you live on your slugging average. You make so much more on the ones that do well than you lose on the ones that do poorly that you don't have to succeed every time."

Surveying the 1980s scene, with its aggressive new venture firms and its nervous public market, Schmidt takes an Olympian view: "We've never been very short-range oriented. We don't have to worry about 1981's investment succeeding in 1984 because we've got 1976's investment to succeed in 1984. We're not so interested in a business being a great success in two or three years. We're not in any hurry to go public."

Schmidt worried when the venture industry sent too many immature companies to the public market at excessive prices in the early 1980s and welcomed the ensuing decline in initial public offerings as a well-deserved correction. He stated his misgivings in Texas-style repartee: "I was expressing astonishment and shock that something was coming out at a particular price, and somebody in the business said to me, 'Well, just remember that in the right wind even turkeys can fly.' And I said, 'You remember that even though they're flying they're still turkeys. And when the wind is no longer right, they're going to fall.' And that is what has happened."

"OUR LOYALTY RUNS DEEP"

Amazingly, not one of the ninety-plus companies Venrock Associates has backed since it was created in 1969, nor any of the sixty investments of Laurance Rockefeller and his organization before that, has ever gone bankrupt. This is partly because Venrock, under no pressure to invest, does only ten or twelve deals in a year and selects them very carefully. Of course, Venrock does lose money on at least a fifth of its investments and some have had to be written off entirely even though the company managed to survive. But once a bet is placed, Venrock is grimly tenacious—a point that is vividly illustrated by the fact that Henry S. Smith, who made his first investment as a Venrock partner in 1976, still sat on the board of that company in 1984 and still hoped to nudge it beyond the fledgling stage.

Venrock, like J. H. Whitney, is never in a hurry to sever its ties with an investment. Laurance Rockefeller has been involved with Eastern Air Lines for over forty years. And Peter Crisp, now Venrock's managing partner, notes that he is the fourth Rockefeller associate to serve on the board of Thermo Electron Corp., a 1960 investment. One Venrock partner, Anthony B. Evnin, admits to thinking, after a 5-year effort with a struggling medical instrument company, that "probably we should have walked away" once it was clear the company was not going to succeed. As it was, Venrock and other investors were able to avoid a total loss by finding a corporate buyer for the miscreant.

By the late 1960s Laurance Rockefeller's venture investment activities were becoming unwieldy. Things had been simple in the early days, when Laurance could write one check to put a company in business or perhaps invite his brothers and his sister Abby to participate. But now many of the cousins, as members of the fourth generation are known, were eager to play Laurance's game. A separate partnership called Kin & Co. (the etymology is obvious) had been set up to allow younger family members to coinvest with their seniors. But the deals were getting bigger, and it became something of a burdensome game at times to round up all the checks. To simplify things, Laurance and all of his siblings except Nelson contributed their interest in eight investments to set up Venrock Associates as a limited partnership that would be a single vehicle for the family's venture capital activities. Cash from twenty-six other Rockefellers brought Venrock's initial capitalization to $7.5 million when it started life in 1969. Crisp will not disclose the results Venrock has achieved, but the combined value of current investments, cash, and distributed gains is well in excess of $300 million. The count of limited partners now is over eighty, including three Rockefeller-connected organizations: Rockefeller Center Inc., Colonial Williamsburg Foundation, and Rockefeller University.

Considering its heritage, Venrock's reputation for investing cautiously and its low-profile image are not surprising. What is surprising is that the reputation and image have been disguising an aggressive dealmaker that is as well-connected in Silicon Valley as it is on Wall Street. Venrock's first general partners were drawn from Laurance Rockefeller's staff of advisers, but additions to the ranks have come from industries in which the investment action is hottest. Ted H. McCourtney, who arrived shortly after the creation of Venrock, shares Crisp's business school background and generalist outlook. But Hank Smith, who was the first microcomputer systems product manager at Intel—the first microcomputer manufacturer—plugs Venrock into high-tech electronics. Tony Evnin, holder of an MIT doctorate in chemistry and a onetime Union Carbide research scientist, looks after biotechnology. David R. Hathaway, once in charge of acquisitions at Automatic Data Processing Inc., covers computers. And Anthony Sun, an MIT-trained electronics engineer with Silicon Valley experience, sniffs out innovations in everything from software to robotics.

Many of Venrock's deals come about as reactions to opportunities. The firm has been making a concerted effort to create more of a strategic underpinning for its investments, and the partners even set aside one day each year to get together and consider long-term technology trends. "We definitely do target areas of interest," Crisp says, "and we have been fairly successful at filling the gaps and doing what we said we wanted to do." But Tony Sun, probably the most diligent of the Venrock partners at seeking out deals at the far fringes of science, is skeptical about placing too much reliance on forecasting: "If I had a crystal ball, I'd be retired by now. I don't. My edge over the rest of the world, if I have any at all, is measured by a hair's breadth. You just have to move a little faster, take a little more risk, see opportunities when most of the world doesn't." To get that hair's breadth advantage, Sun follows as many as 100 periodicals, many of them esoteric journals. When he spots something interesting, he gets on an airplane and talks his way into a deal. "It's up to me to find the stuff that everybody is shying away from," he says, "and try to mold it into something that looks not so bad."

There are advantages and disadvantages, the Venrock partners find, to the Rockefeller connection and their East Coast location. The advantages, obviously, include a range of contacts that few firms can match. "We can lend a lot of credibility to our portfolio companies by virtue of who we are and who we represent," Hathaway boasts. But the Rockefeller name does not ring as many bells among entrepreneurs as it once did, and the younger partners have been chafing at the traditional restrictions on publicity that surround the activities of Room 5600. In the modern environment of intense competition for deals, says one of them, "we need to toot our own horn a bit." Venrock was also slow to think about opening an office on the West Coast even though the focus of its investment activity has long since shifted there. Crisp argued that Venrock may have done a better job of following events in Silicon Valley by traveling there than by opening a local office. "I do believe we know more about what is happening in California than we do about what is happening within the Rockefeller Center complex," he points out. Nevertheless, with half its portfolio companies located west of the Rockies, Venrock finally made the move late in 1984, dispatching Sun to open a Silicon Valley office. "We have tried to do it all from the East Coast," says Smith, who commutes regularly from his home in Vermont to California, "but that is physically very difficult."

Not even Venrock can afford to sit at home waiting for investment opportunities to arrive these days. Smith's travels and his ties to Intel's old-boy network resulted in Venrock's biggest winner of the modern era—a $488,000 investment in Apple Computer that at the $22 price per share at which Apple went public was worth $83.6 million. Later, a casual conversation at an Apple annual meeting led Smith to an investment that launched VisiCorp as a temporary leader in personal computer software. Hathaway, trying to avoid the rut of seeking deals in California and Massachusetts, turned up Mentor Graphics Corp., a comer in computer-aided engineering, on a prospecting trip to Portland, Oregon. And Evnin discovered Native Plants Inc., a promising pioneer in plant genetics, by being in San Francisco when Frank Chambers decided to liquidate Continental Capital, which had invested in Terra Tek Inc., parent of Native Plants. Venrock picked up Continental Capital's position in Terra Tek and then split off Native Plants to give it a chance to grow independently.

Certainly the Apple investment early in 1978 did not spring from any grand design to enter the personal computer business. In fact, Smith recalls, the reaction in Room 5600 after Steve Jobs, Mike Markkula and Apple's then-president Mike Scott had demonstrated their crude little gadget was one of bewilderment. "These were very different guys than we had been used to dealing with," Smith says, "and we had not done a lot of early-stage things during that period." In the end, the decision to invest hinged almost entirely on Smith's recommendation, which in turn was based on his respect for Markkula. To Smith, "it was a case of investing in someone I knew and trusted and in a product that looked interesting."

Venrock had already demonstrated a willingness to experiment by hiring Smith, even though he showed up for his interviews with Laurance and the senior partners looking like a California dropout in full beard and mustache. He had decided if he was going to get the job he should get it just the way he was, although he ended up shaving before he went to work. More importantly, Smith's background as a semiconductor warrior brought an entirely different style to East Coast venture capital, where financial experience was the usual prerequisite. Venrock was looking for electronics expertise because of its experience as an investor in Intel, and Hank Smith had impressed Charlie Smith, Venrock's man on the Intel board, with a presentation on microcomputers. Intel founder Bob Noyce agreed to allow Venrock to approach Smith, with one proviso: "If he wavers, don't coax him." But Smith, an Easterner who had not adapted well to the California scene, did not have to be asked twice.

Hank Smith had worked with Markkula at Fairchild Semiconductor and later at Intel, and when Markkula saw that Apple would need substantial outside capital, he called Smith. After the demonstration in Room 5600, Smith's enthusiasm carried the day for Apple even though the price—$500,000 for 15 percent of the company, valuing it at more than $3 million—seemed high. "We regarded that as a very full valuation," Crisp recalls, "as there was no track record and an incomplete management team." Venrock took $288,000 of the deal and Don Valentine, now convinced that Apple was for real, put up $100,000. Dick Kramlich, Arthur Rock's partner and a classmate of Crisp's at the Harvard Business School, called to see if there was room for Rock to make a small personal investment. And Andrew S. Grove, then Intel's chief operating officer, whom Markkula was attempting to recruit for Apple's board, also invested. Later rounds of private financing brought Apple an additional $7 million, to which Venrock contributed $200,000, and its public offering in December 1980 raised $101 million, including $12 million for some late-round venture investors.

The story of Apple's abrupt rise from obscurity has become a favorite legend of Silicon Valley. Jobs's charisma, Steve Wozniak's creativity, Markkula's savvy, and Scott's discipline turned out to be a very powerful combination. It is worth noting, however, that Apple was perhaps the only one of dozens of microcomputer companies launched in the mid-1970s to obtain adequate financing early enough to make a difference. Most of Apple's competitors in the early "homebrew" computer market tried to bootstrap their growth by getting paid in advance of delivery and using the cash to finance production. When the market shifted gears about 1978, away from hobbyists and toward small-business and professional customers, at least thirty of those companies disappeared.[3] Apple not only had the wherewithal to develop a new generation of products, but it had in Smith and Valentine a braintrust of marketing talent that helped guide the company through the 180-degree turn in strategy that market changes demanded. Apple's most valuable outside director, however, in the opinion of one former insider, was not a professional venture capitalist but Henry Singleton of Teledyne, who made a personal investment of $100,000 and agreed to join the board late in 1978. "Singleton manages more than 100 presidents of the different divisions of Teledyne," says this source, "and he really trained the people in Apple to be presidents."

Just as Venrock's Intel connection led to the Apple deal, Apple in turn, but quite indirectly, provided the opportunity to invest in a company then, in 1979, called Personal Software. Daniel H. Fylstra, who had started Personal Software as an outgrowth of a master's thesis at Harvard, was an Apple stockholder. Hank Smith struck up a conversation with him after an Apple annual meeting, became intrigued with the idea of a software publisher for personal computer users, and persuaded Venrock to join Arthur Rock in a $500,000 financing. Smith went on the board (dropping off the Apple board to avoid potential conflicts of interest), and when Personal Software needed management help he recruited an Intel executive to take over as president.

Personal Software's first product, a "spreadsheet" program called

VisiCalc that allowed businessmen and investors to answer "what if . . ." questions about their finances, was so successful that the company was renamed VisiCorp—even though the product was actually written by others. Many venture firms would have urged the company to go public in the heat of early success, but Venrock in its cautious way decided the time was not right. "The management team had its hands full just managing the growth of the company," Smith explains. "My feeling is when you become a public company you tend to manage differently. You may want to put more money into R&D or building up a distributor organization but you tend not to do that because you are public and your eyes are on the quarterly results." Whether that sound, conservative reasoning is appropriate for the wild and woolly personal computer software business was being severely tested in 1984, however, as VisiCalc lagged and VisiCorp dipped into the red while it struggled to find new growth vehicles.

If Venrock has to wait a while for its return on the VisiCorp investment, that would be nothing new. Smith was still gamely going to board meetings of Caere Corp. eight years after Venrock joined Bob Noyce in backing the maker of wands used in department stores to read price tag information into computers. Other investors have come and gone but Noyce and Smith have hung in through several rounds of bailout financing—Venrock's stake now totals $600,000—and still have hopes that the company will break out of its prolonged startup phase. "Our loyalty runs deep," Crisp says. "We tend to stick around and work with management of both successful and less successful companies." Even after a portfolio company has gone public and Venrock has distributed most of its holdings, a partner may stay on the board.

More impressive still, Venrock will bend over backward to avoid making investments that might damage those longstanding relationships. For example, when Roger Badertscher approached Hathaway about funding Mindset, his personal computer venture, Venrock decided there would be a conflict with Apple and sent Badertscher back to Sand Hill Road. "I think that was the right decision," Hathaway says. "I don't think we would have felt good about the fact that we backed a company that then went out and recruited a lot of Apple people at a time when Apple was going through some pretty rough days." As it turned out, Mindset became an $18 million disaster for its backers.

ADAPTING IN BOSTON

In The Hub, as Bostonians immodestly call the center of their city, angular metal and glass office towers rub uncomfortably against sleek Art Deco buildings of the 1920s and ponderous stacks of stonework from the nineteenth century. Appropriately, the venture firms based in Boston also blend old and new traditions in ways that at first glance seem discordant. Some trace their lineage directly to American Research & Development and its defecting employees, and they still pay homage to Georges Doriot's philosophy of building companies for the long term. Others, with roots in Boston's active community of money managers and investment bankers, stress organization and analysis. All are caught up in the need to respond to massive changes that have swept venture investing in the last decade: the shift of high-technology opportunities to the West Coast, the rush of massive resources into the industry, the push to invest more money at earlier stages. For some Boston firms, the new fast-paced, high-stakes game seems distasteful and dangerous. They play grudgingly and carefully. For others, it is an opportunity to be seized with the same calculating Yankee determination for which their forebears were known.

Boston venturers, like their California counterparts, have tried to forge links to the academic community. John H. Carter, a founder of the Charles River Partnership in 1970, was active in MIT's governing body and worked out an arrangement to involve six professors as special limited partners in the firm. Some were helpful, recalls Charles River partner John T. Neises, but their expertise was too narrow to be of much help in most deals. "We thought it better to be more egalitarian and just hire consultants as we needed them and not have them be part of the action." At any rate, despite the excellence of MIT and Harvard, Boston by the mid-1960s had lost its preeminence as a center of technology-based entrepreneurship to the semiconductor wizards of Silicon Valley. "You could just see the activity swing out there," says a Boston venture capitalist. "Things were still happening in Boston but not nearly to the degree they were in California." Lately, the pendulum has been swinging east again. But except for an occasional minicomputer startup, Boston deals still tend to be smaller, less risky—and less rewarding—than California deals. To be competitive, Boston firms have had to change.

No firm more clearly reflects Boston's clash of cultures than Greylock Management Corp., which is so concerned about being swept along by short-term thinking that it refuses to seek institutional money (other than money that is also managed conservatively, such as Harvard's endowment). Greylock's Chairman, Daniel S. Gregory, a Bostonian's Bostonian in dress and manner, is actually an Ohioan who thinks in national rather than regional terms. But his philosophy is as conservative as his style. Gregory can barely contain his disdain for the idea of trying to compare venture investments by annual rate of return measures. "The quest of the institutions for rates of return is very counterproductive for achieving the long-term results that we are supposed to be after," sniffs Gregory. "I think it is causing venture capital firms to worry far too much about building market values in-

stead of building real values." Gregory even balks at calculating rates
of return for the private investors who back Greylock. How they measure the results, he says, is up to them: "I don't really know how they
figure it nor do I want to go through the arithmetic to help them. I'd
rather have them base the case on their own warm feelings about the
nature of the companies that came out of the process—that they were
good companies with interesting projects—than on rates of return."

Nevertheless, Greylock is acting more and more like a firm to
which rates of return are not unimportant. From a posture of investing
primarily in second-round financings of emerging companies, Greylock has become in the last few years an eager and respected participant in startups such as Masscomp, Priam, and Mentor Graphics. To
keep up its end as important deals have become more expensive,
Greylock has gone back to its investors for ever-larger infusions of
capital. Most recently, it set out to raise $40 million and finally turned
off the flood of offers at $54 million. Greylock has started to add part-
ners with backgrounds in industry. And Greylock has steadily increased its visibility on the West Coast. Not wanting to lose its Boston
image, which sometimes helps gain access to a deal, Greylock still
refuses to open a California office. But Charlie Waite, the ARD graduate who joined Greylock in 1965, finally has taken up residence on
San Francisco's Nob Hill after more than a decade of 300,000-miles-
per-year commuting, and David N. Strohm, another peripatetic Greylock partner, has acquired a permanent desk in the Palo Alto branch
office of a Boston law firm.

These changes are updating a conservative heritage that comes both
from ARD, where Waite and Greylock's founder William Elfers ap-
prenticed, and from investment management, where Gregory got his
start. Greylock was set up from the beginning as a partnership, promising big rewards for its principals that General Doriot could not
match, and the format was quickly copied by others. Fidelity Venture
and Palmer Partners spun out within a few years, and others have
followed to create a tight little band of investors who share at least
some of Doriot's philosophy. Greylock raised its first $9 million from
six wealthy families, including the Cornings of Cleveland (oil, not
glass), Sherman Fairchild, and IBM's Watson clan. Other families and
endowment funds came in later as succeeding Greylock funds raised
over $100 million.

Despite his ARD training, Elfers preferred at first to avoid startup
investing. "We didn't have to do startups," Gregory says, explaining
that in the 1960s and even well into the 1970s competition was so
rare that investors had the luxury of waiting until a company was at
least off the ground to make a commitment that paid off handsomely.
Greylock's second-round investment of $300,000 in Prime Computer,
for example, eventually was worth $30 million. Other winning late-

stage bets were placed on ROLM, Floating Point Systems, Cobe Laboratories, and Apollo Computer. As late as 1980 Greylock was able to put $750,000 into Micom Systems Inc. after the maker of telecommunications equipment was solidly profitable and still reap a tenfold gain on the public offering only a year later.

Waite, a rumpled and casual man with an adventurous spirit, always enjoyed the challenge of backing startups, although the first few he tried ended badly. He recalls talking his partners into a startup in 1968 that was a hair shirt for several years. "We eventually fixed the company and it is today highly profitable," he muses, "but to get there was an incredible voyage of failure and money and mess. Was the return adequate for the effort? Hell, no." But Greylock was finally forced to change its strategy by the growing competition and rising prices for second stage deals. Waite puts it this way: "If we went to do another Micom, for example, people would outbid us. And we saw that those of us who were really good in this business could demonstrate that goodness by doing startups, where we might not do the second stages any better than others."

Although Greylock has joined the startup game, it is inhibited by the background and philosophy of its partners from matching the aggressiveness with which others are playing. Gregory, for one, prefers to take on only one startup at a time because the process is so demanding. "If you do them right," he says, "it is very intensive." Greylock is also careful to avoid the appearance of conflict between its investments. "We perceive things a little differently," Waite says, and he relates a morality tale from Greylock's involvement with Priam Corp., a Silicon Valley maker of Winchester drives—computer memory systems in which the data is stored on rigid disks. Greylock and BankAmerica Corp.'s venture arm were invited into the $1.4 million startup financing for Priam by Paul Wythes of Sutter Hill in 1978. Waite joined the board along with Wythes and BankAmerica's Steven L. Merrill. Two years later, just as Priam was getting off the ground, another Winchester startup called Quantum Corp. came along. Quantum planned to make lower-capacity drives than Priam was then making, and Wythes and Merrill concluded there was no conflict. Waite, on the other hand, ran into Priam cofounder Alonzo A. Wilson at a trade show and said, "Al, my colleagues tell me they are looking at Quantum and that it isn't competitive with you guys. What do you think?" Wilson "went wild," Waite recalls. "So I said, 'If you feel that way, we aren't going to touch it.'" That conversation, Waite estimates, cost Greylock $20 million.

THE POWER OF ORGANIZATION

Passing beneath the arches, columns, and sculpted figures of the turn-of-the-century International Trust Company Building, visitors to TA

Associates receive a sense of Old Boston—power and wealth in a traditional package. TA certainly has power and wealth to spare. *Venture*
magazine ranked its $410 million of paid-in capital at the end of 1983
as the largest venture capital pool of all.[4] That understates the case.
By mid-1984 TA was managing more than $500 million domesti-
cally—including $300 million in cash to be invested within three or
four years—and it had a hand in running five foreign venture funds.
But TA is in no way a traditional operation. To the contrary, founder
Peter A. Brooke has broken with the conventional wisdom in almost
every way in his remarkable effort to institutionalize and internation-
alize the process of risk investment. "Peter is one of the few visionaries
in the venture capital business," says a former partner. "He recognized earlier than most of us that it was not going to be a club forever."

   Under Brooke's guidance, TA has evolved a structure and style that
is more corporate than collegial, more reliant on strategy and analysis
than on intuition. Instead of sitting down at regular partners' meetings
to make collective decisions, TA's twenty professionals work in small
teams that zero in on industry sectors and bring carefully researched
proposals to the three managing partners for approval. Rather than
earmarking all its funds for high-technology deals, TA balances its
portfolio by putting a quarter of its assets into cable television operators and other conventional communications businesses and another
10 percent or so into manufacturing companies. Where other firms
have abandoned the SBIC vehicle, TA has embraced it as a source of
leveraged financing for its more mundane investments. And in an
industry of networks and syndications, TA is a loner, preferring both
out of choice and the necessity of investing some $75 million per year
to go it alone in the deals it finds.

   Not surprisingly, TA's approach is controversial among venture tra-
ditionalists. They argue, for one thing, that a hierarchy is an inappropriate and even dangerous form of organization for a venture capital
firm, because it removes an important element of peer review from
the decision-making process. "There is no check and balance,"
charges a partner in a West Coast firm who includes such other hier-
archical groups as San Francisco's Hambrecht & Quist and Los An-
geles-based Brentwood Associates in this indictment. A similar case is
made against TA's practice of swallowing the whole deal rather than
bringing in other venture groups to share the risks and rewards. Jack
Neises of Charles River states the potential for problems: "You end up
with a two-person board of directors, the entrepreneur and the venture
capitalist, and heaven help you if you ever have a serious disagree-
ment. We believe there is much value in a democratic sharing of
ideas." Purists also criticize the strategy of targeting an industry or
technology and then pouring money into it, as TA has done in data
communications, software, and factory automation. "It's like sowing

a lot of seeds on very fertile soil and hoping the big ones will take care of the ones that don't grow," runs one line of attack.

To some extent, the TA style is a necessary response to the unprecedented resources that it has attracted. "We prefer to work in syndicates," says C. Kevin Landry, Brooke's second in command. "It's nice to have some partners in a deal. However, given the fact that many of the deals are only $2 million in size and the fact that we'd like to have an average investment of $3 million, there isn't much room to do things with partners." But the go-it-alone policy also reflects TA's independent spirit. Others in the business have solved the problem of too much money by creating, in effect, two portfolios—one of companies in which they do the usual homework and get actively involved and the other of deals that are found and managed by other firms. "We are not going to do that," Landry declares. "We are still going to be reliant on our own decisions and not get comfort from the fact that someone else is doing the deal."

Given that philosophy and the amount of money TA is trying to find homes for every year, there is probably no alternative to a more structured approach to investing than the venture industry is used to. And Peter Brooke was certainly the man to perfect it. Brooke is a Harvard College and Business School graduate who carried away a fervent belief in the virtues of strategic planning, organization, and analysis. Initially at First National Bank of Boston and later at Bessemer Securities, a family-funded venture firm in New York, Brooke rose by setting up smooth-running operations that put high-technology lending and investing on a firm analytical footing. Soon Brooke was running his own show, an investment banking operation he established with a Boston brokerage firm called Tucker, Anthony & R. L. Day to arrange private placements of securities for small companies. That was so successful, Brooke says matter-of-factly, that the business had to be liquidated to avoid paying prohibitive taxes. Brooke then persuaded his Tucker, Anthony partners to plough the proceeds, about $1.8 million, back into a venture capital partnership. He raised another $5 million from Tucker, Anthony clients and in 1968 launched the first Advent fund under an umbrella organization called TA Associates.

For a few years, Brooke did deals with the same gentlemanly reserve that then characterized many Boston firms. "An attractive guy would come in the office with a project and you'd invest in it," he recalls. "We were responding to things that came in rather than identifying what we wanted to do." The first Advent fund was only modestly successful—a 13 percent annual rate of return over ten years—but Brooke was able to put together another fund, this time for $10 million, in 1972. Advent II compounded at better than 30 percent per year, and after that raising money was the least of Brooke's problems.

Advent III was a $15 million fund, Advent IV came in at $60 million, and in 1983 Advent V was closed at an impressive $165 million.

An important reason for this flood of support was the strategy Brooke adopted in the mid-1970s to focus TA's partners on a few growth sectors—to become "a seeker of opportunity rather than a responder to opportunity," as he puts it. Brooke organized TA into teams, each concentrating on one industry and traveling constantly to develop contacts and find investment opportunities. One favorite trick, says William P. Egan, who left TA in 1979 to start his own venture firm, was to seek out financial reports on companies in a targeted industry and track down private investors who might be willing to sell out. "We could always find a shareholder who was illiquid from real estate investments," Egan recalls. "We'd buy the shares for five times earnings and assuming earnings doubled and we could sell to a large company at ten times earnings, we'd quadruple our investment."

As prices for later-stage investments escalated, TA has been forced to include more startups in its strategic assaults, and it sometimes plays a catalytic role in getting a company started if it finds none that meet its criteria in a targeted sector. Landry, for example, began talking to Harvard Professor and Nobel Laureate Walter Gilbert about starting a biotechnology company in the Boston area in 1977. Nothing came of that initiative, but TA's partner in the talks, the venture arm of International Nickel Co., succeeded the next year in organizing a company called Biogen around European scientists. Gilbert agreed to become chairman of Biogen, and TA picked up first-round stock in the company, now considered a leader in the field, at 20¢ per share. It went public in 1983 at $23.

The jury has yet to render a verdict on TA's memorable plunge into computer software. In the course of two years, software specialist Jacqueline C. Morby led a whirlwind investing spree that put over $30 million into a dozen companies including Spinnaker Software, Sierra On-Line and Digital Research. At the time Morby started looking into the field, software companies were considered poor venture bets because, as Landry allows, "your assets drive home every night." But Morby, then a trainee with the firm, saw that an industry was coming of age and began calling on companies until she had the personal contacts and expertise to start investing.

Morby and Jeffrey T. Chambers, head of TA's West Coast office, had almost carte blanche in deciding which horses to back in the software race. Some of their choices were controversial. Others at TA questioned the Spinnaker investment, for example, because founders William Bowman and David Seuss decided to focus on educational programs—a far smaller niche than the business and entertainment markets other companies had picked. "We were sticking our necks out," Chambers recalls, "but Keven (Landry) said if we wanted to do it, go do it." TA invested $800,000 for half the company in April 1982, brought four new investors into a $1.5 million financing nine months later, and organized a $5 million mezzanine round at the end of 1983. At the third-round price of $15.75 per share, TA's original investment was worth more than $15 million—assuming an eventual public offering or acquisition confirms that valuation.

To a greater extent than most other venture firms, TA has tried to balance its portfolio—between industries, between stages of development, and between debt and equity securities. Thus TA became a major investor in prosaic cable television and broadcasting operations, which with the help of SBIC leverage practically guaranteed a four- or fivefold return on 25 percent of its assets. At the same time, Brooke put TA into such long-shot ventures as Federal Express, the biggest and wildest venture capital deal of the 1970s, and Tandon Corp., then operating out of a garage in the San Fernando Valley, which became the leading producer of disk memory devices for personal computers. "Our goal was to show the institutional investor that venture capital was a prudent and safe way to invest money," Brooke explains, "and we did that by convincing them that we would balance the account so that we could mitigate the risk of any one or two investments going sour."

This prudent approach went over especially well abroad. Long before Europe had discovered venture capital, and at a time when even most domestic sources of backing had dried up, Brooke went to France and the Netherlands and raised $15 million for TA to invest in the United States. Since then he has tapped investors in West Germany for over $100 million, in England for $30 million, and in the Middle East for $25 million. Brooke's foreign contacts led him to provide advisory help for French, Dutch, and Swedish efforts to promote venture capital, and by the 1980s TA was directly involved in venture groups in Great Britain, Holland, Germany, Southeast Asia, and Japan. Problems of infrastructure and attitude still inhibit the venture process abroad, Brooke concedes. But he believes that in many countries the supply of new technology and entrepreneurial managers now is great enough to allow venture capital techniques to succeed. "Our first fund in Great Britain will be as successful as our first fund in America was," Brooke predicts. "It won't be a 40 percent compounded rate of return. It will be something like a 15% rate of return. But for a first effort that isn't bad."

Brooke's ultimate goal, one that is pulling him away from day-to-day involvement in the venture business, is to create a central clearing house to assist TA's foreign portfolio companies in penetrating the U.S. market and to help domestic portfolio companies sell and manufacture abroad. What he has in mind, it seems, is a kind of multinational *zaibatsu* that can free TA-backed companies from their dependence on local economies. As an example of the kind of thing that can be done, Brooke mentions a Belgian company making a medical instrument that will be sold in the United States through a joint venture with another TA portfolio company. "That Belgian company would have had no way, probably, ever to address this market while its technology was still competitive," Brooke points out. An independent, centralized organization would allow Brooke to orchestrate this kind of thing on a grand scale. And it would certainly bring a new quality of international sophistication to the venture process. To make it work, of course, Brooke must first prove that venture capital itself can work in foreign environments that have never been friendly to entrepreneurs. That may be the ultimate test of Peter Brooke's considerable powers of organization and persuasion and of Boston's drive to recapture its position of leadership in risk investing.

NOTES

1. Adam Smith, "Behold the Brothers Rockefeller, Bearing Gifts," *Esquire*, December 1983, p. 223.
2. Collier and Horowitz, *The Rockefellers*, pp. 556–575.
3. "Surviving a Microcomputer Shift," *Business Week*, April 16, 1979, p. 104E.
4. Lee Kravitz, "Venture Funds Stop to Catch Their Breath," *Venture*, June 1984, p. 54.

7
UPSTARTS

The year 1978 marked the end of a lean and troubled era for venture capital and the beginning of a cycle of fat years without precedent in the industry's brief history. That the cycle will turn down again—most likely is doing so even now—is beyond question. But the seven years between 1978 and 1984 saw $13 billion added to the pool of capital managed by venture firms, a pool that had stagnated at less than $3 billion since the late 1960s. As if someone had pried open a faucet that was rusted shut, money began gushing into funds run by established venturers and then spilling over into the hands of newcomers. For the first time in a decade, it was possible to launch a venture firm with a reasonable expectation of raising capital for it, and new partnerships naturally proliferated. Where only two new funds were formed in 1977, and managed to raise a grand total of just $20.2 million, five started up in 1978, seven in 1979 and ten in 1980.

Then the real growth began. In the next three years, more than 100 new venture partnerships raised over $2 billion, with half of the action occurring in 1983.[1] Things have cooled off somewhat since then. By early 1984 there were reports that some of the new firms had gone back to the well and come away with buckets only half-full. "There are some people who wanted to go for a much bigger fund on their second time around and couldn't pull it off," a partner in an established firm notes with some satisfaction.

Newcomers to any field must pass through an initiation process, and the difficulty of breaking into venture capital is compounded by the cliquish culture that pervades the industry. While it is no longer the cozy fraternity it was a decade ago, venture capital remains a clubby business where past history, individual reputation, and personal contacts mean more than a distinguished resume. "When you look for coinvestors," says a partner in a leading West Coast firm, "you are very selective about how you expand your circle. It is unusual at this stage in our firm's life to form a close relationship with another firm because we have a web of interrelationships and dependencies and debts and obligations. If we have a good investment, people have to take a number and stand in line." Like members of the baby boom generation who must be exceptionally talented to win the intense competition for jobs, the new venture firms must bring something to the party. Don Valentine offers his wry view: "There is an army of investors out there whose position is, if we are going to be in a deal they'll follow us. That's momentarily very flattering but there is a lot of work to be done in these companies. There are guys out there who are good workers and good helpers and guys who don't help. Very simple-mindedly, we gravitate toward the workers and the helpers."

Not surprisingly, then, most of the new firms count at least one veteran venturer among their partners. Of the sixty-one new venture groups formed between 1977 and mid-1982, two-thirds had at least one partner with seven years of experience and only seven had no experienced hands at all.[2] Commonly, a junior partner in one firm will grow dissatisfied with his lot and leave to form another. "The forces of ego and power lure you to start your own fund," says one young venture capitalist who so far has resisted the urge. "Giant egos are required in this business, and that is one way to test them." Others are seduced by the larger piece of the carried interest that a senior partner normally receives, although that must be weighed against the likelihood that the old firm, if it is well-established, will outperform the new one. "In most venture firms there is a tremendous disparity in the [partnership] share people are given," says one source, "and that pushes them to think about starting something of their own."

For the most part, however, there is little movement between partnerships. By necessity, the newfledged firms are largely filled out with newcomers to the business, a development that has occasioned a fair amount of hand wringing. "Do We Have Too Many Venture Capitalists?" inquired a 1982 *Fortune* article which decried the "number crunchers" who were being attracted to the field. "You wouldn't necessarily want the top people at business school to become venture capitalists," one industry veteran warned.[3] Many of them are doing just that, or at least joining venture firms in relatively low-paying jobs while they wait for the chance to move up to partnership rank. *Venture* reported that twenty of the 700 members of the class of '83 at Harvard Business School had joined venture capital groups, many of them long-established firms staggering under the workload imposed by huge increases in funds to invest.[4] The most important sources of talent for old and new venture firms alike, however, may be the successful companies whose managers have both the contacts and the operating experience to find and help high-tech entrepreneurs. Following the lead of Kleiner Perkins, Venrock, Technology Venture Investors, and others, the best new firms have tapped Intel and its ilk for partners who can make an immediate impact.

Seeking an edge in a crowded field, the newcomers are trying out strategies that make venture capital far more diverse than it was a few years ago. Although a few firms are interested in consumer products and other low-technology fields, the focus for most is still on computers, biotechnology, robots, and other technology-based industries where change and growth are fastest. But many of the new partnerships are specializing along geographic lines, some attempting to build truly national firms while others aim heavily at one neglected region.

And others are dividing up according to the stage of investment they favor, ranging from raw startup or "seed" financing to "mezzanine" deals done just before a public offering. While mezzanine funds are becoming vital to the venture process, they come and go with the vagaries of the public new-issues market and are more closely related to traditional investment vehicles than to this book's venture capital investors. We will meet some of the new seed funds in Chapter 9. This chapter looks at four new firms, one with a strong regional emphasis and all engaged in classic early-stage venture investing. All have already achieved an unusually high profile in the field, although it is far too early to comment on the results they are likely to end up with.

"WHAT DO YOU KNOW ABOUT VENTURE CAPITAL?"

"The way to break into venture capital," says Benjamin M. Rosen, "is to have a success." Rosen is a master of the understated jibe, but he is at least half in earnest on this point. After all, the momentum generated by early winning investments had a lot to do with the subsequent triumphs of Arthur Rock, Fred Adler, Tom Perkins, and other masters of the venture game. Just as gamblers crowd to the machine that has recently spilled out a jackpot, although hopefully for more rational reasons, entrepreneurs seek out investors associated with successful deals. And winners add enormously to the intangible assets—reputation, credibility, contacts—which determine the pecking order among venture capitalists and decide who works with whom, who is invited into which deals. Nothing, indeed, succeeds like success.

Rosen and his partner L. J. Sevin raised $25 million in 1981 and quickly demonstrated the continuing validity of the old French proverb. Of the fifty-odd venture groups raising money that year, Sevin Rosen Management was probably the only one with no prior experience in venture capital. Rosen had been a New York securities analyst, Sevin a Texas entrepreneur. Yet two of their early investments—in Compaq Computer and Lotus Development—became so successful so fast that it was almost anticlimactic when the companies went public late in 1983 and gave the neophytes an overnight gain of more than $100 million. The gain, of course, existed only on paper and fell dramatically the next year as both companies' stock dropped by 50 percent from their peaks. But Sevin and Rosen leaped immediately to the top tier of the venture hierarchy and had no difficulty raising a second fund of $60 million for an expanded partnership even though they increased the partners' carried interest in the profits from the standard 20 to 25 percent. They co-invest regularly with the likes of Kleiner

Perkins and Sequoia Capital and consider themselves with real justi-
fication a branch of the San Francisco Mafia.

The impetuous rise of Ben Rosen and L. J. Sevin proved again the
importance of a tight connection between venture capitalists and the
network of engineers, managers, marketeers, consultants, and journalists who form the inner circle of an industry. As Don Valentine
and others had previously demonstrated, fresh recruits to venture investing often bring along contacts and insights that allow them to pick
the right team with the right technology in their field. In the case of
Rosen and Sevin, notes Frank Caufield of Kleiner Perkins, "their
strengths were really a perfect match for where the market was going."

Rosen, trained as an electrical engineer at California Institute of
Technology and Stanford, built a reputation at Morgan Stanley & Co.
as the foremost electronics industry analyst in the country. For six
straight years in the 1970s he was the top choice in his field on *Institutional Investor's* All-America Research Team. "It was a very comfortable, rewarding experience," he says, "but after a while you can write
only so many reports to clients explaining why TI's earnings were 2¢
above your estimate or 3¢ below. Then it's time to move on." Rosen
departed to start a newsletter and conference business that further
consolidated his position as the leading guru of microelectronics.
Sevin, a former engineering manager at Texas Instruments, had
founded Mostek Corp. in 1969 and made it a leader in semiconductor
memory devices and a $400 million company by the time it was ac-
quired in 1979 by United Technologies.

Neither Rosen nor Sevin had so much as thought about trying venture capital until the subject came up at lunch in New York with investment banker Thomas I. Unterberg. Rosen had tried doing a little
personal investing in the year or so he had been on his own, and when
Sevin left United Technologies the two had discussed starting a semiconductor company of their own. But Rosen was out of money for
such ventures, Sevin was doubtful that anyone could compete with
the onrushing Japanese, and in any event the timing seemed inaus-
picious, with the semiconductor business mired in one of its periodic
slumps. Unterberg's offer to raise a venture fund for them sounded
interesting. "The more we got to talking about it," says Sevin with his
usual note of irony, "the more the delusions of grandeur welled up in
us. We'd be just perfect for this business." Then came the moment of
truth. "I think Ben asked me first," Sevin recalls. "'L. J., what do you
know about venture capital?' I said I didn't know, what did he know?
So we evolved a strategy that we'd go around and try to find some
pretty good looking deals, bring them to Kleiner Perkins and invite
those guys to look at them with us, and go to school on them."

Kleiner Perkins had already initiated the contact—Caufield had an
inspiration to call Sevin for help in evaluating a semiconductor in-

vestment—and agreed to help. Together, they looked at two prospects Sevin found and turned them down. "They weren't real turkeys," says Sevin, "but Kleiner Perkins pointed out some real flaws in both deals." Kleiner Perkins loved the next two ideas, though. One, Compaq Computer, came in through Sevin's contacts in Texas technology circles and involved an attempt to capitalize on the emerging IBM standard in personal computers. The other was Lotus Development, a product of Rosen's extensive network in the world of personal computers, which aimed at integrating the most useful application programs into one software package. The two venture firms put $1.5 million into Compaq and $1 million into Lotus in the spring of 1982 and later in the year helped raise $8.5 million for Compaq and $3.7 million for Lotus. In the next year Compaq racked up sales of $111 million, apparently the fastest takeoff in business history, while Lotus hit $53 million to become the fastest growing software company ever. Encouraged by Sevin and Rosen, both companies went public before they were two years old. "In this business," Rosen says, "money is a weapon. You raise money when you can, not when you have to."

That kind of pragmatism helped keep Compaq from starting off with the wrong product. Founder Rod Canion had left Texas Instruments with the idea of developing a disk drive unit that would attach to the IBM Personal Computer, but Sevin and Rosen rejected it as too easy to do and hence unlikely to be the kind of technical contribution on which major companies are built. Canion returned three months later with the plans for a lightweight, portable computer that would run all the software written for the bulky PC—a project so difficult that a skeptical John Doerr of Kleiner Perkins predicted it would take eighteen months to pull off instead of the nine months Canion projected. It was the kind of product that could only succeed if it got to market first and in time to catch the wave of demand that IBM was creating. To Doerr's amazement, Compaq pulled it off. Within four months of the first financing in March of 1982, Canion's team had developed a basic input-output system—which orchestrates the internal workings of a computer—that mimicked IBM's without copying it. With the technical risk largely removed, the venture investors pumped in enough additional money to allow Canion to attend the big Comdex trade show in November with working prototypes and fully-tooled parts. Sales took off and kept going. "The Compaq idea was not one of the century's alltime greats," Sevin says, "but the way those guys executed it was spectacular."

For Sevin, ability to execute a plan is "nine-tenths of the law," the most important criterion in assessing the quality of management in a new company. "As these startups progress through the first two or three years," says Sevin, "our style is to make them sing for their suppers. If they perform you can come along and do second-round and third-round financings." Two ventures that met Sevin's standards, Convex Computer and Cypress Semiconductor, found their second-round financings in 1984 greatly oversubscribed even though the private capital market was by then far tighter than it had been a year earlier. But Sevin Rosen can take a hard line when the execution does not measure up. The firm had made an early $400,000 investment in Osborne Computer, the pioneer in portable personal computers, but when Compaq came along with a better idea—an IBM-compatible portable—Sevin and Rosen switched horses and offered to sell back their Osborne holding. (The offer, unfortunately for Sevin Rosen's performance, was not accepted.) In the case of Computer Thought Corp., a Texas company developing artificial intelligence systems for use in education, Sevin Rosen sold out its $1 million investment when it became clear the initial product hopes could not be met. "It's not what you've done that counts," says Sevin, "but how it is measured against what you said you'd do originally."

With their diverse backgrounds and contrasting personalities, Sevin and Rosen make a unique Mr. Outside and Mr. Inside combination. Rosen contributes global views of the electronics industry and Sevin a pragmatic familiarity with its inner workings. Yet they have worked up no grand strategies for their investments, other than to look for opportunities where the timing seems perfect. "You want to catch technology at the right point on the wave," says Rosen. "If you catch it too early—like artificial intelligence—you have a technology in search of a market. And if you catch it too late, you end up in a commodity business."

In adding partners, the firm has leaned heavily on the industries it tracks. Roger Borovoy, an engineer and an attorney, was Intel's top legal officer; Jon W. Bayless taught telecommunications at Southern Methodist University and was chief scientist at Arthur Collins Laboratories. The six Sevin Rosen partners in three offices—in New York, Dallas, and Silicon Valley—see twenty-five or thirty proposals every week, look through all of them and invest in virtually none unless they come recommended. "This is 100 percent a contacts business," says New York-based partner Robin Grossman. "We have a real bias against doing a deal that is not prescreened." Some of the best deals have been products of the extensive network of contacts that Rosen brought to venturing. As an analyst, Rosen had been one of the earliest personal computer enthusiasts and owned a very early Apple model. So it was only natural that Trip Hawkins, the former Apple Computer manager who founded Electronic Arts in 1982, should take his involvement for granted. And Rosen got to know Mitchell D. Kapor, founder of Lotus Development, when he bought Tiny Troll, one of Kapor's pre-Lotus programs. Again, it was natural when Kapor encountered Rosen and Sevin at a Las Vegas trade show late in 1981 to confide his plans to strike off on his own. Sevin's reaction: "Let's kidnap this guy."

Rosen's network includes many of the journalists who cover high-technology companies. The connection is due more to the writers' heavy reliance on a few analysts than to any great public relations effort on his part, but he is adept at using it to help spread the word about companies and products Sevin Rosen has backed. When the public relations agency for Lotus was planning the announcement of 1-2-3, the company's fabulously successful first product, it sent out invitations that omitted any mention of Lotus, Mitch Kapor, or 1-2-3. "Ben Rosen invites you to a press conference" was enough to fill the room. Sevin Rosen compounded its reputation as a PR-oriented firm with the addition of Grossman, a former business journalist who is one of only a handful of women working in venture capital. While she and Rosen counsel their companies on public relations, Grossman says, "it's not just a matter of getting press. It's a long, involved process of asking the management to think through what the company is really all about, what its values and culture are. That's how these companies achieve visibility."

One lesson Sevin Rosen learned from Kleiner Perkins was the art of incubation—stockpiling talent until the right idea happens along and then building an enterprise from scratch. That happened with Cypress Semiconductor, which was plotted in Sevin's Dallas office by founder T. J. Rodgers, who had left his job at Advanced Micro Devices in November 1982 with little more than a burning desire to run his own company. Rodgers first had to convince Sevin that there was still hope for U.S. technology. Shortly after it was acquired by United Technologies, Mostek—along with most other American semiconductor memory companies—was hammered by Japanese competition. The Japanese had won the war, Sevin declared bitterly on leaving United Technologies, and he was not going to get involved in another semiconductor company. But Rodgers persuaded him that the right combination of new technology and clever marketing strategies "just might win."

Convex, which is building a high-performance scientific computer, was the product both of Rosen's network and of Sevin's incubator. It began in October 1981 with Rosen engrossed in *The Soul of a New Machine*, Tracy Kidder's riveting account of a product development effort at Data General, in which a team of young engineers works nights and weekends for little reward other than the satisfaction of getting a new computer to market. Rosen finished the book on a flight to California and was just thinking, "I would really love to meet those guys and maybe fund them in a new company," when the telephone rang in his Monterey hotel room. The caller was Rich Rubinstein, a friend Rosen had worked with as an engineer twenty years earlier.

Rubinstein was starting a company—would Rosen be interested? Who was involved, Rosen wanted to know. "Me and a guy named Steve Wallach." It was a clear case of serendipity. Wallach had been the architect of the new machine in Kidder's book, and Rosen all but had his checkbook out before he heard another word. But few venture deals come together that smoothly, and this one came unglued altogether. Rubinstein ended up at Cypress Semiconductor, and Convex only clicked six months later when Robert Paluck, a recent addition to Sevin's stockpile of ex-Mostek managers, joined Wallach's team as chief executive and reconstructed the deal.

As opportunities dwindle in the personal computer area that Sevin Rosen has tapped so effectively, the firm is likely to rely even more on its ability to create its own openings. In software, for example, Sevin Rosen sees more business plans than in any other field, many involving outstanding products. "But we think it is extremely hard to start a software company around a single product today," Rosen says, "because it takes millions of dollars to get your product announced, introduced, distributed, advertised, and all the other things you have to do." One solution to that problem would be to convince several software entrepreneurs to band together, foregoing their independence in order to share the marketing infrastructure they need to survive. Says Rosen: "We have an active project to figure out how to pull a lot of these people in and see if we can start a major software company, something similar to what United Artists did in the movie business fifty years ago."

With offices in three states and investments scattered across the country, Sevin Rosen's partners face a major logistical challenge but still manage to get together every two or three weeks to debate deals. Between meetings, they trade information by electronic mail and use Lotus's Symphony software to stay organized. But it is, by Grossman's testimony, a low-key partnership for all its high-tech trappings. "We're a laid-back, unstructured firm," she says. "Ben and L. J. carry somewhat more weight but you'd never know it. It's never come up where they have said no to a deal." Trying to keep things manageable, Sevin Rosen cut off its second fund at $60 million even though it could have raised far more. And the two senior partners have made it clear that for them at least this is the last hurrah. Sevin explains: "We're both in our fifties now and it's time to do something else. I have nothing but admiration for people who make a lifetime career out of venture capital, but with all the traveling, all the traumatic experiences, it ain't a fun life."

VENTURE CAPITAL IN CLEVELAND?

The Midwest has not been seen as a center of entrepreneurship since the last half of the nineteenth century, when Andrew Carnegie was making steel in Pittsburgh, John D. Rockefeller refining oil in Cleveland, and Henry Ford tinkering with cars in Detroit. But David T. Morgenthaler believes the Midwest can again become a magnet for startup activity, and he is doing his part to energize the process. Morgenthaler, a solidly-built branflakes-for-breakfast Clevelander in his mid-sixties, raised a $21 million venture capital fund in 1981 and three years later was setting out confidently to double the size of his firm and to seek another $50 million to $75 million. "I can raise any amount of money you need in Cleveland for an exciting idea," Morgenthaler declares, "and we are beginning to see more of those."

Morgenthaler's is a familiar face on the venture scene in the Midwest. Trained as a mechanical engineer at MIT, he discovered early in life that he preferred working for small organizations. He joined Delavan Manufacturing Co. in Des Moines when it consisted of twenty-five employees and helped it become the world's largest maker of fuel injection equipment for jet engines. His first exposure to the opportunities in risk capital came in 1957 when J. H. Whitney asked him to take over the infant U.S. subsidiary of Foundry Services, a British company that had bought out its American licensee and then brought in Whitney as a partner in the operation. Morgenthaler built Foseco Inc. into a major supplier of specialized chemicals to the steel industry. The British parent eventually bought out the minority shares and Morgenthaler was a millionaire several times over by the time he left the company in the late 1960s.

Morgenthaler had been making venture-style investments right along, and feeling he had done enough operating for a lifetime he decided to set up shop as a full-time venture capitalist. Cleveland, he decided, was a good location because it was in the industrial heartland and only an hour from New York. Using his own capital, Morgenthaler and his partner Robert Pavey, a recruit from Foseco, built a national reputation with investments in Modular Computer Systems in Florida, Evans & Sutherland Computer in Utah, and Apple Computer in California. But Morgenthaler's biggest winner was a Midwest deal. He was the original backer and largest single shareholder in Manufacturing Data Systems Inc. (MDSI), an Ann Arbor company providing computer services to users of numerically controlled machine tools. Started in 1969 with a total venture commitment of $1.6 million, MDSI went public in 1975 and was acquired by Schlumberger in 1980 for more than $200 million. At the time, Morgenthaler held shares worth $20 million. "It was a hugely profitable transaction," Morgenthaler allows with uncharacteristic self-satisfaction.

By 1981 the MDSI sale and other successes had raised Morgenthaler's holdings twenty-fivefold. (He doesn't disclose financial details but puts the value of his venture investments at "significantly more than $25 million.") But he was reluctant to go on risking only his own money. "It became very clear to me that venture capital was going to

go on a much bigger scale than it had been," he explains. "And it was
also clear that if I wanted to attract other good people to the firm they
would be concerned that if anything happened to me my estate might
not want to continue in venture capital." Money was readily available,
in no small part because Morgenthaler as president of the National
Venture Capital Association had been successful in the drive to cut
the capital gains tax, and he was able to pull his first fund together
with a few calls to wealthy individuals. Later, Morgenthaler added two
partners with strong management experience—Paul Brentlinger, who
had been a senior vice president at Harris Corp., and Robert Bellas,
formerly a marketing manager in two California startups.

Morgenthaler invests wherever in the country he can find an opportunity but he is putting more emphasis than ever on the Midwest.
"We have made more money in the Midwest than people realize," he
says, "because so many of our investments are in companies that people have never heard about." In Pittsburgh Morgenthaler has found
such companies as Dynamet, the leading maker of precision rods for
aircraft fasteners, and Tartan Laboratories, a supplier of advanced automation tools for software production. "People would have doubted
that you could do that in Pittsburgh," says Morgenthaler of Tartan. In
Ohio he has backed Advanced Robotics in arc-welding robots and
Tecmar in personal computer attachments. Many of Morgenthaler's
leads come from East Coast and West Coast venture firms who pass
on investments they feel are too far away to handle. Fortunately, he
finds, "many of the East Coast venture capitalists believe the Midwest
begins at the Hudson River and many West Coast venture capitalists
think it starts at Denver." Morgenthaler gets a look at almost everything in between.

Of course, the Midwest will not quickly rival Silicon Valley as a
hotbed of high-tech entrepreneurship. Still lacking, for one thing, are
the great research and development centers that produce product ideas
and entrepreneurs in Massachusetts and California. "I'm asked repeatedly how to get venture capitalists to come to Ohio," Morgenthaler
says, "and I say I can get as many as you want with a phone call. What
you need first are the institutions that people can spin out from. You
have to start with the opportunities and then the venture capital will
come." Such an institution, Morgenthaler believes, is being built at
Pittsburgh's Carnegie-Mellon University, whose computer science department spawned Tartan Laboratories. Also needed are entrepreneurial role models and clusters of high-technology businesses that can
make the company-formation process self-generating. "We are seeing
more interest in entrepreneurship and we are finding more opportunities that we can work with," Morgenthaler claims. Midwest weather,
he says, is only an excuse, not a reason, for the region's failure to
match California's supply of venture opportunities. "People say how

can we compete with the sunshine? I say nonsense, the sun was brighter from 1900 to 1940 in California than it's been from 1940 to 1980
but where did the Stanford engineers go in 1940? They went East
because there weren't any exciting jobs in California." If David Morgenthaler has his way, they will soon be heading for Cleveland.

THE FOLLOWER PLOY

It was perhaps the most unlikely success story in the short history of
modern venture capital. An engineer and Sorbonne-trained economist studies innovation for the ministère de l'industrie, tries without
notable success to introduce venture capital to France, then arrives in
San Francisco with $2 million to invest. And voilà! The $2 million,
later increased to $6 million, becomes $75 million as the clever and
persuasive Frenchman talks his way into some of the best deals available in the late 1970s—Tandem Computer, Genentech, Dysan, Triad
Systems—and even runs across his own engineer-in-a-garage situation
that becomes one of the biggest winners of the decade. Now it is the
1980s. Jean Deleage has broken his ties to the Old Country and joined
two defecting partners of TA Associates to raise $100 million for a
new venture fund. Can he repeat his achievements of the past?

That was a question raised by some who wondered if Deleage could
adapt to the more competitive conditions now prevailing in venture
capital. Says a partner in a leading firm: "He made good decisions.
Now he has to prove that he can add value by working with the companies. It's one thing to be the doubting, cynical venture capitalist
who negotiates like he plays bridge—and Jean is a world-class bridge
player. It's quite another thing to go into a company and be a mixture
of father confessor and psychiatrist and good drinking buddy." As a
matter of fact, Deleage has not played bridge for years, and he can be
a formidable drinking companion as long as French wine is served.
But no one is more aware than Deleage of the changes in the venture
business and their implications for his strategy. "We are a big organization," he says, "and we have no other choice than to be the lead
investor, sometimes the only investor, and to play a completely different game."

Deleage describes the strategy that worked so successfully when he
arrived in San Franciso in 1976 as a representative of Sofinnova, the
French venture firm: "I got acquainted with the major groups and told
them I was ready to invest at a time when the eagerness to invest was
not too high. We were a European group that could be useful for a
company that already had three or four American investors, and my
asset was the list of investors in Sofinnova, where you would find all
the big names in France." Deleage was also representing TA on the
West Coast—Peter Brooke, an adviser to Sofinnova, had not yet

opened a California office—and could marshall sizable resources when
he had a chance to play a lead role. But when he was not in a position
to be the leader in a deal, which was most of the time, he became the
unassuming follower. "I didn't try to get a board seat, didn't try to be
obnoxious by insisting on changing two sentences in the agreement,
didn't use people's time. We played decisively the follower strategy."

Appropriately, it was a French connection that brought Deleage his
big opportunity to be a leader. A purchasing engineer for a French
company told Deleage over drinks one night in 1976 about Sirjang
Lal "Jugi" Tandon, who was developing magnetic heads for disk memories in a garage in the San Fernando Valley. Deleage went to see him,
came away impressed and started doing reference calls. (It was far easier to get information about people and markets in the U.S. than in
Europe, Deleage had found, and he always did a lot of calling.) A few
months later he invested $300,000 in Tandon Magnetics (now called
Tandon Corp.) and later organized two additional rounds of financing
that allowed him to repay Don Valentine for inviting him into one of
his deals. Tandon became the leading supplier of heads and then of
complete floppy disk drives for personal computers and accounted for
more than half of Sofinnova's U.S. winnings. The total Sofinnova
investment of $600,000 was worth $10 million when Tandon went
public in 1981 and some $40 million even in the distressed market of
1983.

After three years of working for a meagre salary, Deleage discarded
his civil servant mentality in 1979 and launched his own firm with
two partners in TA Associates. Burr, Egan, Deleage & Co. (BEDCO),
reflecting the TA heritage of the Boston-based partners, Craig L. Burr
and William P. Egan, is taking care to balance its portfolio with unex-
citing but hopefully secure investments in radio broadcasting and cable television. "We strongly believe that if we do four or five investments where we are guaranteed a fourfold or fivefold return," Egan
says, "the partnership will make money." But the firm is doing half its
investing in California high-tech companies, and it is Deleage who
must sniff out the big winners. "The fact that my strategy worked so
well in the 1976–80 period has given me great credibility," Deleage
boasts, "and in this business the best deals stem from your past deals."
For example, in 1981 Deleage was alerted to the potential of a lack-
luster company called Telco Systems by an entrepreneur he had
backed during his Sofinnova days. New management and an injection
of capital enabled Telco Systems to go public three years later at a
price that gave BEDCO a sixfold gain on its $2 million investment.

As a lead investor, Deleage will now be measured on his ability to
seek out startups and to help them thrive. He was burned by the bankruptcy of Osborne Computer Corp., in which BEDCO had invested
$800,000. And since 1982 he has been deeply involved in the strug-

gles of Vector Graphic Inc., another personal computer high flyer that fell with a thump when IBM entered the market. Deleage raised $750,000 for the company from Sofinnova and others in 1979, three years after it was founded on a shoestring by two Los Angeles housewives, Lore Harp and Carole B. Ely, and Harp's husband Robert. BEDCO later took a $750,000 position in the company but Deleage played a passive role until 1983, when he took over as chairman and chief financial officer as sales were scraping along at a third their level a year earlier. Deleage pulled together another $5 million in private capital and, he says, pressed president Lore Harp to shift product strategies toward IBM compatibility. Harp, who left the company in 1984, maintains that Deleage's role was confined to raising money. Vector, she adds, was on the right track, "but there were a lot of cooks stirring the broth and in the end no real decisions were made." Whether Vector Graphic could be saved remained an open question late in 1984. Deleage, however, has learned from his baptism of fire. "I know that job somewhat better," he says of the company-building task.

Deleage and his six partners now have moved away from microcomputers, where he says "enough companies have been started," to focus on software, communications, and healthcare. One promising field, they believe, will be mobile telephone service as new cellular radio technology allows vastly expanded operations. Egan expects cellular telephone systems to have many of the same investment characteristics as cable television franchises and is building up expertise "so that when they start looking for money they'll come to us." The Boston and San Francisco offices work almost autonomously, although the firm sticks to a policy that two of the three founding partners have to agree to an investment. It is not three out of three, Egan says, out of concern that "the longer you stay in this business the more biases you carry around." In Deleage's opinion, however, venture capital is a business of individual decisions. "You should have partners and you should collect information and advice," he says. "But trying to reach decisions by consensus can be dangerous. Sometimes in two minutes you can feel you are in front of a sensational deal."

NEA'S BRIGHT BOY

When C. Richard Kramlich was a precocious twelve-year-old in Appleton, Wisconsin, he set himself up as the Bright Boy Light Bulb Co., persuaded Sylvania to give him a wholesale price and made more than pocket money selling light bulbs door to door. It helped, of course, that his grandfather had been a founder of Safeway and that his father ran what had become the biggest independent grocery chain in Wisconsin. But Dick Kramlich has always had plenty of his own enthusiasm—a former colleague calls him "the ultimate cheerleader"—and it is not astonishing that he has gone from light bulbs to venture capital. As managing general partner of New Enterprise Associates (NEA) in San Francisco, Kramlich runs one of the largest of the new private venture partnerships, and he runs it energetically. None of NEA's investments have so far achieved phenomenal success although enough have prospered to produce impressive compounded rates of return for his two funds—40 percent for NEA I and 50 percent for NEA II through late 1984. But NEA is important because Kramlich is constantly trying out innovations, organizational and operational, that could make it a prototype as venture investing goes nationwide and reaches for new sources of capital.

Kramlich came under the influence of Georges Doriot at Harvard in the late 1950s, and after four years as a financial handyman at Kroger Co. in Cincinnati he headed back to Boston to learn the venture capital business. At the old-line investment management house of Preston Moss & Co. he organized a series of early-stage deals, scrambling each time for backers among clients of the firm. "I thought we were in venture capital," he reflects, "but we really weren't." In 1968, Kramlich saw a magazine article describing the windup of Davis & Rock and quoting Arthur Rock to the effect that he was planning to look for a younger partner and start a new fund. Kramlich sat down that night and wrote a longhand letter describing his background and suggesting a partnership. A year later, after Rock in typically thorough fashion had examined all of his accounts and talked to most of his acquaintances, Kramlich was ruled acceptable.

The new partnership, Arthur Rock & Co., got $5 million in cash and pledges for another $5 million largely from Rock's previous backers, but it ultimately invested only $6.5 million. "Those were lean years in our business," Kramlich explains. "We sent out a letter to our partners saying the name of the game is survival and the key to survival is cash." Rock and Kramlich hoarded their cash to help out such long running problem investments as Xynetics, Qantel, and Autotronics, and Kramlich got a crash course in crisis investing. Qantel Corp., a small-business computer company, was particularly instructive. Rock had participated personally in the startup round at $5 per share, but three years later, when the partnership agreed to lead a second round, it was clear that this would be a distress financing, well below the initial price. Kramlich recalls going to William R. Hambrecht, an investment banker who had just orchestrated a distress financing for Shugart Associates. "I was thinking of doing this round at maybe $1 a share," he said. To which Hambrecht replied, "You're not being tough enough. Do it at 10¢." Even at 10¢ a share, a price which effectively diluted the early investors out of any meaningful stake in the company, Kramlich and Rock were barely able to raise the $2 million needed to keep Qantel afloat. It took two more rounds of financing, a change of management, and extended bargaining sessions with banks and suppliers to get the company out of the woods. But Qantel eventually was successful enough to be acquired by Mohawk Data Sciences for a price that gave Rock and Kramlich an eightfold return on their money.

Despite the problems, Rock and Kramlich ultimately distributed some $30 million—a decent return, considering the times, they both felt. But the partners had disagreed on a number of issues and Kramlich was chafing in his subordinate role. He began looking for backers to start his own venture fund and discovered that T. Rowe Price Associates, the Baltimore-based manager of some $16 billion, was trying to find an entree to venture capital. Because of SEC restrictions, Price Associates could not participate directly. But Charles W. Newhall III, who was leading the effort for Price, agreed to join Kramlich as a general partner along with Frank A. Bonsal Jr., a Baltimore investment banker. Cornelius C. "Neil" Bond Jr., Price Associates' chief financial officer and a former fund manager and electronics industry analyst; C. W. "Woody" Rea, a General Signal executive; and Arthur J. Marks, a manager at General Electric, came in later. Starting with $1 million from Price Associates and $4.5 million from a family group based in New York, NEA was able to raise a total of $16.4 million for its first fund in 1978. Subsequent funds of $45 million and $100 million put NEA safely into the venture capital big leagues.

With offices in Baltimore and San Francisco, NEA was a national firm from the beginning. Kramlich has expanded that posture by opening an office in New York and helping to finance an affiliated partnership in Dallas, and he has set up an elaborate communications system based on weekly conference calls backed up by personal computers that swap investment data from office to office. NEA also lays great stress on building a "vertical network" of affiliations, starting with Price Associates industry analysts who pass along deal prospects, and extending to well-heeled limited partners such as CIGNA, the big insurer, who provide mezzanine financing for portfolio companies about to go public. Managers from corporate limited partners, including 3M, Merck, Timken, and Japan's C. Itoh, serve on advisory committees, and representatives of NEA's biggest investors act as an outside board of directors to pass on matters affecting the limited partners.

All of this seems over-organized to many West Coast venturers, who say investment decisions are best made in the heat of face-to-face debate and would not dream of submitting their operations to external scrutiny. "This business is growing from a cottage operation to an industry," Kramlich responds, "and a lot of people are going to have to come to grips with this kind of discipline." And he points out that an independent board allows NEA's new funds to follow up investments made by earlier funds, a tactic frowned on by some firms, by providing a way for investors to participate in that decision. That paid off in the case of 3Com Corp., in which NEA I had a $560,000 investment and NEA II a $690,000 holding when the company went public in early 1984. At the offering price of $6 per share, stock held by NEA I—which was in on the startup round as well as two subsequent financings—was worth $4.9 million while NEA II's position was worth $2.3 million. Some other NEA II follow-ons, such as those in Bethesda Research Laboratories (later known as Life Technologies Inc.) and Chomerics Inc., have not fared as well. Overall, though, Kramlich is sure that this flexibility will pay off. "The great thing about having an investment committee," he says, "is that we can operate with exceptions rather than rules."

Kramlich used a follow-on strategy to good effect in NEA I, which started up at a time when prices for late-stage investments were deeply depressed. In order to hit the ground running, as he explains it, Kramlich put NEA I into a half-dozen companies he knew something about, including Xynetics and Qantel from the Arthur Rock & Co. portfolio. Within two years all those companies had gone public or been acquired and Kramlich's backers had recouped their entire investment. With the subsequent funds, Kramlich has shifted the emphasis to startup investments. Taking stock of his entire portfolio of eighty-five companies he estimates that NEA originated half of them.

NEA at first did not turn up often in the big deals shared by the top San Francisco Mafia firms. As the new kid on the block, Kramlich had to scramble for his own deals and he acquired a reputation of being willing to pay slightly higher prices than his more prestigious competitors. "He negotiates aggressively," says one rival, "but he has never lost a deal on price." Kramlich denies that he is overpaying, but he concedes that he won't haggle over a price. "If something is going to be a big winner," he says, "what difference does 5¢ make going in?" NEA shies away from high-profile deals and is often willing to look at situations that others consider offbeat or limited in potential. Without doubt, few large venture firms would have backed Vectra International Inc., a company in Dayton, Ohio, that was developing cancer detection systems based on thermography—a method of recording temperature differences in body tissues that is widely regarded more as folk art than science. After four years and $800,000 from NEA, Vectra is still in the "might make it" category, and Kramlich admits "we should have been stronger on our intuition about these people." So many problems cropped up at Gavilan Computer, a personal computer startup that soaked up more than $30 million in venture capital in less than three years, $3 million of it from NEA, that Rea was dispatched in mid-1984 to take over as president. The move didn't help: Gavilan filed for Chapter 11 protection a few months later.

NEA's East Coast-West Coast connection paid off in an investment in Digital Communications Associates of Atlanta, a deal that was turned up by Bonsal and then turned around by a manager Kramlich recruited. DCA was puttering along at about $2 million a year with its statistical multiplexers—devices for consolidating telephone conversations or streams of computer data for long-distance transmission—when Bonsal found it in 1981. NEA agreed to organize a financing if founder John Alderman would accept a professional manager as president. Alderman was reluctant until Kramlich introduced him to Bertil Nordin, who had been executive vice president of Qantel and had just moved to Atlanta. With Nordin in charge, NEA raised $3 million that got DCA moving, and a year later the company was performing so well that it was able to go public. Says Kramlich: "That's a case where had we not been on the two coasts and had this proliferation of resources the deal would not have come together nearly as smoothly as it did."

The gem of NEA's portfolio so far is Giga-tronics Inc., an unlikely success story that illustrates the value that can be found in venture situations others dismiss. Several factors made Giga-tronics a questionable bet when Kramlich heard about it in 1981. President John W. Scheck proposed to enter a mature industry, electronic test and measurement equipment, where growth is slow and few startups have succeeded, and he planned to go up against entrenched competitors such as Hewlett-Packard and Systron Donner in the specialized niche of microwave signal generators and counters used to test radar and electronic warfare systems. Furthermore, Scheck was looking for only $600,000—too little to interest most big funds—in hopes of keeping most of the equity for the five founders. "We didn't want to dilute ourselves beyond the amount we needed to get through the first phase," Scheck explains.

Most of the venture firms Scheck talked to wanted to invest $1 million or more and take a high percentage of the company. But Kramlich was willing to meet Scheck's terms because he liked the unusual level of commitment and experience in the founding team. All had bailed out of senior jobs at Systron Donner after it was acquired by British electronics giant Thorn EMI, and only one was under fifty. Their early backer and board chairman was George H. Bruns Jr., the former president of Systron Donner. They had demonstrated their personal commitment to the company by hand-crafting their own furniture and production benches and then proceeding to design an instrument so advanced that it was the only one of its type accepted by the navy for use in calibrating new high-frequency electronic warfare systems. "We thought they had growth potential," Kramlich says, "because they had a lot more experience than the garden-variety Silicon

Valley entrepreneur." NEA invested $480,000 for 29 percent of the company and received its reward two years later when Giga-tronics went public at $16 a share and the stock zoomed immediately to $29. At the higher value, NEA's holding was worth $28 million.

Like others in the venture industry, NEA has attempted to add operating experience to its arsenal, notably by bringing Rea and Marks aboard and by linking up with C. Vincent Prothro, a former president of Mostek, in forming the $25 million Southwest Enterprise Associates fund. Dallas-based SEA gives NEA a source of deals as Texas begins to produce high-technology startups, and Prothro provides invaluable semiconductor industry contacts. But Kramlich maintains that background alone is no measure of a venture capitalist's ability. "To me," he says, "understanding issues, defining goals, being able to communicate policy with people at a board level—that is the role of the venture capitalist. I think it overshadows whether you come from a technical background or an operating background or a financial background. There is no formula for coming into this business."

NOTES

1. Statistics in this paragraph are taken from "The Growth of an Industry 1977–1982," *Venture Capital Journal*, October 1982, pp. 6–11, and "Capital Transfusion 1983," *Venture Capital Journal*, January 1984, pp. 6–12.
2. "The Growth of an Industry 1977–1982," *Venture Capital Journal*, October 1982, p. 10.
3. John W. Dizard, "Do We Have Too Many Venture Capitalists?" *Fortune*, October 4, 1982, pp. 106–119.
4. Udayan Gupta, "Venture Capital's Young MBAs," *Venture*, June 1984, pp. 70–71.

8

MR. FIXIT

"Do most startup companies encounter a crisis at some point?"

"All."

"Is that a Murphy's Law of the venture business?"

"Yes, it's not a question of if something will go wrong, it's just when."

As this snippet of conversation with one venture capitalist suggests, trouble is a dividend he expects with every investment. Most often, the problems are minor. But what to do when a deal really goes sour? Unlike the stockholders of public companies, who can always find an ignorant or optimistic buyer for shares in even the most troubled enterprise, venture capitalists are stuck with the problem. The paper they hold is backed largely by hopes and dreams. When the hopes fade and the dreams turn ugly, the paper is usually worthless. Other venture capitalists are most reluctant to buy into a colleague's problems, and even within a firm the partner responsible for a deal in difficulty may get little but sympathy. "If I tried to turn over a sick company to one of my partners," says Charlie Waite of Greylock, "you'd see the biggest bicycle-riding charade in history."

The venturer saddled with a shaky deal can simply walk away, and at times that is the only course that makes sense. "If the technology doesn't work or if you've missed the market," says Tom Perkins, "there's nothing anybody can do." Most often, though, there is something to be salvaged. If they have control—and usually in aggregate they do—outside investors can press for changes in strategy and management in hopes of hitting on a successful combination. They do that frequently. Neil Bond of New Enterprise Associates estimates that a major change of management is required in 80 percent of the deals NEA originates. The skill with which a venture firm uses its boardroom power can be the most important factor affecting its return on investment. Some try to keep on tap a cadre of venture managers who can be moved into troublespots as the need arises. One of the best of these corporate relief pitchers, Q. T. Wiles, was so effective at salvaging lost causes for Hambrecht & Quist, the San Francisco firm that combines venture capital with high-tech underwriting, that he was brought in as chairman of the firm following the death of its cofounder, George Quist. H&Q immediately sent him to the field again to attempt to save Diasonics and ADAC Laboratories, two troubled medical technology companies it had brought public.

Talent like Wiles's is a scarce commodity, however. And most venture capitalists shrink from taking direct control of a portfolio company. Those with an investment or consulting background may simply not be suited to the task of running a small, fast-growing company. Admits Bond of NEA: "I'd say the worst thing that could happen to a company would be to have me at the controls." The young Turks coming into venture investing from management jobs in industry are more tempted to jump in when they see a problem, although they usually see it as a waste of their precious time. "I'd do it for a while," replied one technologist-turned-venturer when I asked him if he would like to jump the fence to help a struggling company get to its feet. "But I don't think I could convince my partners that it's a worthwhile investment."

Occasionally the urge is irresistible. Tony Sun, the cocky, Malaysian-born engineer who joined Venrock Associates in 1979, felt he had something to prove when one of his first deals, a $250,000 investment in American Robot Corp., nearly fell apart before the company had built so much as a prototype of its high-precision robots. "We considered shutting it down," Sun recalls, "but I'd be damned if I was going to take a loss right away so I took over running the company." Sun started commuting to North Carolina, where American Robot was then based. He cut the company down to three engineers and fed in $15,000 a month, mostly from Venrock, while they tinkered. Finally, armed with a working prototype of a robot arm so accurate that it could put a pin through the eye of a needle, Sun was able to find and fund an entrepreneur to put American Robot in business. "I think it is going to be one of the few success stories in the robot industry," Sun claims.

Probably more typical is the experience of Burt McMurtry of Technology Venture Investors, who early in his venture career was persuaded to step in as chief executive of a portfolio company that was headed down the drain. McMurtry was dubious, but after two weeks at the company he decided to try to save it. "There were only a couple of people there who made any sense at all," he recalls, "both women. One was the executive secretary and bookkeeper and the other was a very young production scheduler. I asked the bookkeeper if she would be willing to be general manager, and we ended up putting another $15,000 in just to clean up some bills. It stabilized, and I backed out as president after about two months." A year later, however, it became clear that this would never be a successful independent company and it was sold to a public company for stock and notes at a price slightly higher than McMurtry's original investment. But the public company promptly went bankrupt and he had a total loss. Those two months, from an investment point of view, had been wasted. "So in general I think it's not a good idea for venture capitalists to run companies," McMurtry concludes. Even to step in on an acting basis, he adds, is usually a mistake. "You can't run a company effectively unless you're essentially there all the time, which takes you out of the venture business. And it's hard to run it effectively if the other people in the company know you're there in a temporary capacity." Even so, TVI's Jim Bochnowski had to take over at Synapse Computer Corp. in mid-1984.

In most cases the venturers work on problems indirectly, first prodding managers to bring out the best in them, but often bringing in new talent if the original team still falters. This is, or should be, a subtle process. Dave Marquardt of TVI describes it this way: "In each situation you have to size up the entrepreneurs involved and figure out early what their strengths and weaknesses are. Once you've got a good assessment of the CEO, you've got to figure out what kind of relationship you have to have with him to make him shine. If he's really creative, throwing out good ideas all the time, you've got to keep him channeled. Look at all these ideas that come flying over the fence and pick out the good ones. In other cases, you're dealing with somebody who may never have been a general manager, somebody who may lack confidence in the functional areas where he doesn't have experience. In those situations you've got to get in there and be real supportive, show the guy it's easier than he thinks."

But a change of management can make all the difference for a venture. Xidex, before Sutter Hill brought in Lester Colbert, was losing money and going nowhere in an attempt to compete with 3M, Kodak, and other big names in too many niches of the microfilm business. "They were mismanaged in the sense that they were not staying focused on trying to do one thing well," says Paul Wythes. "Colbert brought some direction to it." Arthur Rock and Dick Kramlich put Qantel on the right track by bringing in Douglas Baker as president and Bert Nordin as executive vice president, replacing a management team that, according to Kramlich, "could only do one thing well and that was manufacture in volume." Sometimes multiple changes are needed, as at Display Data Corp., a company selling computer systems to automotive dealers, where J. H. Whitney and Greylock tried three CEOs before they were satisfied. Says Waite: "We waited too long to get rid of the first guy, we made a mistake on the second guy, and on the third guy we hit a home run."

The issue of just how forcefully to apply their clout is one that many venturers agonize over. There is always the chance that too violent an approach will make things worse. Arthur Rock, for one, admits that he prefers not to change chief executives, not so much because firing somebody bothers him but because he doubts his ability to find a better replacement. "I find that in changing chief executives," he says, "you are taking a big risk." Fairly often, the problem is not so simple that a single change can solve it. "It boils down to a question of strategy and timing and the right people," says Jim Lally of Kleiner

Perkins, "so there is a whole series of things you have to do to fix it."
Dick Kramlich argues that precipitant action can be counterproductive in the complex environment of a fast-growing company and usually isn't necessary. "You don't have to fire anybody in order to change
the management," he insists. "You can evolve things in a constructive
way instead of going off the deep end and trying to dominate the
situation."

THE ADLER TOUCH

Most venture investors get involved in problem situations reluctantly
and find the experience debilitating. But Frederick R. Adler, a tough
New York trial lawyer turned venture capitalist, calls rescuing a company "a high you can't believe." Adler is a leading backer of high-
technology startups, and his most successful company, Data General
Corp., entered the $1 billion club in 1984. But Adler is also known
for his feats as a turnaround artist and he is indisputably the most
controversial of the top venture capitalists, criticized by some of his
peers for the abrasive and aggressive tactics he has sometimes employed when he decides to take control.

Adler's slight figure and almost elfin features belie a driving personality and unquenchable ego that he can turn loose in a torrent of
words. In troubled situations he uses his command of the language to
establish control of a situation and then to understand it and change
it. "Fred just likes to get in there and pull the prey apart and then
reassemble it," says one admirer of his art. "Other people like to dissect
it as opposed to pulling it apart." Adler is aware that a few venture
firms will not join deals where he is involved, although he says the
number is diminishing. "They consider me to be too tough," he says.
"I'm probably the only person in the field who has that reputation."
Adler says his detractors don't really know him, that they are judging
him on second-hand reports. But in the next breath he admits that
he "doesn't have the greatest tact in the world on occasion." When
he is faced with a situation where a company is fast going under, Adler
acts first and worries later, if at all, about tact. "I probably could do
it better if I took more time," he says, "but I usually feel I don't have
the time. If I'm wrong and I get the chance, I apologize. If they accept
my apology, good. If they don't, there is nothing I can do about it."

RESCUING MICROPRO

After eighteen months of personal confrontation and painful effort
had pulled MicroPro International Corp. from the edge of bankruptcy
and prepared it for a public offering, Adler looked back on it all and
confided: "I would have paid Seymour Rubinstein (MicroPro's found-

er) $100,000 to get his company in trouble because of the fun of turning it around." The MicroPro situation was one that demanded fast action, and Adler delivered it in inimitable style. Adler and the funds he manages put about $1 million into MicroPro in 1981, picking up a 25 percent chunk of the California software company that was already well-known for its best-selling word processing program called WordStar. Adler was impressed by the opportunity to use the success of WordStar as a pipeline to move other products to the shelves of computer retailers, although he says he had reservations about MicroPro's management. In evaluating a deal, says Adler, "I start first with the size of the market and its growth pattern. Second, I go to the value of the product in that market and the barriers to entry to other products that would compete with it. Management to me is the third or fourth item, contrary to the popular view of venture capital."

But management was MicroPro's achilles heel. Despite the astonishing success of WordStar—which sold more than 800,000 copies in the five years after it was introduced in 1978—MicroPro ran into embarrassing problems. In the early summer of 1982, Adler helped MicroPro arrange a $9.5 million private placement in anticipation of going public that fall. The expectation, says Grace H. Gentry, a MicroPro director, was for a pre-tax profit of $3.5 million in the fiscal year ending that August. Instead, the board learned with dismay, sales had begun to level off while expenses continued on a steep upward ramp. The company would in fact *lose* more than $1 million for the year. The difference of $4.5 million in projected profits was especially troubling to William H. Janeway, a director representing F. Eberstadt & Co., the investment banking house that had handled the private placement and sold most of it to institutional clients. The board ordered a 10 percent cut in permanent staff, then standing at 510, but Janeway was not satisfied. It seemed to him that things were out of control, and he appealed to Adler—who had introduced Eberstadt to MicroPro—to take a hand.

The agreement under which Adler had invested in MicroPro gave him the right to two board seats, although he had always been content to allow a partner to represent him. But at the next board meeting, conducted over a telephone link between MicroPro's headquarters near the futuristic Frank Lloyd Wright civic center in suburban Marin County and Adler's office on Park Avenue, Adler made it abundantly clear that he had reclaimed his seat. Before the meeting began, the board learned that although fifty people had indeed been fired, employment was now up to 540. Adler began asking detailed questions about the business and expenses. "How many lawyers are in the room?" Adler demanded to know. Four, he was told. "Do you realize what four lawyers are costing just for this meeting?" And by the way, what were MicroPro's legal fees last month? A vice president on the

California end objected: "Listen my friend. . . ." Adler cut him off: "I pick my friends very carefully, and you are not among them." The vice president, according to Adler, got angry. "So I said the meeting's over and I hung up."

Gentry, who is president of a small computer consulting firm, was attending her second MicroPro board meeting. She found the performance vastly entertaining. "It was very clear what Adler was doing," she recalls. "My father used to tell me this old joke about the man trying to get his mule across a bridge. The mule is not moving, and there is a guy standing there who offers to help. He walks over and picks up a 2 by 4 and hits the mule across the head and the guy says, 'First you have to get his attention.' It was very clear that all he was doing was getting their attention."

If that was the intent, Adler's 2 by 4 certainly got results. Rubinstein quickly agreed to allow Adler to come in and conduct a two-day review of MicroPro's budgets and organization, a marathon session that filled the board room with managers explaining their operations and trying to save their jobs. Rubinstein was present but mainly as an observer. "He tried to participate a few times but when he was called on it he backed off voluntarily," Adler states. By the end of the two days, Adler had approval for a plan to cut employment by more than 50 percent within a week and to start looking for a new president. MicroPro was profitable again by that December, and in the fiscal year that ended August 31, 1983 it netted $4.9 million. The following spring, when Eberstadt joined with Lehman Brothers Kuhn Loeb and E. F. Hutton & Co. to take MicroPro public at $10.50 per share, Adler and his funds emerged not only with holdings worth $20.8 million but with effective control of the company as well. In an unusual stock conversion maneuver written into the public offering agreement, Rubinstein's remaining 3.7 million shares became "founders common stock," with virtually no voting rights.

A MATTER OF DOMINANCE

The shock tactics at MicroPro were typical of a confrontational style that has been an Adler trademark in troubled situations from the beginning of his involvement in venture investing—and before. Adler learned survival on the streets of New York after his Austrian-born father lost everything in the Depression. As a lawyer he became a tough and expensive litigator, and when Wall Street clients asked him to help companies in difficulty he learned to apply a courtroom style to business. The best trial lawyers, Adler believes, succeed by establishing intellectual dominance from the outset. That is what he tries to do, he says, "by sheer force of intellect." Even Adler's admirers, though, say he occasionally resorts to tirades that give him control of a situation as much through emotion as through intellectual superiority.

Herbert J. Richman, a founder of Data General, brought Adler into the startup of what is now the third-largest minicomputer maker first as an attorney and then as an investor. Richman credits him with a crucial role in a massive shakeup that the company went through between 1980 and 1983. "Fred was always able to grab us by our collars, bring us back into reality a little bit and kick us into the absolutely fundamental methods of running the business," Richman recalls. But Data General's executives were able to profit from Adler's counsel partly because they had known him long enough to shrug off the emotional outbursts. "You have to have lived with Fred as long as we have to be able to deal with him and not walk out feeling totally insecure or beat up," Richman says. "You can listen to Fred screaming and shouting at all the other guys and you can take your choice. You can be offended by it, or you can let him keep going and then get him focused again."

The situation that soured some West Coast venture firms on Adler's style was the 1975 turnaround of Intersil Inc., the California semiconductor company started by Fairchild founder Jean Hoerni. The process was so arduous for Marshall G. Cox, then Intersil's president, that he dropped out of the electronics industry for a while with plans to go into the resort business. "I think I was then what they call a burnout," says Cox, now happily running his own semiconductor sales company. Cox harbors no ill feelings toward Adler, although he still questions some of his strategic moves. "My association with Fred was as a very supportive mentor in the first four years at Intersil and as a very tough taskmaster the last two years," Cox says, "but we left as friends." Adler calls Cox "an honest, brilliant entrepreneur" but explains: "when things were in trouble, he could not cut back so I was forced to do the cutting back myself." Still, another Intersil investor was aghast: "He just raked Marshall over the coals so I couldn't believe it. Why Marshall didn't slug him one, I can't understand."

One story, which Adler recounts with relish, goes far toward explaining why the Intersil turnaround assumed almost legendary proportions in Silicon Valley, where egalitarian management styles predominate. Adler, a vehement nonsmoker, had just started commuting weekly from New York as Intersil's losses mounted in 1975. He walked into a meeting exhausted and spotted a vice president smoking. The following exchange took place:

Adler: "Will you please put out the cigarette."
VP: "No, it's personal. I don't have to put out the cigarette."
Adler: "You know, you're really making a mistake."
VP: "I don't care, my personal life will not be infringed on."

Adler: "You're fired."

VP: "What did you say?"

Adler: "You're fired. Get out of here, there'll be a check waiting for you across the street in the cashier's office."

(Exit VP. Five minutes later, re-enter VP)

VP: "I'd like my job back."

Adler: "Why?"

VP: "I made a mistake."

Adler: "You did worse than that, you were trying a power play in order to test me. This company is in trouble and it doesn't need any garbage from you or anybody else."

VP: "I know that. I misestimated my importance, I guess. Can I have my job back?"

Adler: "Do you understand the rules?"

VP: "Yessir."

Adler: "What are the rules?"

VP: "The rules are I do what you tell me."

Adler: "And what will happen the first time you don't?"

VP: "I guess I'll be fired."

Adler: "That's right."

With Adler badgering Cox and his vice presidents, Intersil moved from near-bankruptcy to profitability early in 1976 and then merged with Advanced Memory Systems Inc. (In 1980 the combined company was sold to General Electric Co. for $237 million.) Adler was an intensely active board chairman—and after Cox departed an even more active president for a time—although he held only about 100,000 shares of stock in the company, ultimately worth less than $1 million. Why had he expended so much energy on a relatively minor investment? In large measure, it seems, to defend his name. Intersil had gone public, "and to some degree it was being sold on my reputation." Although he had more at stake in MicroPro, Adler uses a similar rationale to explain his participation in the turnaround there. He had gotten other investors involved, and it was his responsibility to protect them. "You do it because of a combination of pride and obligation," he says.

But in one case, Adler seemed to jump into a troubled situation for no more reason than the challenge it involved. Adler had twice turned down the chance to invest in Bethesda Research Laboratories Inc., a biotechnology startup he felt was trying to be all things to all men. As he expected, BRL began losing money. Janeway, who had raised some $15 million for the company, called Adler in West Palm Beach, where he was nursing a flareup of the chronic osteoarthritis he suffered in both hips, and offered him stock at any price he cared to name if he would get involved. "The weather in Florida was pretty good but I was doing pretty poorly," Adler says, "so I said what the hell do I have to lose." He agreed to buy 10 percent of the company for a token $2,000, added $250,000 for a convertible note and persuaded other investors to put in another $750,000. Within a year, BRL was in shape to be merged with a division of Dexter Chemical Co. amid hopes that the combined company could be taken public.

Adler's watchword whenever he gets involved in running a company is cash flow, a preoccupation he learned during his father's days as a salesman. "He'd leave home with a roll of bills on Monday and he'd come back on Saturday night with another roll of bills. I'd say, 'How did it go, Dad?' And he'd total it up and say, 'Great week, I've got more today after all my expenses than I had on Monday.'" In an Adler company, the focus on cash flow is almost that narrow. Adler's aphorisms on the subject—"Happiness is positive cash flow." "Nobody ever went bankrupt with a lot of cash in the bank."—assume the status of holy writ. To Adler, all the investments that companies make in research, new equipment and new products should be viewed as expenses. The fact that most can be capitalized and written off against profits over several years seems to him a kind of accounting chimera that ignores reality. "What is a capital expense in a growing company that has to keep building plants year after year?" he asks. Looking primarily at cash flow rather than at reported profits or expected growth, Adler may amputate what looks to others like a healthy limb. At Intersil, he ordered Cox to sell off a division making digital watches although it appeared to be making money even during a recession and continued to be profitable after it was sold. By Adler's standards, the division's profits were illusory. "There was no allowance for corporate overhead, no reserve for bad products or warranty expenses, no depreciation of the assets dedicated to this stuff," Adler says. "A seventeen-year-old kid taking an accounting course in high school would have knocked it apart."

HELPING INNOVATION FLOURISH

For all his tough talk and his assertive reputation, Adler has an idealistic, even romantic view of his role and the contribution he believes he is making to society. He left litigation in the late 1960s, he says, because he realized it was a destructive profession. "You were what amounted to a hired gun. I looked at my clients and decided that 40 to 50 percent of them were no damn good. Why spend my life with a lot of people I despised?" Adler moved into venture capital almost by accident, when a group of bankers who had seen him in action as a turnaround expert offered to back him in business deals. A leveraged buyout of a small trucking company clicked, and Adler was on his way as an investor. Reading about the new potential of integrated circuits and minicomputers, Adler began to look for ways to get involved. Innovation, he concluded, was crucial to America's survival. "As far as I'm concerned," Adler says, "innovation flourishes through entrepreneurial behavior. The companies that are making it are making it because people will take on odds and work fifteen hours a day seven days a week. And the key people putting that together are the best of the venture capitalists."

Adler put out the word on Wall Street that he was interested in high-technology deals, and early in 1968 he heard from Richman, then an East Coast marketing manager for Fairchild Semiconductor. Richman, a would-be financier himself, had run across a group of engineers at Digital Equipment Corp. who wanted to start their own minicomputer company and had offered to raise money for them. With almost $900,000 lined up Richman had encountered a snag. A lead investor had demanded that he get an attorney to represent the group, and Richman couldn't find one who had ever done a venture deal. Finally he heard about Adler. "I told him if he wanted to be our attorney the only way he could do it was to put some of his own money in," Richman recalls. "I said if we have any trouble from Digital or anybody else, we wanted his ass on the line right with ours. He thought that was a kind of unique and pragmatic concept." Richman was only talking about a few thousand dollars, but the ante escalated when the largest investor he had found suddenly dropped out. Adler restructured the deal, put in $150,000 of his own money and got Data General in business.

The engineers, led by Edson D. deCastro, who later became president, moved into a former beauty salon and began scribbling designs on pads of yellow paper. Richman, who had resigned from Fairchild to join the startup although he had never sold a computer, moved in as well. "It's just another thing to sell," Richman told himself, "just a little more densely-packed semiconductor." By December the engineers had announced their product, a powerful machine for engineering applications, and by February 1969 Richman had sold and shipped the first model to Mobil Oil. Or tried to ship it. "It went out of here the day after a major blizzard," Richman recalls, "never to be seen again. It disappeared." But another machine was substituted, and business took off. By the fall Adler was able to persuade Bache & Co., then the second largest brokerage firm in the country, to take Data General public. "Getting somebody like Bache to take you out gives you a certain credibility in the marketplace," says Richman, "and Fred was at his best dealing with those guys." But Richman recalls a slightly embarrassing footnote to the public offering: "Fred has this thing about $14 as a magic number when he takes a company public, but demand for the stock was incredible and the market opened at $40. There were a lot of surprised people, but if we were priced at $25 maybe there wouldn't have been that much demand."

Adler's turnaround talents were seldom needed at Data General, but he held onto his stock—480,000 shares worth about $22 million in 1984—and as chairman of the executive committee he still watches the company closely. "Fred's real genius and contribution at Data General was keeping us way ahead in the financing of the company," Richman says. "We never had a nickel and dime kind of worry. What we had to worry about was operating the company, making the product and selling it." For Adler, the Data General connection provided the entree he had been seeking to the world of high technology. Richman introduced him to Michael McNeilly, who was starting Applied Materials Inc. to make semiconductor manufacturing equipment, and that investment in turn led him to Intersil.

Jean Hoerni, who also served on the Applied Materials board, invited Adler to invest in Intersil but Adler was leery of the management situation. Hoerni was brilliant but he shouldn't be running a company, Adler decided. At about the same time, Marshall Cox asked Adler for help in starting a new semiconductor memory company. Adler, then investing only as an individual, could not provide enough capital to swing the deal alone but he sold Hoerni on the idea of backing Cox and merging the two companies. Not only would the move strengthen Intersil's product line, he figured, but it would go a long way toward solving the management problem. Adler went on the Intersil board, replacing Arthur Rock, whose ties to Intel created a conflict as Intersil moved into the metal-oxide-silicon (MOS) technology that was becoming important in memory applications. But Cox could not get along with Hoerni, whom he calls "the most emotional man I ever met," and Adler ultimately felt he had to jump in to preserve his investment.

MELLOWING

After the exhausting Intersil battle, his marriage on the rocks, Adler went into a period of inactivity that lasted until mid-1978. By then he had missed the opportunity to invest in the big wave of microcomputer startups, and he had begun to question his ability to operate alone in a field increasingly dominated by large funds. Looking at the future direction of venture capital, Adler decided that to be effective his "value added" had to go up. In the past, he had added value to an investment mainly by helping out in management. Now he wanted to tie in market research, executive search, and technical consulting services to do a better job of finding deals. "You may still do the investment," he explains, "but at least you know the nature of the beast before you get into the cage."

Partly to pay for all this overhead, Adler gave up his loner status for the first time and raised a series of funds, which by early 1984 totaled $100 million, from foreign and domestic institutions. The first

three funds showed an annual compound rate of return through 1983
of around 50 percent, which Adler says approximates his record as an
individual investor, with a series of successful deals including Daisy
Systems, Monolithic Memories, Lexidata and Ungermann-Bass. One
reason for those impressive returns is Adler's ability to hold down
losses. Through 1983, he calculates, writeoffs and writedowns of failed
or troubled deals totaled less than $4 million on about $70 million
invested by his funds. Adler's conclusion: "I really don't think that
this business is a risk business in the financial sense—if you do your
work, if you really focus, if you have a high energy level." In addition,
Richman believes, Adler has a unique attribute: "He is willing to
throw his body in front of a train to make a deal work. Nobody loses
money on his deals because he is willing to get in there and tear the
place apart, restructure it, get it moving, then find somebody to take
it and start running with it again. Most of the venture guys won't do
that."

Adler brings some of his assertive style to the management of his
partnership. Every investment has to be justified in detail to the managing partner, and subordinates must stand up to a withering cross-
examination. "Fred, being a litigator by background, has a very logical
mindset," says James Harrison, a California-based partner. "He very
definitely takes positions, but they are not off-the-cuff positions." Two
of Adler's partners departed in 1983 to start their own fund. There
were differences in investment philosophy, Adler explains, but he
adds: "These fellows came out of Citicorp where they were quite senior
and they didn't go through that sort of intense interrogation." Adler's
partnership is somewhat unusual in another regard: He has the right
to invest personally, as much or as little as he likes, in any of the deals
he finds. Some other groups allow partners to coinvest, but the
amounts are usually small. Adler may put as much individually into a
deal as his funds do, and his rate of investment—including family
funds—has varied from a high of $10 million annually when his funds
invested $30 million to about $7 million in a year when the funds
invested $22 million.

There is a streak of religious and altruistic sentiment that colors
Adler's investment record. Although he has never been confirmed
and doubts that he would even be considered Jewish under Jewish law,
Adler holds to a personal Judaism that includes fervent support for
Israel. "As far as I'm concerned," he says, "it's an island of civilization
in a sea of anarchy." Adler is deeply committed also to aiding medical
research, which he does both through philanthropy and by directing
about a third of his investments into healthcare and medical technology. While the medical investments may not do as well financially as
other alternatives, Adler explains, they give him "psychic income."
Adler's two passions came together in the early 1970s when backers

of Elscint Ltd., an Israeli instrumentation company, approached him about generating support for the venture in the United States. Adler liked the entrepreneurs involved in the company, and he saw it as a vehicle to enter the field of diagnostic imaging. He put in $35,000 to begin a series of personal investments in Israeli companies that now totals about $5 million. With Adler's help, several, including Elscint, Sci-Tex and Biotechnology General, have gone public in the United States. "Israel doesn't have the sort of market where you can raise enough capital to finance high-growth export companies," Adler explains, "and they are all basically binational companies."

Adler went to unprecedented lengths in 1983 to assuage the distress of investors who bought shares in BTG, which were offered at $13 and quickly fell to about $8. As chairman and largest stockholder, Adler rammed through a 25 percent stock dividend that went only to buyers of the public shares, in effect giving them a price of $10.40 per share. "If I hadn't been sick at the time," Adler explains, "I could have done a much better job on the public offering." Actually, since BTG's stock was hit both by a general collapse of biotechnology shares and a currency in crisis in Israel, there seems to be little he could have done. But Adler has a phrase to describe his response to embarrassing situations: "Pay the two dollars." Which means, roughly, stop complaining and clean up the mess even if your first tendency is to blame somebody else for it.

With gestures like the BTG dividend Adler may also be attempting to correct impressions about his style and motivations that he feels are either inaccurate or outdated. "There are all sorts of legends about me," he says, "and when I try to trace them down invariably people say they heard it from somebody else." Looking back on the Intersil episode, Adler admits that he could have been more tactful. He avoids confrontations now, he says, and he has tried to make his firm less structured and himself less dominant. "I have to force myself nowadays to be nondominant, to take a back seat a lot," he says. As he nears sixty, Adler is also concerned, apparently, with the judgment of history. If he can persuade Congress to change the laws governing foundations, allowing them to reinvest income in new ventures, he hopes to create a kind of Venture Foundation that would fund new companies in applied medical research and "really do some good in the world." After all, he says, there is no such thing as immortality. "The only thing you can hope for is to be remembered by those acts that are either so horrible that people can't forget them or so good that people don't want to forget them."

9

THE SEED MONEY MEN

Great venture successes of the past were often built around entrepreneurs with at best modest credentials to run a company. The founders of Digital Equipment, Fairchild Semiconductor, Data General, Apple Computer and ROLM, to name five we have looked at briefly, were youthful engineers and scientists with little or no general management experience. Their business plans were sketchy and their product ideas unproven. There may have been a marketing or financial expert on the team but almost never an individual who by training or work history was obviously qualified to be a chief executive. Spotting a Ken Olsen or a Bob Noyce as an immensely gifted future manager was a matter of instinct, intuition—or just luck. By the standards of the venture capital megafunds of the 1980s, theirs would be "incomplete teams" that could not be financed until a proven president and all the important staff officers had been found and substantial progress on a product had been demonstrated.

Today's big funds, by virtue of their size, must concentrate their resources and attention on complete, experienced teams that can readily absorb large amounts of capital. Gib Myers of Mayfield Fund: "The teams are much better than they were ten years ago. We're not seeing the old classic entrepreneurs who raise half a million and try to make a go of it. We're seeing a very professional manager leaving HP and IBM and DEC. They can't bootstrap it, they don't know how to do that. But if you give them $3 million and twenty people, they're quite effective. And today they can raise that kind of money easily."

Building an organization from scratch, designing and developing the first product, researching and planning a marketing strategy—all this requires a substantial commitment of time from the investors as well as from the entrepreneurs. Spreading $100 million over 200 raw startup deals would dilute the effort of a handful of partners, or require an increase in staff that would dilute their compensation. The same logic impels the megafunds to focus as much as possible on deals that have a chance to produce sizable returns. "If you make a $1 million investment in a company that you think is going to be a $10 million company," points out Jim Lally of Kleiner Perkins, "it takes the same amount of work as a $1 million investment in a company that's going to be a $100 million or $200 million company. If we made a host of investments in companies we felt would be small companies, all our time would be consumed working with those companies and the returns would be small relative to the returns we're expecting to make."

The reasoning is certainly sound, and the instant success of such complete-team, high-capitalization startups as Compaq Computer and LSI Logic seems to prove it in practice. On the other hand, some entrepreneurs are not above requesting more money than they need, just to ensure that they fall above the cutoff point. Dan Gregory of Greylock asked one applicant why he wanted to start with $4 million and was told baldly, "that is the amount you need to attract the venture capitalists." All but lost in this waltz of the elephants is the lonely scientist who really needs only a few thousand dollars and a lot of advice to get started. The big funds will back a few of them every year if their ideas have significant potential. Some have set aside office space in hopes of recreating the incubation process that worked so well for Kleiner Perkins. But there are many more would-be entrepreneurs whose capital requirement is simply too small or whose growth plans are too limited to interest a major venture group. And it is not surprising in a field as dynamic as venture capital that a new style of fund—a "seed capital" fund—has appeared to fill this gap in the market.

It was a concept whose time definitely had arrived. By the end of 1983 at least two dozen professionally-run venture funds specializing in seed investments had been created, altogether representing well over $100 million in backing for deals too small, entrepreneurs too callow and ideas too risky for most other venture firms. So many irresistible deals flooded in that one of the new firms, Crosspoint Venture Partners, launched twenty-two companies and ran through $18 million in fifteen months, then started on a new $42 million fund early in 1984. Alpha Partners, another busy seed investor, set up shop with $13 million in 1982 and raised another $22.5 million less than two years later. Wally Davis, who left Mayfield Fund to start Alpha, expected to start slowly but was bowled over by proposals and inquiries that came in at a rate of 1,000 per year.

Far from looking on the newcomers as competition, megafund venturers often welcome them as farm clubs for deals that can graduate to the big leagues. Some 90 percent of Crosspoint's individual backers are venture capitalists. Three of the biggest California venture firms—Kleiner Perkins, Mayfield, and New Enterprise Associates—got together in 1984 to create a $5 million seed fund of their own called Onset Partners. Cleverly, they built Onset around the talents of the twenty-five design engineers at David Kelley Design, a Palo Alto firm that specializes in the nitty-gritty work of turning great ideas into great products. Instead of cash, entrepreneurs backed by Onset get as much as $500,000 worth of product design work at Kelley Design, enough to prove the value of even the vaguest notion and emerge with a prototype product. "It is very difficult to add value to a deal at the seed stage," says Mike Levinthal of Mayfield. "Asking the tough tech-

nical questions at the beginning is extremely important, so we hope
that Onset will be a great value-added incubator."

"WALLY TAKES A HARD LINE"

To deal with the higher level of risk associated with seed deals, Alpha
Fund has evolved a disciplined approach to picking investments.
Wally Davis is a graying, professorial "engineer's engineer," as a former
partner calls him, who keeps a slide rule on his desk and likes nothing
better than to hear somebody describe a new gadget or technical idea.
Unlike most senior venture capitalists, who often hire assistants to
read through the piles of business plans, Davis does the initial screening on most of the four or five proposals that come to Alpha every
day, replying to most supplicants that they are too far away from his
Sand Hill Road office or too large or just not technically interesting.
If the concept piques his interest, Davis brings in partner Brian J.
Grossi, a former research engineer at Hewlett-Packard and SRI International, who delves into the technology in real depth. If both Davis
and Grossi still like the deal, Alpha's two other partners pass on its
organizational, personnel, and financial aspects before an investment
decision is made.

To further limit his exposure to risk, Davis then works out a detailed
schedule for investing in three or four increments, each of which is
contingent on milestones in product development or corporate organization. "If they don't hit the milestones," says Davis, "we don't have
the obligation to go on." And despite an avuncular disposition, Davis
is a hard-liner when it comes to meeting those deadlines. Says one
entrepreneur: "If you can't meet your milestone, Wally's attitude is to
say, 'call me up when you get there.' If you say you're running out of
money and can't meet the payroll, he kind of says, 'that's your
problem.'"

The Davis approach is well illustrated in the short history of a company called Deka Inc., founded in 1982 to develop and sell telephone
equipment that could be manufactured in the Far East. James E. Herlinger, who had been in charge of a similar strategy at Plantronics, an
established telecommunications company, took the idea to Davis after
borrowing $100,000 to start work on the prototype of a new light-
weight headset. "I had about five employees and very little money left
by the time Wally funded us," Herlinger says. Davis liked the idea of
capitalizing on the deregulation of the telecommunications industry
and he and Grossi liked the team of engineers Herlinger had pulled
together. "A lot of people say the telephone business is a commodity
business," Davis says, "but I don't believe that. Building a many-fea-
tured telephone is as difficult as building a disk drive."

Alpha agreed to put in $670,000 on the usual incremental basis, and Deka worked frantically to finish the first product and get it to a trade show—the milestone event that would release another allotment of Alpha's cash—by the end of 1982. To meet that schedule, Deka had to go with a version of the headset that used discrete components instead of a custom-designed integrated circuit to transmit voice signals, which "didn't work really well," Herlinger admits. Although Deka sold a number of early headsets to large distributors, it wound up being forced to take most of them back once the advanced version was ready. "That is one of the dangers of taking a product to market too soon," Herlinger says. "Sometimes the venture capitalists have the attitude that even if your product doesn't work as well as you'd hoped, you should get it to market, see if it will sell and work nights to fix it."

Despite its startup problems, Deka was doing well enough late in 1983 to raise another $1.9 million at a modest two and one-half times the price of 87¢ per share at which Alpha invested. Alpha did not participate in the financing, although several of Alpha's limited partners did come in on their own. "As a matter of principle," Davis explains, "we're doing only seed investments." With the larger fund Alpha raised in 1984, Davis has been able to increase the average commitment in order to carry companies a bit beyond the product development stage. But he does not plan to be a second-round investor, even though this policy might damage a startup's credibility with some potential new investors, who usually like to see old investors upping the ante as a demonstration of support. "That's not our role," he tells investors who wonder why he hangs back. Davis does help in subsequent fundings by providing strong contacts in the financial community. "We get to talk to a lot of people just because they are impressed that Wally funded us in the first place," Herlinger says. But Herlinger was unable to convince Davis that he should change his antireinvestment policy, even though it might have helped Deka raise its next crucial round of capital. "Wally takes a hard line," he reports. "Wally is going to run his business the way he runs his business."

"NEVER PAY RETAIL"

John B. Mumford of Crosspoint Venture Partners in Palo Alto is another seed investor whose motto is "never pay retail" for stock in the companies he backs. Mumford made an exception, however, by investing personally at a one hundredfold markup in a later-stage financing for CXC Corp., a company that stands a chance of being one of the big winners of the 1980s and as a startup provided the template for Crosspoint's seed strategy. CXC is spending $45 million in a bold attempt to develop an exotic family of office telephone equipment that can handle voice and data messages in huge volumes. With a backlog of orders well in excess of $100 million before it had finished a delay-plagued development effort in 1984, CXC had the potential to become a major company. In Mumford's book, it was also a classic example of how a seed deal can be turned into a significant investment opportunity.

The genesis of CXC was a few pages of notes and diagrams scribbled in 1980 by James F. Willenborg, a brilliant engineer who is also a self-described malcontent, full of ideas but usually unwilling to endure the drudgery of implementing them. Mumford, a sometime management consultant and entrepreneur who was then running a small invest-ment firm, had helped Willenborg raise money in the mid-1970s for one of his brighter ideas, a mail order house for computer supplies that grew into a $100 million company called INMAC. Later he backed other Willenborg notions, but cautiously. "Jim is one of the most pro-lific idea people around," Mumford says, "but you have to use him properly or he will take you down fifteen paths."

When Willenborg scrawled his inspiration for an advanced private branch exchange (PBX), Mumford was interested but not enthusiastic until other engineers had verified the concept. One was Joseph R. Leonardi, a top manager at Pertec Computer Corp., who spent ninety days researching the market opportunity and the technology that would be required. Willenborg, he discovered, was at least half right about what could be done technically. And the market, in view of the regulatory changes that were coming in the telecommunications in-dustry, looked wide open. Leonardi quit his job to head CXC and joined Mumford, Willenborg, and a few others in a $200,000 seed financing that allowed him to write a business plan and do the addi-tional engineering that would prepare the company for major funding. Kleiner Perkins, which saw in CXC a situation analogous to Tandem's technologically audacious beginning, led a first-round financing of $1.5 million in June of 1981 while investment banker Sandy Robert-son put together an R&D partnership—an investment vehicle allow-ing outside investors to share the costs, risks, and rewards of corporate research projects—that added $3.5 million.

CXC finally developed its complex product, one year late and 50 percent over budget. Three years and an additional $30 million after the company's birth there was still no assurance that CXC would suc-ceed, although Leonardi believed the delay did not hurt its chances. But partners in Kleiner Perkins and in Robertson's firm were impressed from the start with the role Mumford and Willenborg had played in CXC and other seed deals, and they offered to back them in raising a fund. As Eugene Kleiner, who invested as an individual and acts as an adviser to Crosspoint's startups, points out: "There is a need for smaller groups because some things are more difficult when you have $150 million than when you have $20 million." As partners in a major seed-capital fund, Mumford and Willenborg were inundated with more than 100 proposals per month. But they read everything that comes in. "You have to make it easy for people to contact you," Willenborg says, "and when they do contact you you have to treat them with respect."

Few of the proposals Crosspoint sees share the CXC potential. But those that are too small for the major venture capital funds can look like substantial opportunities for investors getting in on the ground floor. One such deal, in the summer of 1983, originated with three engineers who had worked together at Intel and decided to approach Jim Lally, the ex-Intel manager at Kleiner Perkins, for $100,000 to start a company making productivity aids for writers of commercial software. Lally persuaded them to raise the ante, but even the $250,000 they decided was the maximum they could use made the deal far too small for Kleiner Perkins to consider. And besides, the team was incomplete because no president was aboard. Lally called Mumford, who was delighted to take over the deal. This was a business area that he and Willenborg had been thinking about, and they agreed within a day to back the threesome in a company called Atron. Their first product was snapped up eagerly by the biggest names in software and the company was profitable only two months after shipments began. But Atron's founders showed no interest in seeking the kind of growth that most venture investors demand. "We've had experience with companies going through the trauma of rapid growth," explains founder Terry Fowler, "and the second time around we want to take it slow."

Whether Crosspoint could make Atron attractive to other investors in a second round of financing was still in doubt at mid-summer of 1984, and certainly the go-slow attitude of the founders was no help in that regard. "One problem is getting them to think bigger," Mumford admits. Like Wally Davis, Mumford is reluctant to invest in later rounds. But Crosspoint has already proved, he claims, that most seed investments can get later-stage funding even if the original investor stays out. "From what we have seen," Mumford says, "the only difficulty comes from the fact that we are usually the only investor in the first round so we have no built-in syndication network. It takes longer than we expected to get the second-round financings done because we have to educate people about the deal." Mumford put Crosspoint into only three of the first ten second rounds he arranged, and then only because he wanted to do it. But he has taken the precaution of recruiting well-heeled institutional backers, including General Electric Co.'s venture subsidiary, for Crosspoint's second fund.

RECYCLING ENTREPRENEURSHIP

A large and growing source of seed capital is the community of "business angels" who invest occasionally and informally, usually in fields related to their background. One study of the phenomenon of informal venture capital turned up 133 angels in New England alone and determined that they had committed a total of more than $16 million to 320 ventures between 1976 and 1980.[1] Many successful entrepreneurs become angels. For some it is like sacrificing to the gods a portion of the harvest, for others it is just another investment and better than most. Motivations differ, but the beneficiaries of the first wave of venture investment are themselves becoming an important source of seed capital for new companies of the next generation. Bob Noyce of Intel, Ken Oshman of ROLM, and Max Palevsky of Scientific Data Systems are among the successful entrepreneurs who have become active investors in startup companies, and legions of lesser lights have followed their example. For the most part, these are isolated individuals backing acquaintances or ideas that catch their fancy. But there is a birds-of-a-feather trend stirring. Formal investment funds based on groups of high-tech entrepreneurs and executives are springing up and adding an element of recycled experience to the venture capital process.

Noyce, who held three million shares of Intel stock with a market value of $125 million at the end of 1983, clearly has no financial need to back risky new companies. He explains: "I always justified it by saying people put money into the crazy ideas that I had, I might as well plough some of it back in. The first experiences that I had in making small venture investments were pretty good, and after that I found I was getting an awful lot of people wanting me to come in and look at this, invest in that." Oshman started investing in the 1970s out of a sense of obligation to the new crop of entrepreneurs and concern about the then-shortage of venture capital. "These days entrepreneurs don't need my money," Oshman says. "There's too much money already out there for them. But I enjoy the excitement of little companies and I enjoy seeing entrepreneurs have a chance to do their thing." Palevsky, who at one time invested in virtually every deal organized by Arthur Rock, now works with other venture groups and jumps in independently "if the technology interests me and the people seem to be bright."

Despite their technical expertise and skills at judging people, great entrepreneurs don't always make great venture capital decisions. Noyce backed such modestly successful companies as Coherent Radiation and Data Technology but also was the founding investor in Caere, which after almost a decade still had not achieved real success with its character reading devices. Noyce admits that he invested in Caere

mainly because he was intrigued by the notion of developing an inexpensive way to feed written material into computers and conceded
in 1984 that "it's still not an idea whose time has come." The prospect
of applying Intel's microelectronics technology to solving society's
problems also led Noyce to join Arthur Rock in backing Diasonics
Inc., which became a leader in medical diagnostic equipment but
managed to lose $60 million in 1983, the year it went public. Oshman
has ASK Computer Systems to his credit but was also an investor in
Osborne Computer and served on the board of directors as Osborne
plunged toward bankruptcy. If there is a lesson in that experience,
Oshman says, it is that outsiders have little control over the success
or failure of a company. "The board really can't do much," he insists.

Neophyte entrepreneurs welcome the backing of seasoned veterans,
partly for the aura of authority they can lend to a new business and
partly because they are often motivated by more than financial goals.
Fred M. Gibbons, founder of Software Publishing Corp., talked to four
venture groups before choosing Jack Melchor's Page Mill Group to
make the initial $250,000 outside investment in his company. Page
Mill, bankrolled by Noyce, Oshman, and other big names in Silicon
Valley, would bring an operating perspective to the deal, Gibbons
thought. "My concern was if we stumbled it would be better to have
an understanding operating group instead of somebody going by the
numbers," Gibbons explains.

The idea of enlisting entrepreneurs as limited partners in a venture
fund dates at least to 1961, when Arthur Rock and Tommy Davis
invited the founders of Fairchild Semiconductor to invest and to help
investigate deals. A decade later, Don Valentine reinvented the concept in the form of a parallel fund that could accept small investments
and go into deals alongside his big institutional funds. In the 1980s,
the trend may be for groups of entrepreneurs to take the initiative and
form their own professionally managed funds. A prototype for this evolutionary development is Eastech Associates, a partnership set up in
1981 with $8.1 million from thirty-five executives and entrepreneurs
in the high-technology centers along Route 128 outside Boston. Two
years later Eastech raised a second entrepreneur's fund, $13.2 million
from sixty-five investors, and in a neat twist on the usual arrangement
launched a parallel fund for institutions.

The driving force behind Eastech is G. Bickley Stevens II, a flamboyant former real estate developer who drifted into venture capital
in the late 1970s. Stevens was approached in early 1981 by a group
that included Benjamin F. Robelen, who had been financial vice president of Prime Computer, and Michael J. Cronin and John J. Dias,
founders of Automatix. Like most top executives of successful high-
technology companies, they were all seeing a lot of business plans and
occasionally making small investments, but they wanted to formalize

things. Stevens saw the chance to start a major new venture fund that could use its unique network of investors to break into a crowded field. "We spent several months strategizing this," Stevens recalls, "and what we found was a real market need. If you look at Eastech as a small company, it has to compete against companies with more dollars, more longevity, more established networks. The key in this business is to have a deal flow, and we provided a network of people who know people."

Eastech's limited partners, who invest between $150,000 and $1 million, provide the leads for half its deals and frequently serve on boards of directors. Eastech makes sure that all its limited partners get a chance to comment on every deal it does, usually by sending out a two-page summary of the proposed investment. "It's a lightning rod we stick out to focus their attention," says Michael H. Shanahan, an Eastech associate. "We either get no response at all or a violent response." A rotating advisory committee meets once a month to go over the portfolio and give advice. "But the general partners make all the decisions," Stevens says. "They can't really influence our decision overtly because that would destroy their ability to be limited partners."

Robelen was the source for Autographix Inc., a company that automates 35 mm slide production, when he was called by a founder who had known him at Prime and wanted help preparing a business plan. Robelen steered him to Eastech, which ended up investing $750,000 and bringing in other venture investments totaling $9 million. With sales running at an annual rate of more than $10 million by mid-1984, Autographix looked like a winner. But a $250,000 investment in a luckless home computer software enterprise called Mindware Inc. showed that outside their areas of expertise Eastech's backers may be no smarter than anybody else. Mindware planned to build inexpensive printers for the Sinclair personal computer marketed in the United States by Timex. "We brought that company before our advisory group and the one objection a couple of people had was they couldn't build the product," Robelen recalls. "The fact is, they did produce them and sold 5,000 of the things but we never collected any money for a bunch of them because the Timex market went to hell." Mindware tried to shift gears to produce software for Coleco's much-delayed Adam home computer and again found it had backed the wrong horse. So had Eastech, which ended up liquidating Mindware in 1984. "If anybody comes to us now with a consumer electronics product," Robelen says, "we are going to be a little bit gunshy."

A potential for conflicts may appear when the executives of one company invest in another, but Eastech's backers are satisfied that they have set up safeguards to prevent such occurrences. No information on a portfolio company goes out to the limited partners until it has been cleared by the entrepreneur. The limited partners advise but make no investment decisions. And there is a firm prohibition on talking deals with employees of an investor's company. But there are no strictures on recruiting. Indeed, the limited partners can often help find a key manager for an Eastech company, and Stevens relishes his new ability to get straight answers about people he is trying to hire. "I used to call up somebody like Ben Robelen and get something like 'We were sorry to see him go, we wish him well.' Now I can ask about John Jones and they'll say, 'That SOB . . .'" Typically, executives in the high-tech industries see nothing wrong and a lot right with helping others get started in business. "We all like to make money," says Robelen, "but it's more than that. Deep down, we're saying we got our chance and we ought to give somebody else a chance."

NOTE

1. William E. Wetzel, Jr., "Angels and Informal Risk Capital," *Sloan Management Review*, Summer 1983, p. 23.

10

CORPORATE VENTURERS

Toward the end of the 1960s American businessmen developed one of their periodic infatuations with a new management tool. By creating new ventures divisions, as many of these organizations styled themselves, big companies hoped to stimulate external investments and internal entrepreneurship that would catapult them into exciting new growth areas. Within a few years, however, virtually all of the venturing groups were out of business with little to show for their efforts. General Electric's Technology Ventures Operation, set up in 1970 to spin out unexploited technical ideas, ran out of steam after ten deals that produced only a few modest successes. Another GE venture vehicle, created in 1969 to back small companies as a prelude to acquisition, managed to lose $10 million in seven years, and the one portfolio company for which GE made a serious takeover bid turned it down. Ford dropped $14 million into startup deals between 1968 and 1971 and within two years had sold everything off at a loss. Monsanto tried an internal venture operation for about three years and ended up, as a former executive recalls, "with a warehouse full of plastic hobbyhorses we couldn't sell."

These were not great moments in business history. But the lessons learned have helped a new generation of corporate venturers use the venture capital process in a disciplined, pragmatic way that has made big business again a significant factor in the financing of small business. Between 1977 and 1983, according to Venture Economics, resources available to corporate venture capitalists jumped from $1 billion to $2.5 billion. Norman D. Fast, who is president of Venture Economics, believes that the resurgence of interest is not just another fad. "It's different than it was the last time around," he declares, "in that companies are thinking much more long-term about it. I just don't see them turning this off like they did before."

MISADVENTURES

The first, ill-fated foray by big business into venturing was motivated in large measure by the drive to diversify that swept over corporate America as the growth prospects for many established product lines appeared to fade. The old businesses in many cases were still highly profitable, but the outlook for them because of demographic changes or market saturation or (in the case of oil, for example) dwindling resources seemed too limited to justify heavy new investment. As Fast puts it, there was a "financial investment gap" between the cash flow being generated by old businesses and the investment opportunities those businesses seemed to provide. Related to this phenomenon was a surplus of intriguing product ideas turned up by the widespread enthusiasm for basic research in the 1950s and early 1960s. As companies began to reappraise their research activities and to question projects that had no immediate internal payoff, the idea of spinning them off as independent ventures came into vogue. In most cases, there was another factor present: a senior executive who was looking for ways to make the company more entrepreneurial would get behind the idea of creating a venturing organization.

Despite the cheers with which they were launched, most of the new ventures divisions sank without a trace before they had a chance to prove their worth. Clearly, there was a mismatch between the short-term focus of corporate managers and the patience required in venture capital. New ventures normally require several years to reach a level where they can be considered self-sustaining, and the evidence is that those nurtured inside big companies have a longer infancy than those that are forced to grow up on their own. One study showed that the average independent startup takes three and a half years to reach profitability while corporate ventures, for a variety of reasons, require seven years to break even.[1] But in a sample of twenty corporate venture development groups Fast studied, the average lifespan was only four and a half years. "There is a basic problem in setting up a unit that is going to be in operation for four years and giving it a mission that will take it six or eight years," Fast points out. "What happens is the venture groups get shut down and the babies are thrown out with the bath water."

Often, the venture organizations were closed down for internal corporate reasons that had little to do with the success or failure of the investments they were making. Fast cites as typical the case of a company he calls Standard Chemical, which set up a venture group in 1968 when its entrepreneurial president hoped to diversify out of a commodity chemicals business that appeared at the time to have little prospect for profitable growth. Within two years, however, demand for two of Standard's commodity products began to take off as new applications emerged. To remain a leading producer of those chemicals, Standard had to build capacity. Between 1971 and 1973, capital expenditures tripled and the debt-equity ratio doubled. "So all of a sudden they started saying what are we doing with all these crazy new ventures, let's get back to basics," Fast reports. "And independent of that the chief executive retired. It is absolutely uncanny how many times that exact same progression of events took place. The corporate situation changes, the venture group's mission is out of sync with that, and the venture group is shut down."

The rise and fall of GE's ambitious TVO experiment followed a

somewhat different scenario. The idea was to comb through a supposed treasure trove of technology that GE divisions could not use,
and build independent companies around the ideas that seemed to
make commercial sense. Between 1970 and 1975 GE did about ten of
these "sponsored spinoffs," in fields ranging from superconductivity to
membrane filters, then quietly shut down the operation. According to
David J. BenDaniel, the scientist who developed and implemented
the concept for GE and now is a private venture capitalist, TVO simply
ran out of opportunities as GE tightened its control of research work.
"By 1975," BenDaniel says, "research and development was in a new
era of management, not just at GE but everywhere. There was a lot
more analysis earlier in the game of commercial feasibility, and projects were cut off if there wasn't significant potential. As a result, the
mine of projects we had was relatively limited, even though GE had
one of the largest and most diversified research activities in the
world."

Where venturing really fell down was as a means for corporate diversification. At first glance, venture investing appears to be an ideal
method of identifying products or technologies as candidates for future
acquisition, and an early ownership position in a young company
would seem to improve the chances of executing a takeover on favorable terms. But the results have not lived up to such expectations.
Writing in the *Harvard Business Review*, three seasoned observers of
the venture scene offered this debunking opinion: "The unsystematic
nature of new business formation, the difficulty of acquiring venture
capital investments, the problems of obtaining technology from portfolio companies, and the organizational independence required to
make good investments—all these factors combine to undermine venture capital-based efforts to reinforce or extend competitive strengths
or to alter significantly a risk/return profile."[2]

The biggest problem in using venture capital as a diversification
tool may lie in reconciling the objectives of the large company with
those of the startup it has invested in. Says a veteran of one corporate
effort to acquire its portfolio companies: "The moment the company
starts saying it may acquire these things it runs into conflicts between
the strategic goals of the large corporation and those of the small one.
You are dealing with people who are always thinking about what you
have in mind and whether the decisions you are helping them make
are in your interest or their interest."

A classic example of how not to acquire a portfolio company was
GE's clumsy bid for Applicon Inc., a pioneering maker of computer-
aided design systems. Applicon was started in 1969 by four young
Ph.D.s from MIT and backed initially by W. R. Grace & Co. When
Grace declined to invest further, GE's Business Development Services
Inc. stepped up and eventually became the company's largest share-

holder with 27.7 percent of the equity. By 1980 Applicon was a $50 million success and had just filed to go public when GE offered to buy the company for $20 a share. Not only was the bid $2 lower than the eventual offering price, notes a former Applicon board member, but it left the company open to charges that GE was trying to aggrandize its own position by driving up the public share price. The board rejected GE's bid and then was vindicated when Applicon's stock more than doubled within a few weeks of the offering. GE ended up entering the computer-aided design field a year later by acquiring Calma Co., a move that required the company to divest its Applicon holding entirely.

Another visible example of the pitfalls in diversification through venture capital was the painful effort by Exxon Corp. to gain a foothold in the office automation market. After abortive moves to diversify through more traditional means in the 1960s, Exxon began investing in startup companies in 1971. Ten years and $100 million later the oil giant had a collection of fifteen small companies all boring away like so many high-tech drilling rigs at isolated niches of the information systems market. "It was an oil gusher mentality," reported one former insider. But what came up was red ink. Exxon stopped investing and started concentrating on managing its stable of startups in the late 1970s but operating losses of the new ventures hit $150 million in 1980 alone, according to one estimate, as conflicts between Exxon executives and entrepreneurs led to faltering performance and management defections.[3] By 1984, Exxon had its office equipment businesses up for sale.

A problem for many of the ventures, apparently, was reconciling Exxon's need to become a significant factor in the market with their immediate goals of generating cash. "You spent a lot of money pioneering drastically innovative technologies and attacking large markets," one entrepreneur said of his experience with Exxon.[4] Others complained that they were being forced to use big-company personnel and accounting procedures that were awkward and inappropriate for startups. A former manager at Exxon Enterprises, the company's venture investment group, believes that serious problems flowed from the ambivalence of Exxon's original strategy. "Originally Exxon thought of itself as a venture capitalist," this source says, "but then it either changed its mind or brought to the surface its real strategic posture by essentially saying 'we are really investing in order to acquire some of these for Exxon.' That's a whole different kettle of fish." In some cases, entrepreneurs began trying to hold Exxon at arm's length. At the opposite extreme, according to the former Exxon manager, other investors in companies that were not doing well tried to coerce Exxon into acquiring them by raising the issue of conflict of interest. "People were going into the deep pockets of Exxon in order to unwind their investment," he says, "and the traditional management of Exxon began pulling back support from this [venture capital] activity because they recognized it exposed Exxon to this type of blackmail."

DOING IT RIGHT

By keeping their goals realistic and by borrowing techniques and assistance from the private venture capital industry, a few corporations are venturing profitably and successfully. Partly because of the short-term orientation of the institutional money managers who control 60 percent of corporate securities, most big companies shrink from the risks and prolonged uncertainties associated with venture investments. A partner at Goldman, Sachs & Co. told *Business Week*: "I don't think any company can afford a long-term investment today unless its managers own 51 percent of it."[5] In 1983 there were only thirty-four industrial companies with venture capital subsidiaries, an increase of just four in six years.

But those who do play the venture game have sharply increased their commitment to it. The biggest financial rewards, they have found, come from operations in which the investing is done by independent or quasi-independent organizations that are free of short-term performance demands and not constrained by strategies and policies of the parent company. Taking that discovery to its logical conclusion, companies quadrupled their annual backing for independent private venture firms after 1980 to $415 million in 1983. At the same time, support for internal venture operations was growing. Venture affiliates of industrial companies had $1.3 billion under management at the end of 1983, up from $268 million in 1977. (All these figures are estimates of Venture Economics.) Some of the best-managed companies in America are on the brief list of corporate venturers: Xerox, Allied, 3M, Grace, Textron, GE, Monsanto, Sohio, Emerson Electric, NCR, Control Data, and Lubrizol all invest, directly or indirectly, in venture deals.

Looked at purely from a financial perspective, the most successful relationship between an industrial company and a venture organization is probably that between Genstar and Sutter Hill Ventures, the pioneering Silicon Valley firm. Genstar is primarily involved in the highly cyclical construction industry, and gains from Sutter Hill investments have at times contributed more than half the parent's earnings. Aside from occasional calls for additional profits, however, Genstar plays no role in Sutter Hill's business. "They don't attempt to impose a philosophy of how to function or the type of investments to make," says Sutter Hill partner Dave Anderson. "We just send them a quarterly report of what our activities have been."

Few companies have been willing to settle for so tenuous a connection with their venture investments. Most corporate managers who promote venture capital cling to the belief that active investing in new enterprises can be a "window on technology" that provides an early, intimate glimpse of new markets and opportunities. There are other ways to peer into the future, of course. And getting information from venture to investor in usable form is not easy. As Howard H. Stevenson, a skeptical Harvard Business School professor, remarks, "Wouldn't it be cheaper to just buy magazines?" But there is something about having capital at risk that focuses corporate attention on an area and almost automatically ensures that it will be exploited. "It's like buying a puppy instead of getting one free," says James Tait Elder, head of Allied Corp.'s New Ventures Group. "If you want to sensitize your people to an area, you have to put some money in."

A case can be made that the nature of today's business world demands a strategy for turning up opportunities outside mainstream product areas. Through most of the postwar era, American managers could prosper by making Olympian decisions to increase production and improve efficiency. But in the 1970s several factors converged to undermine that approach: Energy and raw material costs rose, foreign competitors achieved equal or higher levels of productivity, markets reached saturation. In short, says William F. Miller, the thoughtful president of SRI International, many industries reached a level of maturity at which their centralized organizations and their traditional management science techniques no longer sufficed to achieve growth. "The strategy has to be to de-mature those industries," Miller concludes. "Now it's the search for new ideas and new products that becomes important as opposed to using your organizational theory and finance theory to make the thing run better."

At the same time, the surge of progress in electronics, computer science, biotechnology, and other disciplines has set the stage for the emergence of new industries that will either supplant or vastly change the old ones. For the most part, the process of experimentation and competition that decides which products and organizations will survive to dominate tomorrow's industries is taking place outside the domain of today's established corporate giants. Somehow, connections between the two worlds must be made and venture investing is one obvious method.

It is possible to make these connections even when the investing is done second-hand, through an independent venture organization. Some venture capital groups, such as Oxford Partners of Stamford, Conn., specialize in seeking out and catering to corporate limited partners. Oxford, organized in 1981 by former Xerox and GTE venture managers, tries to promote contacts between its twenty-five corporate backers and its portfolio of technology-related portfolio companies by holding quarterly meetings at which entrepreneurs and investors can mingle. As an example of the kind of synergy such encounters can generate, Oxford's William R. Lonergan points to Theta-J Corp., a Wakefield, Mass., company making small power supplies that can help shrink the size of electronic systems. "That's a case where IBM and Xerox (both investors in Oxford) invested alongside us because they were sufficiently interested in the technology," Lonergan says. "Theta-J has a good working relationship with both companies as a result of this, and its products will be in both companies' product lines."

The key to deriving real value from a venture investing strategy lies in establishing an individual or organization to act as a gatekeeper for the ideas and products that it generates. "Venture capital is analogous to exploratory research," says L. Edward Klein, who headed Monsanto's New Ventures Group in the 1970s and now does consulting on corporate venturing. "The real problem is coupling it to those people who can actually use this tool and turn it into something useful." Monsanto, the St. Louis-based chemical giant, has been more successful than most major companies at this coupling process. After an unsuccessful stab at direct venture investing in the late 1960s, then-chairman Charles H. Sommer encouraged Klein and others in the New Ventures Group—charged with providing direction for corporate research activities—to try again. As a result, Monsanto joined with Emerson Electric in 1972 to form InnoVen Capital, an independent venture partnership, and Klein set about establishing an internal network of Monsanto managers and scientists who had confidence in the validity of venture capital. As Klein recalls, this paid off in 1977 when Ernest Jaworski, a biochemist who held the title of Distinguished Monsanto Fellow, called his attention to Herb Boyer's progress in genetic engineering. "Within two weeks," Klein says, "InnoVen had an investment in Genentech. If I had decided to make that investment directly, it would have taken six to nine months to write a proposal, sell it up two levels, and get it approved by the board."

Monsanto has acquired only one of InnoVen's portfolio companies, but it has worked closely with several. The relationship with Boyer and Genentech, for example, helped the company to closely monitor the development of biotechnology and to gauge its own leap into the field. By 1983 it was pouring $30 million a year into biotechnology research and was building a $150 million laboratory to house the effort. "All of that activity has come about principally because of what we were able to learn initially about biotechnology through our venture capital activity," remarked a company spokesman.[6] Monsanto bought out Emerson's share to pick up a 25 percent stake in Collagen, the Reid Dennis-backed pioneer in skin-treatment technology, which it considers a beachhead in pharmaceuticals. And it used its indirect connection with Physical Acoustics Corp. to develop a new way to detect flaws in the tanks and vessels of its chemical plants. But Monsanto does not try to steer InnoVen's investment strategy into obviously related niches. "We told InnoVen to make money," Klein recalls. "If it turns out that none of the growth areas they go into are relevant to Monsanto, that tells you something. But we let them go where the growth is and said we'll figure out whether it's relevant or not after the fact."

GENERATING PROFITS

For all the talk about windows on technology and other payoffs, the fact is that most well-run companies will not engage in any activity if it does not make money. And General Electric, which was one of the earliest experimenters with window-on-technology and pre-acquisition investing, has now come full circle to emphasizing profit over all other considerations in its venture capital effort. "You can talk a good game," says Harry T. Rein, the fast-rising young GE manager who became president of General Electric Venture Capital Corp. in 1983, "but at the end of the day making money has historically been the way to attract resources to a business."

GE learned that lesson the hard way. Business Development Services Inc., its original venture investment organization, started out in 1969 with $10 million and, as Rein says with distaste, "ran it to zero in relatively short order." Rather than throw in the towel, GE in 1976 brought in Pedro A. Castillo, an investment professional, and gave him a fresh $10 million with orders to concentrate on making money. By investing in such winners as Tandem Computer and Applicon, Castillo pyramided the $10 million to $100 million in five years. He may have been too successful. When Castillo presented GE's management with a proposal for spinning the venture operation off as an independent fund, the company decided not only to keep it but to give it another $300 million, allowing a big increase in its investment clout. Castillo went off to form his own partnership, with GE as a limited partner, and GE managers took over the newly expanded internal group.

GEVENCO, as the operation is known, rapidly became one of the largest investors on the venture scene. In 1983 it placed $88 million in twenty-three private companies and one that was publicly held, and it is prepared to invest between $40 million and $60 million a year in venture deals. Rather than viewing GEVENCO as a source of technology for the rest of the company, GE turns the relationship on its head and emphasizes the ability of GEVENCO to supply GE knowhow to its portfolio companies. "We can make available to an entrepreneurial company the resources that are available to a general manager running a GE business," Rein explains. "That is the thing that we

bring to the party." As an example, GEVENCO sent in GE manufacturing experts to work out plant layout, equipment, and staffing plans
when ZTEL Inc., one of its portfolio companies, was getting ready to
produce a new computer-based switchboard. And GE was planning to
serve as a beta site, an early test installation, for ZTEL's equipment.
But Rein discounts the value of any reverse flow of technology or
information. "We are not unmindful that because we have guys out
slogging through the tumbleweeds we occasionally learn things that
may be useful," he says. "But if you think of it in terms of six or seven
investment officers and a $27 billion corporation and try to imagine a
mechanism that would be a successful window, I don't think it would
work."

Why, then, is GE in venture capital? For the same reason that it
runs a major asset-based lending operation—to make money in a fast-
growing financial service business. In Rein's view, venture capital has
become a multibillion-dollar industry dominated by professional entrepreneurs and funded by professional investors. Inevitably, he believes, it must become an institutional game. His conclusion: "As the
dollars get bigger, as the managerial task gets more complex, as the
value demanded by the entrepreneurs from their venture capitalists is
greater, it's my contention that we are very well positioned to play in
that game over the longer term."

BANKING ON VENTURE CAPITAL

Bankers, like businessmen, had to learn the hard way how to go
aventuring. In the 1960s banks led the rush to form SBICs and provided much of the seed capital that fueled the growth of California's
Silicon Valley and Boston's Route 128 industries. But in the 1970s
such prominent banking names as Chase Manhattan and Morgan
Guaranty led a stampede of institutions out of risk investing as markets
dried up and ventures withered. In the 1980s the banks have returned
to venture capital with renewed optimism.

The number of bank-owned SBICs almost doubled in five years—to
seventy—by the end of 1983, according to NASBIC. And Venture
Economics estimates that commitments by banks and insurance companies to their SBICs and other venture affiliates rose from $900 mil-
lion to $1.6 billion between 1977 and 1983. This time around, the
bankers hope to avoid the problems that arose when their cautious,
risk-avoiding culture clashed with the fast-track world of venture capital, where risk is the name of the game.

The two largest American bank holding companies, Citicorp in
New York and BankAmerica Corp. in San Francisco, also set the pace
in venture capital. Although they entered the field for different reasons and with different strategies, Citicorp and BankAmerica have

demonstrated that banks can succeed in this newest of financial service industries. Since the mid-1970s, both banks have apparently
achieved annual rates of return above 30 percent in their venture capital activities. Citicorp, which by early 1984 had placed $170 million
in venture deals, had converted $100 million of its venture winnings
to profits and still had another $600 million in unrealized gains sitting
in its portfolio. BankAmerica does not reveal its total holdings, but it
hints at their size when it periodically reports the effect on earnings
of marking the portfolio up or down to reflect significant changes in
its market value. (Citicorp does not "mark to market." It is an accounting elective.) In the last quarter of 1982 BankAmerica got a
$27.1 million gain from this source; in the second quarter of 1983,
$44 million. (It failed to quantify the effect of steep declines in the
market for high-tech stocks late in 1983.) "Our returns have been
significantly higher than for the rest of the corporation," allows Lloyd
Segaski, the executive who oversees BankAmerica's venture
activities.

Many banks got into venture capital with two goals in mind. They
hoped to show a profit on the appreciation of equity investments, of
course, but they had another agenda that some considered just as important. By getting in on the ground floor of new companies and industries, they expected to build future customers for the lending side
of the bank. Not many have been able to get much payoff from that
strategy. And Citicorp never has tried. "We wouldn't want to be in a
position of forcing loans on people," says William T. Comfort, chairman and president of Citicorp Venture Capital Ltd. "If a company
wants to be connected to the bank or wants an introduction to the
bank, we would do that for them. But we have never tied this activity
and the loan activity together. In fact, it's been just the opposite."

Citicorp entered the field in 1967, long after banks in Massachusetts and California—and archrival Chase Manhattan—had seized the
opportunity created by the SBIC act. Prodded by the threat of legislation that would prohibit banks from wholly owning their SBICs,
Citicorp finally jumped in just as a cycle was cresting. "I really respect
their guts to stay with it," comments a former executive of a rival bank
venture operation. "They bought right at the top and went to the
bottom. They were in the hole a huge amount of money." In part, the
losses resulted from a deliberate strategy of investing in as broad a
spectrum of companies as possible in order to develop a feel for the
venture process. The idea was to put out a lot of money in many small
deals that gave Citicorp an almost actuarial spread of risks and quickly
developed a cadre of experienced venturers. Citicorp remains a far
more diversified investor than most venture operations with holdings
in manufacturing, energy, transportation and healthcare as well as in
high technology. As much as a third of its deals are leveraged buyouts,

with the remainder spread across startup and later-stage venture investments. The strategy has produced no winners in the $100 million class, but Citicorp's $2.5 million equity investment in the leveraged buyout that created James River Corp. has been worth as much as $75 million, and its $1.5 million flier on Federal Express grew to more than $50 million.

An example of Citicorp's continuing effort to diversify is a new push to do more in the oil patch, where it started backing independent producers and service companies as oil prices were peaking and hopes eventually to ride another cycle of price increases. "Once again we're putting a number of investments out," Comfort says. "We'll look at them, see what goes right and what goes wrong, what types of companies work, and then put out more. There is no hurry." Citicorp has also diversified geographically. It was the first East Coast venture firm to open a West Coast office and now has five professionals in California as well as two in Texas. And it is pushing abroad again with operations in Canada, Britain, France, Italy, Australia and Japan after pulling back on foreign adventures during the dark days of the early 1970s. Even now, Comfort admits, the bank is "way early" in terms of the prospects for significant returns on venture investments outside the United States, but it is willing to pay a price to learn how to operate in emerging markets.

To do well in venture capital, banks must train and retain a cadre of specialists who differ markedly in background, skills, and temperament from most of their employees. "I don't think there's any question," says one banker-turned-venturer, "that someone whose basic business is based on conservatism and low-risk situations is a world apart from evaluating venture capital deals." As Citicorp's record attests, it has done well at finding and training venture professionals. Some have come in from the banking side but increasingly Citicorp, like others in the business, has recruited talent from technology companies and consultants. What it has failed to do, at least during the recent explosion of opportunities for experienced venture capitalists, is keep the talent from leaving. By Comfort's count, twenty-three Citicorp venturers have gone on to form their own firms or to work for others, creating "the wealthiest alumni base of any entity in the country," he says proudly. Others say this is nothing to be proud of, since experience is a vital ingredient to success in venture capital. One observer points out that Citicorp had the courage to keep investing in Federal Express partly because Larry J. Lawrence, then president of Citicorp Venture Capital, was close to the company from the beginning. Lawrence left Citicorp in 1980 to head his own fund. "If Larry had not been there, if he had left five years earlier, who could have been the advocate for continuing support of Federal Express?"

By 1984 Citicorp was finally moving on plans, already adopted in various versions by other bank venture groups, to allow its venture capitalists to share in the profits they generate. Old concerns about creating hostility among other bank employees have faded in the new entrepreneurial environment of the 1980s, Comfort maintains. "What's happening in the world today," he says, "is that people are being compensated according to the standards on which their industries are compensated. Everybody has gone back to the incentive system."

PIONEERING IN CALIFORNIA

BankAmerica Corp., holding company for the Bank of America, has moved still farther in the direction of entrepreneurship. In 1980 BankAmerica took the unprecedented step of spinning out three of its top venture capitalists in a $38 million limited partnership and then contributed 24 percent of a $55 million follow-on fund. As in any other private venture partnership, the partners of Merrill, Pickard, Anderson & Eyre share a 20 percent carried interest in the profits, and they keep their former employer at arm's length. "Our identity is more our own than the bank's," says Steven L. Merrill, who was president of BankAmerica Capital Corp. before the spinout. The move was all the more extraordinary because BankAmerica had been early and unusually successful at using venture capital activities to build banking relationships. Lending officers found most of the bank's early venture deals, and the venture activity helped it become California's leading lender to the electronics industry. But the bank saw several key people walk away from its venture subsidiary in the late 1970s and it stood to lose more. "They were not interested in working for a salary," says Lloyd Segaski. "A venture capitalist has to have a unique set of talents and when you have those talents you should be exceptionally well compensated."

BankAmerica was pushed into venture capital in 1959 by an eager-beaver group of young corporate lending officers, including Segaski and Alden W. "Tom" Clausen, later the bank's president and then president of the World Bank, who saw the 1958 SBIC act as an opportunity to capture banking relationships early in a company's life. "Probably one of the easiest ways to get a good corporate relationship is to have been there as a founding parent," Segaski says, "and the SBIC thing came along just about at the same time that the electronics industry was getting a lot of visibility." Segaski, Clausen, and the dozen or so others who constituted the corporate finance department then, were constantly running across companies in need of equity, and they put BankAmerica's SBIC into some of the biggest winners of the early 1960s. Dataproducts, Memorex, and Teledyne all got startup backing from the bank and the SBIC was profitable very early. The lending side profited as well. By 1970, according to one source, BankAmerica was doing a good three quarters of the lending to California electronics companies.

After a few years of running the venture operation out of its lending officers' hip pockets, BankAmerica tried to give it a bit of independence. George Quist, the bank's first fulltime venture capitalist, was an aggressive dealmaker who overcame increasing caution on the banking side to invest in Tymshare, American Microsystems, and other important deals, but he soon departed to help start Hambrecht & Quist, the investment banking firm. The bankers who rotated through the presidency of the operation after that kept things together through the grim times of the early 1970s but discouraged risk-taking. As Merrill recalls, "there was the oil crisis and interest rates shooting up and the stock market going to hell and no new-issues market. And bankers are human." In addition, one of the bank's big venture capital winners was turning into a lender's nightmare. Although the bank eventually recouped its $150 million lending exposure to Memorex, Merrill points out that the situation had the bankers "scared to death of any computer company." As a result of all this, it was hard for Merrill and the other inexperienced venturers to get deals approved. "We were turned down on Cray Research [now a leader in scientific computers] because of the Memorex situation," Merrill recalls, "although they were not directly related."

W. Jeffers Pickard, who joined BankAmerica's venture group in 1970, recalls the red tape involved in selling a deal in those days: "We were young and the president liked having every rock turned over. You put together very lengthy written reports, detailing the pros and cons and all the reference checks you made. Then you had to sell it to a committee of senior credit officers." In retrospect, Merrill believes, the bank would have been better off to have brought in an experienced venture capitalist to head the organization. "We would have been more aggressive at a time when it would have been very good to be more aggressive," he suggests. Even so, Merrill and the others were able to persuade the bank to back Advanced Micro Devices, Avantek, Federal Express, Four Phase Systems, and other eventual winners. As some of these began to go public, the bank's confidence returned and it handed more authority to Merrill's group. But the bank could not match the allure of private funds, and after a few defections the spinout plan seemed the only way for the bank to remain an important player in venture capital.

BankAmerica may now have the best of both worlds. As a limited partner not only in Merrill Pickard but in several other private funds as well, the holding company profits from the investment results turned in by venture capitalists it could not have retained in any case. It still operates two internal venture vehicles, one an SBIC, to accom-

modate deals of special interest to the bank. "We've got some investments in high-tech companies that are in businesses that intrigue us
as a bank," Segaski says mysteriously. At the same time, Bank-
America's bankers still look on the venture funds as significant sources
of new business even though the connection now is indirect. "We
have no more claim on that business than any other bank," Segaski
admits, "but we certainly keep asking the funds to keep us in mind as
the companies in which they've invested need bank financing.
They've got to write their checks someplace."

The arms-length relationship also prevents allegations of conflict of
interest that can arise whenever an institution is both a lender and a
shareholder. After its early days in venture investing, BankAmerica
tried to erect a Chinese wall between lenders and investors. "We
would never permit the venture capitalists to go over to the lending
side and say, 'help me out,'" Segaski insists. The problem with that
policy, of course, is that venture capitalists are often placed in the
position of asking lenders to "help them out." A more subtle conflict
comes about, Segaski points out, if a lending customer gets into trouble that requires an injection of equity: "It could always be a contention that what we're really doing is putting the screws to them just to
get a piece of the company." As a result, Bank of America in the past
would send such customers to other venture firms. Now, with nothing
to say about investment decisions of its venture affiliates, the bank has
no such inhibitions.

SPINNING OUT TO FREEDOM

Thrust suddenly from their cozy nest in one of the world's biggest
banks, Steve Merrill and Jeff Pickard had to develop drastically different approaches to venturing—and life—in order to fly on their own.
BankAmerica had been a leader of the California venture capital network from the beginning and almost automatically saw every important deal that came along. Not all of that heritage was transportable.
Merrill and Pickard had to sell their new firm to entrepreneurs and
other venture groups, and one way to do that was to add partners who
complemented their financial backgrounds. In choosing new partners
for the firm they picked one former bank colleague, Chris A. Eyre,
but then pulled James C. Anderson and Stephen E. Coit from high-
technology marketing jobs. They completed the metamorphosis by
moving from San Francisco's financial district to an office building
near the Hewlett-Packard headquarters in Palo Alto.

They found themselves working far longer hours than they were
used to, and their relationship with each other changed abruptly. Merrill, accustomed to managing a team of junior associates and passing
judgment on their ideas, now was a partner with—technically—no

more authority than the others. Pickard, detached and analytical by nature, had to learn to stand up to his former boss in the crossfire of a partner's meeting and argue for his ideas. "At first," recalls Anderson, "if Steve wanted to do something it got done and if Steve didn't want to do it it generally didn't get done." Now, although Merrill's experience and debating skills still carry weight, a more egalitarian style prevails. "If the rest of us want to do a deal," Anderson says, "it'll get done."

Starting with the bank's $38 million, including $11 million in investments made before the spinout, Merrill Pickard achieved about a 70 percent internal rate of return on its portfolio in the first three years of independence. The gains came in part from such prespinout winners as Priam and Quantum, the disk drive makers, and Pizza Time Theatre, Nolan Bushnell's initially successful but eventually bankrupt chain of high-tech fast-food emporiums. (The partnership distributed all its Pizza Time holdings long before the crash.) There were some fast results from partnership deals as well. Merrill Pickard's $750,000 investment in LSI Logic, for example, was worth $20 million when LSI went public less than three years later.

Merrill Pickard finds deals through a network as broadly based as any in venture capital. A Bank of America lending officer called with the tip that led to a $600,000 investment in Acrian Inc., a maker of specialized semiconductors; an accountant suggested Flextronics, a high-technology service company, and a lawyer recommended Quantum Corp., the disk-drive maker that so far is the most successful of the investments carried over from the bank. At one point, Merrill totted up the coinvestors in Merrill Pickard's deals and found ten firms with which his partnership had worked more than five times. Anderson and Coit, both former Hewlett-Packard managers, are well-connected in the high-technology community. "I was really shocked at my ability to develop business," Anderson says. "I still have people at HP, whom I never really knew, calling me up to tell me about offers they've had."

Anderson used those contacts to good effect in helping to build a company called Covalent Systems, which is at least the third venture-financed attempt to sell shopfloor information systems to the job printing industry. Anderson became intrigued with the concept as he watched one of the earlier efforts in the field fail for lack of engineering and management skill. He had been interested in investing and stayed by the death bed even though his partners had vetoed any involvement. "I actually paid for their first couple of appointments with the bankruptcy attorney because I had visions of maybe pulling it out and restarting it," he recalls. After six months of melodrama, Anderson had to give up on that company, but two Hewlett-Packard engineers he had interested in the business decided to pursue the idea on their own. Anderson rounded up $1.8 million from Merrill Pickard and two other Silicon Valley funds, and he served as chief executive of the new company for the first few months. Covalent introduced its first product about a year later, late in 1983, and then raised its second round of venture financing at a handsome 3.75-to-1 markup over the first-round price. "I'm proud of that," Anderson commented.

Reflecting its banking heritage, Merrill Pickard takes an analytical approach to most of its deals. Jeff Pickard, whose horn-rimmed glasses and formal manner make him appear the most bankerly of the partners, admits that his bank training still influences his style as a venture capitalist. "That kind of lengthy analysis would be unworkable today," Pickard says, "but the experience gives me a good framework to check the elements of a deal against." Surprisingly, despite his standoffish air, Pickard comes down more often than not on the positive side of a close decision over an investment. "Looking at history," he explains, "if we had done all those marginal deals we turned down we'd have been better off." An example he cites is Tandem Computer, which Pickard and others then at the bank looked at as a second-round investment in 1976. "We agonized and debated and finally decided the price was too high," he recalled. "We rationalized the decision by saying that we could come in later if the company had to raise more money than it was planning. But Tandem got a long way on a little money."

Chris Eyre, more ebullient than Pickard but also a banker by training, balances the ingrained optimism of his Mormon pioneer heritage with a cautious and balanced approach to every investment. "You can always tell where Chris stands on a deal," says Anderson. "He sort of comes in at a 6-degree glide slope and just lands." Eyre even held back when the bank was considering its investment in Pizza Time Theatre, although he had been following Bushnell's career since both were students and fraternity brothers at Utah State. Bushnell had opened just one restaurant at the time, but he was holding out for a valuation of more than $20 million on his new company, Eyre recalls. He and other venturers waited until Pizza Time had several locations going and was generating annual sales of more than $3 million before investing. The clincher for Eyre was a visit to his children's school open house, where he spotted a bulletin board showing the results of voting for "my favorite restaurant." Although the closest Pizza Time was several miles away, Eyre recalls, "it won hands down."

The partners in Merrill Pickard are very different people. But to some extent at least they all mirror Steve Merrill's judgment of the qualities that must be present in a successful venture capitalist. It is not enough simply to recruit managers who have been successful in finance or industry, Merrill believes. "We are in a very different world," he says. "Some people can adapt to it and others wouldn't at all." A prime characteristic—and one that Merrill himself seems to possess in abundance—is intellectual curiosity. Using engineering jargon, Merrill describes this as "an ability to multiplex," by which he means switching from one subject to another rapidly and effortlessly. "We are very unstructured in how we find deals, how we market, how we evaluate things. Typically we are looking at two or three different deals at a time, so you have to pass from one to the other many times in the course of a day."

NOTES

1. Leo A. Weiss, "Start-up Businesses: A Comparison of Performances," *Sloan Management Review*, Fall 1981, p. 37.
2. G. Felda Hardymon, Mark J. DeNino and Malcolm S. Salter, "When Corporate Venture Capital Doesn't Work," *Harvard Business Review*, May–June 1983, p. 114.
3. "What's Wrong at Exxon Enterprises," *Business Week*, August 24, 1981, p. 87.
4. Jon Levine, "Exxon's Exes Try It Alone," *Venture*, August 1982, p. 59.
5. "Will Money Managers Wreck the Economy?" *Business Week*, August 13, 1984, p. 86.
6. "How to Be a Winner with Venture Capital," *Chemical Week*, December 14, 1983, p. 38.

11

THE PARTNERS

It is three o'clock on a January afternoon in Palo Alto, and outside
the windowless fourth-floor boardroom on Page Mill Road a hazy win-
ter sun is already slanting toward the range of hills that bounds the
Santa Clara Valley on the west. A few decades ago, when prunes were
the primary product of this valley, investment decisions that were
made here had to do mostly with land prices and harvest yields. Now
the area is known globally as Silicon Valley. With the highest concen-
tration of high-technology entrepreneurs in the world, it produces
semiconductors, computers, telecommunications equipment, electronic instruments, software—and a huge crop of new companies.

The shirtsleeved men seated around the oval table that almost fills
the room speak a new language, a jargon-filled technobabble that em-
braces engineering concepts, marketplace forecasting, management
psychology, and financial structuring. For a week they have been gathering information about infant businesses from a network of engineers,
managers, consultants, attorneys, accountants and bankers. In the
next two hours they will spill out what they know or assume or feel in
a bantering, informal, gossipy marathon of words as they consider
which new ventures to back and how much to pay, whom to invite
into new deals, how to resolve problems in previous deals, when to
get out and when to stay put. A venture capital partners' meeting is
about to start.

Venture capitalists are always talking. There are a few exceptions,
but most of the venturers I know are forever on the phone, in meetings, en route to meetings or, with the help of a mobile telephone, all
three at once. They read voluminously, but information on the people
and concepts involved in high-technology venture deals is both sensitive and perishable. The way to get it, usually, is in person. And the
way to use it, at least in the small private partnerships that have come
to dominate the field, is in free-wheeling debate among partners. As
venture firms expand and open new offices they are learning to sup-
plement the face-to-face confrontation with electronic mail, conference calls, even video conferences. Still, most firms set aside a morning or an afternoon every week or every few weeks for a partners'
meeting at which deals can be discussed, criticized or applauded, and
consensus achieved. The meeting also provides a forum where partners with troubled investments can seek advice or comfort, where strategic directions can be set and where intelligence can be passed along.
But its primary function is to guide the partnership toward investment

decisions, often through a process of advocacy and attack that can turn into table-pounding shouting matches.

I had the opportunity in January 1984 to sit in on a partners' meeting at Merrill, Pickard, Anderson & Eyre, the group that spun out of BankAmerica to become an independent private partnership with $90 million under management. Perhaps because of the inhibiting presence of an outsider, this was a calm session. No histrionics, no impassioned challenges—but nevertheless a fascinating exercise in group decision making. Actually, the partners of Merrill Pickard are more cerebral than passionate, perhaps too considerate of each others' feelings, as one of them admitted to me later. Steve Merrill is in his early forties but seems somehow both older and younger. There is a self-deflating humor that is unexpected in the senior role that Merrill plays, but also an air of confidence that comes from long and painful experience. He is articulate, confident, slightly cynical but easily roused to enthusiasm. Accustomed to authority in his days as president of the bank's venture organization, he easily dominates the meeting but then checks himself, defers to the others, even acts as his own devil's advocate when he senses a need for balance. "If something's black Steve will argue that it's white just to be sure you're sure it's black," says one of his partners. Jeff Pickard, barely forty, approaches things with the analytical detachment of an investment banker, which he once was. He says little but gets immediately to the point when he has something to contribute, and he makes up his mind quickly. Once he has taken a position, he is not easily moved from it. Chris Eyre, in his mid-thirties and probably the most organized of the partners, sets the agenda for the meetings and tries to keep them moving. Jim Anderson, the youngest of the four partners present at thirty-three and the only one with a technical background, rivals Merrill for debating skill. But he seems to oscillate during the discussion between positive and negative poles, as if the optimistic engineer that he was and the skeptical investor he is trying to become were engaged in their own private debate.

There are others in the cherrywood-paneled room: John Russo, a research associate, and Steve Coit, newly recruited as a partner, are attending as observers but occasionally chime in. Before the meeting gets serious, Anderson is the victim of a mild roasting over his suggestion to install mobile telephones in the partners' cars and Eyre is congratulated for finally exiting from the first venture investment he ever made—with a profit, he estimates, of $83,000. "That'll pay for a car phone," remarks Merrill. Quickly, Eyre brings up the subject of a second-round financing for a fast-growing portfolio company that now wants to raise $7 million instead of the $5 million the partners had agreed to support.

"We initially talked about taking our pro rata portion on the $5 million, which is $350,000," Eyre says. "My suggestion is to probably not increase that even though they are going to raise more money. The company continues to do well. They are pretty well on track to do $30 million this year and they're projecting $80 million for the following year. They claim to have an $80 million backlog. My concern is that they are growing fast, it is a young and bright management team, but we continue to see some signs of naivete there that are a little bit concerning." "There's always a risk of them getting out of control," nods Merrill.

Anderson moves on to a portfolio company that needs both a new chief executive and an injection of cash. "I just wanted everybody to keep in the front of their minds any candidates [for the chief executive's job]. Right now we have three guys and I think all three are 30 percent possibilities. They are all interested and going through the motions, but when push comes to shove they're not going to move. Meanwhile we are proceeding with a $2 to $3 million financing of which we will be asked for about a $500,000 shot." Anderson mentions that he is planning to show the deal to six other venture firms, an idea that doesn't sit well with Eyre. "Are we comfortable showing it to that many players?" he demands. Anderson responds: "I think this thing is either going to start to go and it'll turn into a hot deal, or else it'll drag on. I won't show it to more than six people, or it would be on the street. These six were sort of strategically picked."

Pickard mentions a company making a novel computer memory device: "It was funded by a couple of other groups and I think it has been a big disappointment. This might be a sort of third-round type financing, certainly at a lowball price. Reason to bring it up at this point in time is twofold. Number one, to the extent you have heard of it, maybe get some input on it. Number two, it represents perhaps the type of situation that we might have more and more opportunity with in terms of venture deals that have gone south and there's some investment weariness, but that might still have some good upside potential. The risk-reward situations might be attractive to us. These people have a prototype but they have not yet proven they can produce it in volume." Anderson is skeptical. "They had a prototype last time." But Merrill takes an upbeat tack. "It's a very low-cost device. And I think everybody acknowledges you can now come up with this kind of storage device and make it very reliable." Anderson is still negative. "I can't think of anyone who has made it in nonstandard storage media." After some discussion of the technical merits of the approach, Eyre asks whether early manufacturing problems have been solved. "It may well boil down to a case where you're not going to get a definitive handle as to whether or not they can really make it," Pickard points out. "It's an investment of faith." But the partners agree it is worth looking into.

The rest of the meeting is largely given over to discussion of The
Learning Company, a promising specialist in educational software that
is seeking to raise $2 million. At this point, Steve Merrill has just
returned from the annual Consumer Electronics Show, where he has
seen enough of the competition to satisfy himself that this company
indeed has an outstanding product line. Whether it has a strong
enough management team and whether it can grow fast enough to
produce a satisfactory return are questions still to be answered. In the
partners' meeting, Merrill cautiously builds a case for making the investment. The others venture a few caveats but in the end seem to
join the bandwagon. With only a few abridgements, this is how the
partners work toward consensus:

Merrill: "Let me give a quick summary of the company. It was started by a
Ph.D. educator out of Berkeley and a few of her friends. They wrote one
program that's turned out to be very well-recognized in academic circles as a
great program, but the company was a disaster as far as I can tell. Jack Melchor and a group of his friends put in $300,000 about a year and a half ago,
but the thing kind of floundered after that. Jack got some good people on
the board, and they went to work trying to get things back in order, primarily
concerning themselves with finding a CEO. They found Marcia Klein, who
has done quite a good job of focusing the company on its products, defining
its purpose, restructuring some of the marketing agreements and pricing—
very basic stuff. So they did $1 million in their first year, made a little money,
and they are now running at $2 million and projecting $8 million in two
years. They are raising $2 million now. I went around at the show, and I led
the tour. I didn't rely on her to pick out competitive products. I must say, I
was absolutely flabbergasted at how terrible those products were compared
with hers."
Anderson: "Well, the others are all entertainment."
Merrill: "It's a dangerous kind of research, but I think it's a fair assumption
that they have built the best reputation in education circles for quality software for children. And that is their philosophy. They want to build a product
line, stick exclusively to education. Ann [Piestrup, the founder] sets the tone
for the company. She is an educator, a crusader, and she believes in certain
kinds of education and she's probably right. Only recently, and because I
think she's been programmed a bit, has she also started talking about trying
to make money at it. But there's no question where her heart really lies when
push comes to shove. And that has to permeate the company to a certain
degree. The second characteristic that permeates the company is that these
people are all very nice and very decent and very bright and therefore probably not very tough and maybe not too effective in the dog-eat-dog world of
selling software."
Pickard: "Does that include Marcia?"
Merrill: "That's a question. Marcia clearly has gone in there and been able

to work with that environment. The few checks I've done on her, they said that's one of her capabilities, she seems to be able to span that environment and the outside world very well. I could do some more checks on her. Even if you were satisfied that Marcia is aware of the need to do that and be tough in the outside world, what will she do to her credibility inside the company? She can't change the entire culture of the company. I don't want to get this thing out of proportion, but the fact is they are not the kind of opportunistic, aggressive people who are running Spinnaker [at the time, the leader in educational software]."

Eyre: "If they are marketing to get shelfspace at the local Computerland, that's one thing, but if they are marketing through schools . . ."

Merrill: "A third to a half of their business will be through schools. The plus side of this, and one of the arguments in favor of this company, is it's exactly that kind of culture that would not work in a video game environment or even in a business software environment, but it's exactly suited to the educational software business. All the other people are trying to act like video game people and apply it to the educational field, and that's a field it's not going to fly in."

Anderson: "Who are the other managers?"

Merrill: "If you look at the whole management team, there is really only one man. This is not a group of feminists, that's not the problem."

Anderson: "You know my bias. [Anderson's wife is a manager at Hewlett-Packard.] I think if you have a group of women with a track record in industry that's one thing, but the problem is they haven't been in industry."

Merrill: "They don't have much of a management team. They have got to hire the number two person in the company, which is going to be a marketing person, and a number three, the finance person."

Anderson: "So they are still building the company."

Merrill: "Absolutely. It's not a Class A management team. It may be a group of Class A educators applying their talents to educational software."

Anderson: "The next question I ask is even at a $5 million valuation, how much money can they make? Let's say they exceed their plan and do $10 million in '85, what's that worth?"

Merrill: "$25 million [a fivefold increase in the value of the company, reflecting a fivefold increase in sales]. But the most appealing thing about this from a gut point of view is that, ignoring the numbers, this kind of philosophy will be very attractive to the kind of company that would be interested in this deal. They're going to like these people and they'll pay a premium over what the numbers show."

Anderson: "One appeal is that products in education just keep on going. People are still buying Tinker Toys."

Merrill: "That's a bet. It certainly applies more here than anywhere else in software."

Pickard: "It would have to. I have no feel for their ability or anybody else's ability to come up with new products in this area."

Anderson: "That's a good question. Wasn't Imagic the one that had the formula they were going to test-market everything and do all that market research?"

Merrill: "These guys have a product that's already won."

Pickard: "To me, measuring the risks on this thing, one of them is how much we're betting on new products."

Merrill: "I think any way you look at it, we're betting a lot on new products. They couldn't quantify that, but they are not saying they will get to $8 million by converting existing products."

Eyre: "The other thing you're saying is that hopefully this marketplace is a little more stable and if you get a product there and people like it they'll hold on to it for a while as opposed to a video game."

Merrill: "The financial issue here is very simple. The bottom line is price-cutting. They're selling these things for forty or fifty bucks apiece and the cost of goods is $4. Is this business going to be one where a high quality product can command a premium price? And second of all, what is the price of talent? Is it going to turn into having to give a $1 million advance to the authors or can they build a stable of inhouse talent to generate product of high quality without paying through the nose for it? Probably the answer is, there are enough people out there in the educational field who want to work on these things."

Anderson: "There's something about it I like, I have to admit. But the thing I'm uncomfortable with is whether we're in effect betting against Spinnaker. If Spinnaker is successful, and they're suddenly a $100 million company, and we're sitting here at $10 million to $15 million, and it's a capital-intensive industry . . . I just wonder if we can survive."

Merrill: "That's a risk."

Eyre: "Isn't the real question here whether these guys are going to be an author or a publisher?"

Merrill: "My perception is that with their talent pool and their orientation, they strike me as quality authors."

Eyre: "If you're going to be a publisher, you have to have a huge line to cover the costs."

Anderson: "Is this going to be time-intensive? We still have to build a team here."

Merrill: "Yeah, it's relatively time-intensive. Not as time-intensive as it might be. We don't need a CEO. I wouldn't want to make this bet if I wasn't comfortable that Marcia was going to work out. But Marcia needs help."

Anderson: "So you'd go on the board?"

Merrill: "Yeah, we'd have to go on the board."

Pickard: "Where do you stand on this? Are you advocating it?"

Merrill: "No, I'm having a discussion on this case. I still have some work to do. I guess the question I am asking myself is should I spend more time on this or drop it."

Anderson: "Two observations I'd make. This is starting to sound more and

more like a price-sensitive deal. And secondly it concerns me a little allo-
cating your time to a board seat on a deal that has at best a 3 or 5 times
upside to it. I'd like to have you working on a deal with a little more blue
sky [meaning one with more upside potential]."
Eyre: "I'd be a lot more crazy about the deal if we could simply park some
money in it."
Merrill: "Or if they would give us a price break. But they are very price-
sensitive."
Anderson: "How much is she raising?"
Merrill: "$2 million."
Anderson: "What is she doing with it?"
Merrill: "Marketing, promotion, new management. It's a partnership decision, not mine. It would be an easy thing to do. The bottom line is, it's low
risk but it's not going to be a huge winner."
Pickard: "Is anybody else looking at it that if they go on the board you'd feel
comfortable parking some money there?"
Merrill: "Unfortunately, I don't think there is."
Anderson: "You know what bugs me? Something tells me if we got the right
couple of managers in there it just takes off and they suddenly dominate
educational software and the market blooms and the sun comes out and all
is wonderful."
Merrill: "It's still not going to be a $500 million company. But what you do
is you cultivate this little jewel and somebody comes along and says we want
to be in the software business and we want a quality acquisition."
Pickard: "You're going to do some more work on it, right?"
Merrill: "Well, I sort of get a sense that we kind of like it. I don't hear any
strong objections. Every deal we do doesn't have to have the potential of
being a $500 million company."

A final investment proposal, involving a company with a new kind
of computer printer, is shot down as a the partners question the fundamentals of the deal. One interchange illustrates the frustration of
dealing with technical concepts that are essentially unpredictable:

Pickard: "We had the technology reviewed by a consultant who in essence
didn't come up with anything that would throw up red flags."
Eyre: "Did he say wow?"
Pickard: "No, I don't know if he ever gets excited."
Eyre: "Why is he a consultant then? He does a thorough review and it's
thoroughly unintelligible."
Merrill: "He tells us it doesn't defy the laws of physics. Two strikes and he's
out, I think."
Eyre: "There's no one on the team or anyone else we've talked to who will
endorse the manufacturing side of this thing. There is no way to intuitively
be comfortable with the producibility. If they can produce it at that price

and with that capability, the market is probably not a big question."

Pickard: "Yeah, producibility and reliability, they're related. Can you produce it and can it stay in alignment and whatnot. I don't know what the answer to that is . . ."

But an even greater obstacle to the investment, seemingly, is the background and reputation of the entrepreneurs.

Anderson: "Any feedback on the people?"

Pickard: "I've done some checks. The president has not had a line job before, he's basically been staff. In these staff roles, he's had a great deal of difficulty. When you talk to people who are not on his reference list you get comments to the effect that he's very political, he doesn't inspire people to get their jobs done. On the other hand, entrepreneurs can be very demanding people. But this personality quirk was more than that and he hasn't proven himself in a line position. The engineering fellow has always been in advanced development. Two people mentioned feedback that he didn't get jobs done, which was a disturbing thing."

Merrill: "I'm not so bothered by that. I don't know any company that really screwed up because the entrepreneur turned people off in another company. Startup companies are so focused that that quality shows up later, after a lot of value has been created, and you can solve it. But when you have an engineering manager and a president, and the president is from staff and the engineering manager doesn't have a reputation for properly assessing a task and completing it, that to me is a key management issue in this deal. Trying to assess whether they can do this thing with $X million in fifteen months is beyond our capability. It's really a bet on this guy's ability to properly assess the task, and he doesn't have a record of having done that."

Pickard: "I'm not hearing a lot of unbridled enthusiasm. I'd be happy if we could get enthusiastic over one aspect of this thing."

And so it went. Decisions were not so much made as discovered, as if the partners were sorting through a haystack of conjecture and warnings to find the kernels of opportunity that had to be there. But a few months later the decisions still seemed sound. The company seeking $7 million raised it easily and by late 1984 was progressing on schedule. The company needing cash and a chief executive got both—and half the financing came from the first group to look at it. Merrill Pickard did not invest in the new memory company, which ultimately wheedled financing from its original investors and kept plugging away on the technology. The printer company, too, finally found financing as well as a new chief executive while Merrill Pickard stayed on the sidelines.

As for The Learning Company, Steve Merrill's optimism ultimately prevailed. Whether it was justified or not remained an open question.

Shortly after the partners' meeting, Merrill Pickard offered to invest about $1 million at a relatively low valuation. In the meantime, though, Dick Kramlich of New Enterprise Associates had discovered the company and offered to finance it at a higher price. Rather than bow out entirely, Merrill Pickard scaled back its investment to $500,000 and agreed to accept John Glynn, an experienced venture capitalist, as a director in place of Merrill. The Learning Company made solid progress for a time but then Marcia Klein, the new chief executive, became ill and was forced to leave active management. At the same time the entire market for educational software began to soften as sales of home computers slipped far behind the industry's forecasts. By late 1984 an acting president had been found and a search launched for a full-time chief executive. The Learning Company was not meeting its sales plan, but it successfully launched a new product that appeared to reinforce its reputation for quality software, and it was conserving cash at a time when many competitors were falling by the wayside. Like most venture capital investments, it appeared to be neither a failure nor an amazing success, but a promising company with an uncertain future.

12

A QUESTION OF PRICE

How do venture capitalists determine the price they will pay for stock in a company with no sales and no profits and assets consisting mainly of brainpower and ambition? Robert M. Metcalfe thinks he has the answer. "It's all negotiable," he says. "There are no rules of thumb. A lot of it is bluffing, a lot of it is muscling, but the essential truth is, everything is negotiable."

Metcalfe is a brilliant computer scientist, a plucky entrepreneur, and a slightly cynical veteran of what might be called a venture price war over 3Com Corp., the company he founded in 1979. He researched the venture capital process thoroughly, and he employed every strategy he learned to add value to the company before he set out to raise money. But Metcalfe was deeply disappointed when the first-round price valued 3Com at less than $3 million, about half what he thought the company was worth. As it has turned out so far, both the venture investors and Metcalfe appear to have won. 3Com went public three years after the initial investment, in the depressed new-issues market of early 1984, at a price of only $6 per share. But that translated to a market valuation of $80 million and a fourteenfold return on the equivalent price of 43¢ per share paid by the first-round investors. And Metcalfe wound up with 1.6 million shares worth almost $10 million after the offering. In all, Metcalfe says, he is grateful that the venture community exists "but also skeptical and bitter about how it works."

The saga of Bob Metcalfe and the venture capitalists began in November 1978, when he attended a luncheon organized by the MIT alumni group in Silicon Valley. The topic was how to start a company, and Metcalfe was impressed by the glowing prospects being painted by Dave Anderson, Tom Perkins, and the other venture capital proselytizers in attendance. An extroverted, cocky New Yorker who had done some entrepreneuring during his undergraduate days at MIT, Metcalfe was frustrated with his job at Xerox Corp. As a scientist, Metcalfe had been the principal inventor of Xerox's Ethernet system for linking computers, word processors, and other equipment in a local network. But a move into engineering management was not going well. "I developed the feeling that to be successful I couldn't be buried inside an engineering organization," he recalls. "So I gave Xerox seven months' notice and said I want to either be a general manager or report to a general manager." Not surprisingly, the job that Xerox finally came up with failed to meet Metcalfe's criteria. "Xerox was really right," he admits. "I had no qualifications to be a general manager of any kind. So I decided to give myself permission to do it."

After the MIT gathering had opened his eyes to the possibilities, Metcalfe started making the rounds of the venture community. At first, he asked only for advice. His idea was to start a company that could exploit the Ethernet standard for local area networks. There would be a big market, he was sure, for the hardware and software to provide digital communications links in an office environment once Ethernet became an accepted standard. It was not until September 1980 that Xerox, Digital Equipment, and Intel announced an agreement on specifications that made Ethernet a true industry standard. But 3Com was already a going concern on the strength of technology development and consulting contracts. At that point, Metcalfe went back to his venture capital mentors with a business plan that painted 3Com as a candidate for second-round financing. "We've got this business going," Metcalfe told them. "We've got the technology handled, and what we need is marketing and manufacturing so we'd like to raise some money."

The venture people disagreed. For one thing, they too thought Metcalfe was not qualified to be a general manager. And they found his business plan laughable. Its centerpiece was what looked like a series of clouds, showing the possible applications of Ethernet, drawn on yellow paper. "The first few times we showed it to people," Metcalfe concedes, "they didn't think it was a plan." Furthermore, recalls Dick Kramlich of New Enterprise Associates, "he was asking for too little money to get the job done and valuing the founders' share at too great a level."

The first real offer came from Wally Davis, then at Mayfield, who suggested doing a seed financing at $7 per share (a figure not traceable to present share values). Metcalfe, still thinking in terms of a second-round deal in the $20 range, saw that as a step in the wrong direction. He turned Davis down. Then Kramlich put together a group that was willing to pay $13. And Metcalfe could find no West Coast firm willing to go higher, a development he ascribed bitterly to collusion. "We had this notion of a free market thing, of competitors competing for our stock, when in fact there was a fairly strong communications channel among investors," Metcalfe charges.

Metcalfe decided to break the cartel. A Boston firm, which he will not identify, offered to do the deal at $21 and Metcalfe accepted. He called Kramlich back: "Dick, we have somebody who thinks we're worth what we're worth. They just want a month to do their due diligence. So if you insist that this is the deal and you won't wait a month, we're going to walk away." But the Boston deal proved too good to be true. Metcalfe began to notice what he calls the Oh-By-The-Way Syndrome, as in "by the way, a condition of the deal is that we have some other investors." Metcalfe found another investor willing to join the deal at the highest price, but it was a New York firm. "Actually, we need a *West Coast* firm in order to close this deal." He found a West Coast firm. "No, it has to be a *major* West Coast firm. He found a major West Coast firm willing to put up $100,000. "What we really want is a *significant* participation of a major West Coast firm or we can't close this deal." The structure of the agreement began to change as well. "New terms and conditions came out of the woodwork," Metcalfe recalls. Suddenly there was an "exploding board" clause that gave the investors power to appoint all directors of the company. And a "ratchet-down" clause, protecting them against possible dilution in case 3Com was ever forced to sell stock at a lower price.

Metcalfe knew he was beaten. He had already said no to Kramlich, but he called Jack Melchor, who at one point had also offered $13. "I need this deal closed," he told Melchor. "I'd like you to do it at $13 and I have only one stipulation." What was the stipulation, Melchor wanted to know. "I do not want this Boston firm to participate." Melchor quickly agreed to put in $450,000, NEA and Mayfield contributed $300,000 each, and 3Com had its financing. And Metcalfe had the pleasure of calling his erstwhile backer in Boston to tell him he was out of the deal. "Why?" was the injured response. "We supported you when no one else would." "No," said Metcalfe, "you lied to me when no one else would."

THE PRICING BAZAAR

Clearly, pricing and structure can be sore points between venture investors and entrepreneurs. That should not be surprising. The process of establishing a value for something as insubstantial as a startup company involves subjective judgments on a host of factors. In contrast to transactions involving public securities, where buyers and sellers have approximately equal access to considerable information about corporate performance on the one hand and the state of the market on the other, startup prices are set in a veritable knowledge vacuum. Typically, the entrepreneurs know more than the investors about their own capabilities and the markets they are proposing to enter, and the investors know most about trends in the private securities market. Both sides do what they can to reduce their own ignorance but in the absence of a true market mechanism prices must inevitably be set by a process of bargaining or, as Metcalfe would have it, "muscle." It is a deaf-and-dumb bazaar, with buyers and sellers frantically signalling their claims and intentions. That it works at all is something of a miracle.

What is meant by price in the bazaar of startup investing is not the price per share of stock, but the price for a share of the whole company. Obviously, at this point, share prices are completely arbitrary. What matters is the value of the company and the percentage of its ownership that can be purchased for a given investment. Venture capitalists speak of "pre-money" valuation, meaning the value assigned to the management team and any assets it may have accumulated before the injection of equity, and "post-money" valuation, which takes into account the new capital that has come into the company.

In an investment model used by Wally Davis of Alpha Partners, a typical two-stage seed investment of $1.5 million would purchase half of a company with a post-money value of $3 million (Table 2). The value is actually $3,150,000 and Alpha's share only 47.5 percent because creation of a pool of stock options is assumed to dilute all holdings by 5 percent. At the next stage, which Davis calls the first round, the company has achieved a pre-money value of $9.45 million and a $2 million investment buys a sixth of it. (In the model, additional option shares raise the post-money value to $12.15 million and dilute the new investor's share to 16.4 percent.) In the second round, $3 million buys 10.9 percent of a company now worth $27.6 million, and in the third round $10 million buys 12.5 percent of an $80 million enterprise. Jackpot! The original investors have increased their investment fifteenfold, the founders and other employees hold stock and options worth more than $30 million. Both sides can feel they negotiated a good opening-round "price."

In the real world, of course, prices can vary enormously even between deals that look quite similar. In software, Fred M. Gibbons gave up 25 percent of Software Publishing Corp. for $250,000 in 1981, while a year later William M. (Trip) Hawkins collected $2 million for 40 percent of Electronic Arts. Software Publishing, in other words, had a post-money startup valuation of $1 million; Electronic Arts was valued at $5 million. In computers, the venture arm of Hambrecht & Quist valued Metaphor Computer Systems at $10 million post-money in December 1982, then three months later decided Sequent Computer Systems was worth $15 million. In all these cases, well-regarded young executives had little to offer beyond a team of engineers and a business concept. The difference in valuation lay in subjective readings of their skills and ideas, in the individual goals and strategies of the investing groups, in the ebb and flow of market conditions, and in the bargaining ability of the parties to the deal. Tommy Davis likens the process to buying a race horse or a painting: "Nobody can put a valuation on it and say this is the price. What we try to do is figure out as carefully as we can what the thing really seems to be worth to us and try to get the price in that general target."

The key factors are no secret. "You don't have to be in the business too long before you develop a sense for what the venture market looks like," says Jim Anderson of Merrill Pickard. "They do or do not have a fully-staffed management team: they are or are not in a large market; they do or do not have technical risks associated with the product; they are potentially a $50 million or a $150 million company." Frank Caufield of Kleiner Perkins points out that the amount of money a venture requires also affects the investor's leverage in an important way. "The more attractive the deal, the less equity you'll tend to get," he says, "and the more money they need the more you'll tend to get."

Well aware of this unwritten law of venturing, many entrepreneurs try hard to minimize their need for cash initially, although few carry the effort as far as Giga-tronics, whose founders built their own workbenches and even handcrafted the sign in front of their building to keep costs down and their share of the equity high. Sometimes the bootstrapping is unintended. Philip Hwang, a Korean immigrant who decided to start a company in the highly competitive computer terminals business, was turned down flat in 1978 when he approached three venture capitalists, including Don Valentine. He kept TeleVideo Systems Inc. afloat by taking a second mortgage on his home, and three years later had made the company so successful that Valentine called him to offer $2 million. "He asked what he'd get for that and I said 0.9 percent," Hwang later told the San Francisco Chronicle. "I told him a few years ago he could have had 50 percent for $200,000. He was so mad he never talked to me again."

An inescapable element of any price negotiation is the investor's rate-of-return goal, although it is more likely to be an implicit factor than one that is precisely calculated. It is certainly possible to work back from a set of assumptions about the future sales and earnings of a company and the price/earnings multiple that it is likely to obtain in an acquisition or a public offering, and extrapolate the valuation required for an adequate rate of return. In one example of such modeling, an investor seeks a 44 percent compounded rate of return on a $500,000 investment. If he expects the company to be valued at $7.8 million in five years he would need a 41 percent equity interest at that time to reach his goal.[1] Some investors pile on even more complexities with formulas that try to calculate the probability of success or failure in a given deal or that allow for a range of eventual price-earnings multiples that the company might attain.

Steve Merrill of Merrill Pickard believes that this kind of calculation generally "applies too much science to what is really a very subjective analysis." His approach is to compare and categorize companies, watching the flow of venture deals and saying, in effect, "this kind of company in this stage with these kinds of problems should be worth in this range of valuations." In a general way, though, Merrill must figure the growth potential in every deal. Merrill Pickard's goal is to achieve at least a 30 percent compounded rate of return over the

TABLE 2
Alpha Partners Investment Model

	Seed I	Seed II	Round 1	Round 2	Round 3	Value of Holdings
Month	0	6	18	30	48	
Capitalized Value	$2,000,000	$3,150,000	$12,151,446	$27,632,205	$80,176,229	
Funds Raised	500,000	1,000,000	2,000,000	3,000,000	10,000,000	
Financing Step-up		1.00	3.00	2.00	2.50	
Cum. Funds Raised	500,000	1,500,000	3,500,000	6,500,000	16,500,000	
Founders/Engrs.	55.0%	28.5%	22.1%	19.4%	16.7%	$13,411,184
CEO	10.0	9.5	7.4	6.5	5.6	4,470,395
VP Marketing	5.0	4.8	3.7	3.2	2.8	2,235,197
VP Finance	2.0	1.9	1.5	1.3	1.1	894,079
VP Operations	3.0	2.9	2.2	1.9	1.7	1,341,118
Option Pool*		5.0	10.0	10.0	10.0	8,017,623
Subtotal Company	75.0%	52.5%	46.8%	42.4%	37.9%	$30,369,597

183

Seed Investors	25.0%	47.5%	36.8%	32.4%	27.9%	$22,351,974
Investors Round 1			16.4	14.4	12.4	9,959,108
Investors Round 2				10.9	9.4	7,497,469
Investors Round 3					12.5	9,998,080
Check:	100.00%	100.00%	100.00%	100.00%	100.00%	
*Diluted Option Pool		5.0%	4.1%	8.9%	8.7%	
*New Options			6.1	1.2	1.4	

long haul, a performance that Merrill believes will be required to continue attracting money into venture capital. This means that Merrill
Pickard cannot afford to invest where the potential return is less than
that. "If we earn 20 percent in our business," Merrill says, "we won't
ever raise any more money." To David Morgenthaler of Morgenthaler
Partners, the arithmetic is simple: "You get a lot of people trying to
sell you things at a $50 million valuation. If I want ten times my
money on that round, it's got to become a $500 million company.
How many companies are going to end up worth $500 million?"

BUILDING IN PROTECTION

Some venture firms attempt to compensate for the uncertainties of
the pricing process by structuring the deal in a way that seems to
protect their investment. As Metcalfe learned, there is a difference
between East Coast and West Coast firms in these matters, although
some Easterners have adopted the more casual Western approach. Don
Ackerman of J. H. Whitney, for example: "I don't worry too much
about control and building in a return and all that sort of thing. What
I'm really interested in is what that equity is worth and how do we
make it worth more. Probably I'm like the West Coast guys." But to
William Comfort of Citicorp, West Coast deals seem undisciplined:
"They just throw money at them and let them go, whereas the East
Coast is more rational. You put in more restrictions and more financial
engineering."

The first level of protection lies in the choice of financial instrument. While common stock is the security of choice in some deals,
many investors like the relative security of a preferred stock that is
convertible into common, which ranks ahead of common when the
company is sold. Even more secure would be a debt instrument, typically a note convertible into stock, which provides a graceful way out
of the deal if the prospects for a public offering seem dim. Then there
are conditions and provisions that can run on for pages: ratchets that
retroactively reduce the price of an early investment if the company
subsequently raises money at a lower price; registration rights that allow investors to force a public offering; earn-out arrangements that tie
management's participation in ownership to progress in earnings and
stock prices.

It is all a bit much for a traditionalist like Peter Crisp of Venrock,
who prefers the simplest of purchase agreements but finds himself in
the minority. "In the informal world we grew up in," says Crisp, "you
bet on the people and didn't rely on registration rights and things like
that. If ten years ago we received a purchase document like that we
would have taken issue with it and said we needed a much simpler
document. But now it's the plain-vanilla agreement that has every-

body's-kitchen-sink provisions in it." Once such provisions become accepted, they are almost impossible to eliminate. Lawyers have a way of asking, as Crisp points out, "are you sure you don't want this protection?" As fiduciaries for corporations and huge pension funds with armies of lawyers of their own, today's venture capitalists feel they have little choice but to include the kitchen sink in their agreements.

THE UNITED FRONT

What about Metcalfe's complaint that venture firms in effect fix prices by deciding jointly what the valuation should be? One partner in a distinguished firm agrees that this was a common practice when the venture industry was smaller and less competitive than it is in the 1980s. "In the old days," he recalls, "people were begging us to invest. We'd all call each other up and say, 'what do you want to offer them?' Now they have a whole palette of people to choose from." Another venturer insists there is no need to coordinate prices, since similar firms generally reach similar conclusions. "There have been several deals where we independently submitted bids to a company that were right on top of each other," he says. "We're rarely off by more than 25 percent unless somebody has a stupid reason for doing it."

Among the top-tier venture firms, however, there is still a strong sense of obligation to the club, or at least to the lead investor on a deal. Don Valentine explains how the system works when his firm takes the lead in organizing a deal: "We set the price and the deal terms and decide how much money is going to be raised. Then we select the investors. But the investors know ahead of time what the deal is and they never talk to the president about the deal. You either like it or you don't but the terms are not variable."

Only rarely can an entrepreneur crack this united front once a deal is coming together. Valentine is vehement on the sanctity of the deal: "If I have shaken hands and said I'm going to give you a million dollars, that's it. If you come back to me next week and say, 'hey, we've got an offer from somebody in Toledo and he's going to pay 20 percent more,' my position is you've got a real problem. I would like to know now, before you have my million dollars, whether I am dealing with an ethical person or not. I'm only going to pay what we agreed to pay and if you want to take the money from Toledo, you take it but we're out."

Before the handshake, the entrepreneur can sometimes win surprisingly large improvements in the terms of the deal, as Casey Powell proved by persuading Reid Dennis and his partners to value Sequent at $15 million. That was 50 percent more than Kleiner Perkins and other firms interested in Sequent had been willing to go for, but the deal seemed so important and they had committed themselves so deeply that most could not back away. Brook Byers of Kleiner Perkins explains: "I guess we made our decision from an emotional point of view. We had decided we were going to invest, we had decided how much we were going to invest, and the price changed. We didn't want to call their bluff. We had about two hours to decide before they were going to open it up to five other firms that had offers on the table. If we called their bluff and we were wrong, the hand would have been over and there would have been no reopening it. So we said okay, we'll make an exception."

Trip Hawkins's experience in winning a $5 million post-money valuation for Electronic Arts was less dramatic but probably more typical of the limits of entrepreneurial leverage. Hawkins left his job at Apple Computer in May 1982 to start laying plans for a company that would act as a publisher for independent developers of educational software. Don Valentine liked the idea enough to offer Hawkins the use of a spare office while he worked on a business plan, and before long there were more would-be Electronic Arts employees than venture capitalists in the 3000 Sand Hill Road suite. But Hawkins decided not to talk price right away. "Don is a very shrewd bargainer and the last thing in the world I wanted to do was set price with him," Hawkins explains. Instead, he moved out of Valentine's office and began to talk to other groups to get a sense of what the company might be worth. Hawkins took a price back to Valentine and met resistance. "We finally decided we wanted to talk turkey with Kleiner Perkins," says Hawkins, "and we came up with a price that was somewhat lower than what we asked for originally but quite a bit higher than some of the unsolicited offers we had seen. And we just went back to Valentine and said, 'this is what the price is.'" But Valentine saw no significant difference between his offer and the new one, and he agreed to take half the deal.

WHAT GOES UP

In the final analysis, it is the invisible hand of supply and demand that has the biggest effect on prices. Until recently, the venture capital market was highly imperfect in the economist's sense of a market where buyers or sellers have enough power to control prices. During most of the 1970s, venture capital was so scarce that those who had it could easily dictate terms to those who wanted it. That situation changed dramatically as billions of dollars flooded the field, and although the number of entrepreneurs seeking funds increased along with the supply of capital, the market forces moved closer to balance. The venture capital market also tracks but often lags the swings of the public stock market, especially the market for technology stocks and for new issues, and it reacts as well to the emergence of new technologies or trends that seem ripe for exploitation. Neither buyers nor sellers are ever quite sure where this market is headed because details of most deals are usually closely guarded. Venture capitalists have the advantage, of course, because information is traded freely among groups that work together. "The entrepreneurs have no idea what the market looks like," says Jim Anderson of Merrill Pickard, "but we do." Some firms, in fact, have computerized their files of data on prices and valuations, while entrepreneurs must rely on rumor and guesswork to counter the investors' arguments on market trends.

Market forces are most evident in the pricing of second-round and later investments, where the connection with prices of initial public offerings, or IPOs, is obvious. Pricing of such deals is often expressed in terms of the "step-up" from previous valuations. A step-up of 2.5 times over the first-round price was considered adequate until the early 1980s, when a combination of booming demand for IPOs and a huge increase in the capital committed to venture investing pushed the multiple as high as 5 to 1 in some deals. One example was Gavilan Computer, whose president, Manny A. Fernandez, started discussing a $6 million second-round investment with his startup investors late in 1982. The price first proposed, according to Dick Kramlich of New Enterprise Associates, Gavilan's lead investor, represented a conservative 2.5-times step-up from the first-round price. But a third party, a financial institution, stepped in and offered to take the entire offering at 4.3-to-1. After some debate the original investors agreed to meet the new price and kept the offering themselves. In retrospect, after Gavilan went into bankruptcy late in 1984, price was an irrelevancy in this case.

Some kind of world record for second-round deals was recorded in early 1982 by Wilfred J. Corrigan, the Liverpool slum kid who became a semiconductor engineer and battled his way to the top of Fairchild Camera & Instrument before he was forty. Corrigan left Fairchild after it was acquired by Schlumberger Ltd. and founded LSI Logic Inc in 1980. Corrigan launched his Silicon Valley startup with $6 million from such top California venturers as Tom Perkins, Don Valentine, and Reid Dennis at what Dennis calls a "very full" valuation of $10 million. When it came time for the second round, Corrigan listened politely to the advice of his first-round backers and then totally ignored it. With the help of British investors, Corrigan raised another $10 million in equity at a staggering eightfold step-up in valuation. In this case, Corrigan's audacity was more than justified the following year when a public offering valued LSI Logic in excess of $500 million.

The inflation in later-stage prices never really infected startup valuations, although it drove many firms to concentrate more heavily on startup investing. A few deals, including Electronic Arts, Metaphor, and Sequent, probably fetched higher prices than they would have in normal times. But these were exceptions. In most startups investors continued to insist on a 50 percent or greater stake in the equity, with an average California deal perhaps involving $3 million for 60 percent of the company. "If you look at the average price we pay for the twelve or so investments we make in a year," says Dave Anderson of Sutter Hill, which is mainly a startup investor, "I don't think there has been a big change." By late 1983, as the IPO market began to fade, venture firms were attempting to pull all prices down again. "I don't think you can buy private securities on the assumption that you can sell them in a market like the one we had in the spring of 1983," says Kevin Landry of TA Associates. "I've been in the business fifteen years and I've never seen a market quite like that market." The problem, as Landry notes, is that private prices are slow to reflect the declines in public prices. As a result, it seemed to Landry in early 1984, "now is not a good time to sell but it is also, ironically, not a good time to buy."

As 1985 approached, the cycle appeared to be moving again. Prices of later-round financings were coming down as company after company encountered resistance at exalted valuations. It seemed unlikely that the inflationary ebullience of the early 1980s would be repeated soon, but experienced venture capitalists found nothing in that prospect to cry over. David Morgenthaler tells of meeting a young entrepreneur in mid-1984 and being asked "Do you think the business is going to get back to normal?" "God, I hope not," replied Morgenthaler, recalling all those years when little or no money was available. "What do you think is normal?" "You know, the spring of 1983." Morgenthaler laughed. "I haven't seen anything like the spring of 1983 since the summer of 1968. In my opinion, mid-1984 is not only normal, it's pretty good. The public market for the crap has dried up, and the overpriced offerings are having difficulty, but this isn't bad." In venturing, as in other areas of life, a sense of perspective is helpful.

NOTE

1. Calculated by Stanley C. Golder in "Structuring and Pricing the Financing," *Guide to Venture Capital Sources*. Capital Publishing Corp., Wellesley Hills, Mass., 1983, p. 79.

13

VULTURE CAPITALISTS

An ominous side of the venture capital process was exposed to public view when investment activity and new-company formations reached excessive levels in the early 1980s. As talent poured out of established companies into scores of startups, as aggressive newcomers to venture capital threw money at marginal deals, as seemingly mindless competition killed profits for entire industries, a backlash developed. For the first time in memory, opinion leaders in Silicon Valley—themselves, often, the beneficiaries of venture financing—began to wonder aloud if there could be such a thing as an oversupply of venture capital. Gordon Moore, the chairman of Intel, told me in 1983: "There is some optimum amount of venture capital. It's clearly not zero, because at zero a lot of things die without seeing the light of day. But the possibility exists of there being too much venture capital, in which case everything gets fragmented and all the continuity in things that established companies can do gets lost. From the mid-1970s to now, we've gone from one extreme to the other."[1]

William J. Perry, a successful entrepreneur and former Defense Department official who now is with Hambrecht & Quist, expressed similar concerns in early 1984 at an advisory board meeting of the Stanford Center for Economic Policy Research: "I believe firmly that venture activity has been a tremendous catalyst in innovation. But I'm also willing to believe there's some level at which it could become problematic, given the exponential increase since 1978."[2] Even David Packard, perhaps the most respected entrepreneur in Silicon Valley, said in a BBC Radio interview in March 1984: "I think there's a little too much venture capital available today, which makes it possible for some people to get into things when they're really not quite properly prepared for it." Reduced venture activity has rendered some of the complaints temporarily moot. But the ethical and professional questions raised are too important to ignore. They boil down to two sweeping charges against the venture capital community:

- that by draining a few successful companies of their most productive managers and engineers, by pirating their technology, and by disrupting key departments and projects, venture capitalists damage the ability of those companies to innovate and to compete in international markets;

- that by funding excessive numbers of similar companies, many with less than outstanding leadership, they are wasting money and talent, adding little to the progress of technology, and artificially creating overcompetitive situations where no participant can make money.

Intel has been the company perhaps most heavily impacted by the allure of venture capital. In part, this is testimony to the excellence of the organization constructed by Bob Noyce, Gordon Moore, and Andrew Grove, the Hungarian-born scientist who took charge of Intel's manufacturing organization in the early days and made good on the slogan "Intel delivers." It was, without much doubt, the leading technology-based company of the last decade. Intel pioneered two of the most important products of the decade—the semiconductor memory and the microprocessor—and parlayed them into hundredfold growth. And it consistently attracted the best managers and engineers. As one engineering manager explained his move from Digital Equipment Corp. to Intel: "I was planning to get an MBA and then get a master's in computer science. I didn't want to go back to school but I wanted to achieve the same effect. Intel represented a graduate school of business and a graduate school of engineering."

But in the 1980s the venture capital revolution came along, and many of the startup opportunities it created either competed with Intel or relied heavily on its expertise in microcomputers. As Arthur Rock points out: "This is a very unique period in American industry because the great majority of these companies are all based on the microprocessor." At the same time, Intel's size—it crossed the $1 billion barrier in 1983—and the stern discipline with which Andy Grove, by now president of the company, kept the organization locked on course collided with the entrepreneurial spirit of its employees. As Intel bumped through the recession-plagued early 1980s some began to look for greener pastures. For the first time in its history, Intel began losing people. The numbers alone were not impressive, perhaps a hundred or two hundred people who either started companies or joined startups out of more than 20,000 employees, but the cumulative impact was painful and some individual departments were hit hard. Intel was not alone. At least ten new companies were formed by ex-employees of Hewlett-Packard between 1980 and 1982. And Tektronix, National Semiconductor, Advanced Micro Devices, and Texas Instruments all suffered major defections.

Most infuriating to Intel and other large companies were the cases in which managers and engineers from one department launched companies making products that competed with the products for which they were responsible at the old company. L. J. Sevin, now a venture capitalist, was a victim of this scenario in the late 1970s when, as chief executive of Mostek, he watched key members of his 64K RAM team defect to Inmos, a semiconductor memory startup funded by Britain's Labor government. Charlie Sporck of National Semiconductor witnessed a similar melodrama when Robert H. Swanson, who had headed National's work in linear circuits, was joined by two top designers from the same group in forming Linear Technology. And Noyce and Moore watched five managers of Intel's Special Products Division, responsible for a line of erasable memory components, walk out to form Seeq Technology with plans to develop their own erasable memory chips.

A QUESTION OF ETHICS

Reluctantly, because they were among the earliest entrepreneurs to profit from venture investment and because they themselves are informal venture investors, the founders of Intel began to speak out on what some wag called the "vulture capital" issue. Noyce puts the matter in dire terms: "If we get into a situation where Company A puts an enormous amount of money into an R&D project and Company B can simply appropriate that, then the first project will never be done again. That becomes the destruction of the American industrial base, to put it simply. And that is what a number of the venture capitalists have really used as a strategy. They wait until the development is done and then exploit it, instead of contributing to the development." Noyce agrees that there is an enormous advantage to the U.S. economy in encouraging entrepreneurial activity that creates new ideas. "But there is also an enormous disadvantage in the destruction of existing teams who are carrying [those ideas] the next step further."

Noyce worries that this trend is already making it impossible for American companies to take the long-term attitude toward training that characterizes their Japanese competitors: "The Japanese company knows that it is going to have the benefit of that training for the rest of the man's life, basically." Noyce is not suggesting that American companies should expect lifetime employment commitments. "You should have a reasonably good assurance that you will get the training investment paid back but you certainly don't want it to the extent that the employee is a slave laborer and does not have the opportunity to go out and exploit a new idea." And Noyce puts the ethical question squarely in the lap of the venture capitalist: "I don't think it is legitimate for people to reach into existing companies where there is a technology they want to exploit and drag it out. If the individual is unhappy in the company and wants to leave, that's one thing. But to have outside influences come in and create dissatisfactions feels uncomfortable to me."

Similar complaints were aired on university campuses as faculty members rushed to seize venture opportunities and ran into conflicts over the ownership of research findings and their ability to combine academic roles with entrepreneurship. Some universities have tried to

clamp down on commercial activities of their faculty members, pushing many out of teaching altogether, out of fear that commercial interests will pervert their academic work. Responding more to the dollar than to the student, one department chairman warned, could
precipitate "a deterioration in the educational process."[3]

Most, or all, venture capitalists would reply that they do not entice
employees to leave companies or professors to leave academia, that
they only respond to the inquiries of people who have already decided
to leave, often because they have been treated badly or thwarted in
attempts to implement their ideas. But the proliferation of venture
capitalists recruited from top technology companies such as Intel, National, Hewlett-Packard, and Burroughs encourages a close, informal
relationship with likely entrepreneurs in those and other companies.
And many venture capitalists freely admit that they engage in the
practice of "cold calling"—contacting researchers, managers, or engineers they have not met and giving a sales pitch for their firm on
the off-chance the person is thinking of leaving. There is normally
nothing illegal about such activities, but they raise the hackles of
managers in the affected companies. And increasingly, established
companies have turned to the courts to fight what they see as raids on
employees, technology, and proprietary information by venture-
backed entrepreneurs.

James H. Pooley, a Palo Alto attorney who handles trade secret
litigation for many Silicon Valley companies, estimates that the inci-
dence of such cases has at least doubled and probably tripled over the
last five years. "The linchpin of a startup is often a successful manager
or scientist from another company," Pooley explains. "In the eyes of
the established company, the venture investment can look like payoff
money for theft. And the venture capitalist is often seen as the bad
guy who dangles the money." Normally, it is the new company that is
sued. But in one highly publicized case, *Intel* vs *Seeq*, the venture
capitalists themselves were added to the list of defendants. Among the
several ironies of that case, Gordon Moore in effect was suing himself:
he was a limited partner in a fund managed by Kleiner Perkins, the
lead venture firm backing Seeq. The Seeq suit, like virtually every
other trade secret case, was settled long before it got to trial and the
terms of the settlement, along with the evidence produced by laywers
on both sides, were put under seal. Seeq made an undisclosed payment
to Intel and agreed not to hire more Intel people for a time, and an
independent expert was appointed to ensure that Seeq used no proprietary Intel technology. "The payment was far less than it would
have cost Seeq to take it through the courts," says John Doerr of
Kleiner Perkins, "and we got back all the management attention."
Seeq survived, went public, and had sales of over $40 million in 1984,
its fourth year in business.

Because most of these cases are settled quietly, after closed hearings, the public has no direct view of an important body of law that affects the right of individuals to start their own ventures as well as the ability of established companies to protect their technology. A trade secrets case is won or lost in the few weeks between the time a complaint is filed and the hearing on the plaintiff's request for a preliminary injunction that, if ordered, could put the defendants out of business. "The trial really occurs at the preliminary injunction hearing," Pooley says. "You have a discovery process that might take two or three years compressed into six weeks to two months." Neither plaintiff nor defendant can normally afford to let the case go to trial because both companies would be damaged by the disruptions and costs involved in prolonged litigation. By the time of the first hearing, lawyers for both sides will have developed enough evidence to determine the "winner" in a settlement. Out of such settlements has come a broad consensus on what is acceptable behavior and what is not, and in some cases the agreements reached between entrepreneurs and their former employers have been quite amicable.

One thing venture capitalists have learned is to be wary of talking to entrepreneurs who have not severed their employment ties, especially if a competitive product is involved. Says Roger S. Borovoy, formerly Intel's general counsel and now a venture capitalist with Sevin Rosen: "We will not talk to a group that is still employed and has a product that is going to compete. Period." It was the competitive nature of the Seeq product that made that group's departure actionable, in Borovoy's opinion. Just agreeing to leave is no different than if the people had decided to quit independently, he says, and is unlikely by itself to be the basis of a successful suit. Even if the defectors plan a product that competes with one of the employer's products, they do not necessarily face legal problems. If the Seeq group had left to form a company making microprocessors—anything other than erasable memories—Intel may have had what is called a wrong without a remedy, Borovoy believes. "It is hard to make these suits stick without a flavor of trade secrets," he says. The similarity between what the group had been working on at Intel and the products planned for the new company created at least the possibility that Intel's trade secrets were at risk. Even so, Intel did not push for an injunction until it was able to show there was a threat that Seeq would disclose its technology to another company. "The strategy of moving the focus to a third party was a good one," Pooley comments. "That was a chief reason Intel was able to get the order it got."

Occasionally, a trade secrets suit is an open-and-shut case that can be resolved without legal action. That happened in mid-1984 when Cypress Semiconductor, the startup backed by Sevin Rosen, agreed to refrain from using a circuit which four of its engineers had proudly described in a trade magazine article. The circuit, it seemed, had been created first at Intel by one of the co-authors who later moved to Cypress. "Engineers sort of feel that the circuitry is all theirs," remarks Borovoy, who helped Cypress settle the case. "It was bizarre and unfortunate."

Even where no trade secrets are involved, companies can be damaged by actions that fall under the general heading of "unfair competition." And this is truly a legal no-man's land. As Pooley points out in his lively manual for defecting entrepreneurs and outraged employers, most of the lawsuits alleging unfair competition revolve around "raids" on employees and taking customer lists. But where expert testimony can often establish what a trade secret is and whether it has been misappropriated, there are few objective tests of whether a recruiting drive or any other business practice is "unfair." Court decisions in this area, Pooley writes, "are often inconsistent and are characterized by a heavy reliance on the 'peculiar facts' of each case."[4]

Despite the legal fuzziness surrounding the issue, losing talent to a startup seems for many executives to be the most galling aspect of "vulture capitalism." Casey Powell's departure with sixteen Intel co-workers to form Sequent drew even more criticism from Intel executives than the Seeq case. "That was a bad one in terms of its disruptive nature," Noyce says. "They took a high percentage of our total capability in an area." Moore was concerned enough about Sequent to lay into Powell in his remarks to shareholders at Intel's 1983 annual meeting: "A newspaper interview with their leader indicated that he followed what he thinks to be 'the rules to get around litigation.' I want to assure you that we do not accept that view. To the contrary, it seems to me evident that a group departure such as that cannot be secretly arranged by an Intel manager without breaking all legal and ethical rules."[5]

For all the sound and fury, Intel never sued Sequent, no doubt in part because Powell was careful to hire no more than three additional Intel employees, long after the initial defection. "By the time Intel knew the first thing about it," Borovoy says, "the damage had been done. Intel was better off with a legal Sword of Damocles over Casey's head." There remains the question of whether Powell and the others abused the "fiduciary duty" that binds any manager entrusted with confidential information by, for example, selecting the best employees and enticing them to leave while still employed. Borovoy is skeptical that any such claim—without trade secret involvement—would hold up in court, and Powell took great pains to avoid even the appearance of predatory recruiting. At least three months before he left, Powell says, he warned Intel that he was considering options outside the company, including a startup. Conversations with Scott Gibson and Larry Wade convinced him that they were interested—"quite unsolicited"—

in doing something similar. Others who joined the group, with the exception of Powell's secretary, came from other parts of Intel's Oregon operation. "I can't conceive of a case where we damaged Intel in any way," insists Wade. "People came from all over the organization, and Intel has incredible depth."

It would not be easy to demonstrate that Intel, National Semiconductor, Advanced Micro Devices, IBM, Hewlett-Packard, or any other major technology company has sustained severe, long-term damage as a result of venture capital inroads on their people or technology. Most have prospered in the sustained growth in demand for computer-related products of the mid-1980s, a boom stimulated at least in part by the product development and marketing efforts of startups. Daisy Systems, a pioneer in engineering workstations, recruited at least fifty Intel engineers. But Daisy's product, by helping companies speed up the design of complex integrated circuits, may have helped Intel more than the loss of talent hurt. And the established companies have a formidable weapon in the use or threat of a lawsuit, which typically is brutally disrupting to a new company. In fact, some attorneys charge that the trade secret litigation undertaken by large companies against startups increasingly is aimed as much at dampening competition or seeking revenge as at protecting their technology. "A trade secrets case is easy to bring and easy to justify," says Jim Pooley, "and the potential for abuse is large because a startup is as vulnerable as a turtle on its back." John Larson, a partner in Brobeck, Phleger & Harrison, a San Francisco law firm that represents many startups, agrees: "A lot of these cases involve heavy-handed behavior by the employer; even the threat of litigation can produce a chilling effect."

THE FEEDING FRENZY

It is a complaint on which venture capitalists and their critics can agree: Far too many companies were formed in the early 1980s with far too little regard for their viability. Gordon Moore repeated his warnings at Intel's 1984 annual meeting: "The sopping up of resources by multiple startups trying to solve the same problem is detracting from the competitiveness of U.S. industry." Don Valentine, one of the most thoughtful venture capitalists, points out that the proliferation of startups has profoundly changed the venture business. "It used to be that the only competition we ever faced was from larger, well-established companies that didn't recognize a market niche or an opportunity," Valentine recalls. "It took most of us to finance one company into business, two at the most. Now because of the overwhelming amount of money available, each venture group feels it has to have every kind of an investment. And the competition is the little companies we are financing." Noel J. Fenton, an experienced Silicon

Valley executive, describes the spectacle of too much money chasing too few worthy deals as a "feeding frenzy" that has resulted in "companies being launched with management teams that are woefully inexperienced."

Venture capitalists began suffering the after-effects of their binge in 1984 as company after company fell short of its targets, disappeared into bankruptcy, or dragged out a miserable existence as "living dead," soaking up money and attention but never really succeeding. Some of the companies got almost to the point of going public before their flaws surfaced. In other cases, perhaps even more damaging to the reputation of the venture business, the defects were not discovered until after the public offering. Disgruntled shareholders began suing companies and underwriters when heavily promoted new issues turned sour, and Reid Dennis warned a meeting of the National Venture Capital Association: "Public securities of venture-backed companies are the product of the venture investment process. What would happen to our portfolio companies if only one out of every four products they manufactured worked?"[6]

Some markets or product niches became so overcrowded with startups that even the best of the lot have found it difficult to make money, a circumstance that bodes ill for their ability to survive the inevitable onslaught by major companies. A prime example is the business of making "Winchesters"—memory devices that spin coated metal disks to store information—for the minicomputer and microcomputer industries. Winchester technology was developed by IBM for its mainframe systems in the mid-1970s, and it was quickly seized and scaled down in size and cost by fast-moving new companies. Robert R. Gaskin, who keeps track of the rotating memory industry for Dataquest Inc., the market research firm, counted fifty startups making rigid disk drives in mid-1984, plus about fifty more making the disks alone. The market for their products has grown dramatically as users of small computer systems have demanded more and more memory capacity. Yet only a few of these companies were profitable in 1984, a situation that William J. Schroeder, president of Priam Corp., blames on the proliferating competition. Priam—with backing from Sutter Hill and other venture firms—was a well-financed pioneer in the Winchester business. Its sales jumped from $6 million in 1981 to over $60 million in 1983. But by 1984 Priam found its margins under severe pressure and growth prospects for many of its products already fading. Average gross margins in the industry had dropped from 40 to around 20 percent. "It's a shakeout in a growth industry," Schroeder says, "because the number of participants grew faster than the ability of the industry to support them."

Another shakeout with similar causes is under way in microcomputer software, a field so easy to enter that an estimated 3,000 participants were in it at one point. Fred Gibbons, the former Hewlett-Packard manager who founded Software Publishing Corp. in 1981 and built the company to an annual sales level of $20 million in three years, is appalled by the devastation wrought by a flood of venture money. "In software more than any other area," Gibbons asserts, "money can fragment the industry beyond your wildest dreams because it doesn't take a lot of money to get started. It may make it impossible for anybody to get to a critical mass, or we may have to go through a painful coalescing of the industry." Signs that such a process was starting were plentiful in late 1984 as losses, bankruptcies, mergers, and price cutting dominated news reports on the personal software business. Gibbons, who with disciplined management has kept Software Publishing profitable, questions whether the dozens of unprofitable companies spending millions of venture capital dollars on advertising and promotion can overcome their fundamental weaknesses: "I see no way, if a company has been unprofitable in our industry for one or two years, that they are ever going to make it up."

The personal computer industry, meanwhile, is well into the second shakeout of its brief history. The first had little to do with venture capital. Most of the pioneers in the field were self-financed and simply too short of cash to adapt to changes in markets and the arrival of formidable new competitors. Stars of the 1970s such as Polymorphic Systems, Imsai, and Digital Group vanished before most professional venture capitalists had discovered the potential of computers for individuals. When the venture money did start to flow, it became a kind of sorcerer's apprentice, creating in the neighborhood of 300 companies by 1984 with a wide range of management competence and technical strengths before it was finally slowed down by a series of massive failures. As the collapse of Osborne Computer and Victor Technologies proved, reaching $100 million in sales does not guarantee success in this volatile field.

It is not a shortage of money that has caused this second shakeout but management shortcomings and technical glitches. The bankruptcy of Gavilan Computer demonstrated that even an investment of more than $30 million cannot guarantee successful development of a complex product. Gavilan, then called Cosmos Computer, started life early in 1982 when Manny Fernandez raised $8.5 million from a venture group led by Dick Kramlich's NEA. Fernandez, a persuasive Cuban refugee who studied engineering at the University of Florida, rose to managerial rank at Fairchild Semiconductor and for a time was president of Zilog Inc., one of the Exxon Enterprises brood of startups. He had ambitious plans for a powerful portable computer which would weigh only 9 lb. and fit inside a briefcase. Many other companies had recognized the same opportunity, and Gavilan's only hope was to move faster than the competition. But Fernandez bet on the wrong technological horses for this race. Japan's Hitachi could not deliver the 3″ disk drives he selected, and he had to redesign the computer to use 3.5″ drives from Sony. "That could have made the difference," he told *Forbes*.[7] But Gavilan also ran into huge snags in trying to develop its own software for the machine, and Fernandez seemed unable to come to grips with the situation. "It was difficult to get [Fernandez] to understand the seriousness of the problems," a former Gavilan manager told *Business Week*, "which he needed to do in order to address them."[8] Fernandez was more successful at raising money and selling computers. By March 1984 he had accumulated $31 million in venture capital and $85 million in orders. But he was still unable to deliver products in any volume and Gavilan's backers finally reacted. Woody Rea from NEA replaced Fernandez as president in July, but his efforts to slash costs and refocus the product strategy came too late. Gavilan filed for bankruptcy protection on October 1.

Gavilan's trials may be only a preview of the shakeout that will occur as giants such as IBM, AT&T, ITT, and Hewlett-Packard flex their muscles in personal computers. Dataquest forecasts that fully 75 percent of the newcomers will be gone by 1986. "Part of the reason we see so many shakeouts in the industry," says Lore Harp, a founder of Vector Graphic Inc., "is that a lot of schlockey deals were funded. People who should never had money in the first place got funded and because of the enormous appetite in the marketplace were able to sustain a certain momentum for a little while."

The feeding frenzy seems to be over. Disappointing results turned in by such venture-supported companies as Diasonics, Activision, and Pizza Time Theatre following their public offerings helped dry up the market for new issues after late 1983. By 1984 that development had chilled the interest of institutions and foreign investors in "mezzanine" financings and forced venture firms to use more of their own resources to support existing portfolio companies. Many of those companies were in bad shape—victims of the overcrowding in their industries or of bad management—and required handholding that most venture capitalists would otherwise devote to startups. As problem companies surfaced and as prices paid in late-stage financings declined, the growth of portfolio values slowed and many venture firms found it difficult to raise new capital. An industry that a year earlier had had money to burn was suddenly struggling with a liquidity crisis.

The situation was far from desperate. Most of the top venture firms had built such a cushion of capital gains in the early years of the decade that a year or two of disappointment would put only a minor dent in their long-term returns. They had plenty of cash and commitments to nurse their promising portfolio companies through a rocky period. But the industry had clearly returned to the cautious and careful investment posture of the 1970s. Late in 1984 Richard

J. Matlack, president of computer industry consultant InfoCorp, scanned the Silicon Valley horizon and remarked: "There are a lot of deals floating around. They aren't bad deals, but they aren't great deals and nobody will fund them. From now on, maybe for a three-year cycle, the deals that are funded will be much more competitive and will make the industry they are involved in much more competitive."

Clearly, the laws of economics are at work to correct the oversupply of capital that was at the root of the excesses. To the experienced Paul Wythes of Sutter Hill Ventures, this is as natural as the ebb and flow of the tides: "We'll all have some problems in our portfolios in the next few years that were created in this euphoric cycle. Some of the money that's come into our business is going to wish it hadn't come in. We'll see the spigot turn off rather dramatically. And those of us who are in it for the long haul will work with the money we've got until we can prove again that we are ready for that next uptick in the cycle."

NOTES

1. "The Dark Side of Venture Capital," *Business Week*, April 18, 1983, p. 86.
2. Reported in "CEPR Perspectives," *The Stanford Observer*, April 1984.
3. "The Tempest Raging Over Profit-Minded Professors," *Business Week*, November 7, 1983, p. 86.
4. James Pooley, *Trade Secrets*. Osborne/McGraw-Hill, Berkeley, 1982, p. 69.
5. Sabin Russell, "Spin-Off Execs 'Unethical': Intel CEO," *Electronic News*, April 4, 1983, p. 44.
6. "Soothsayers Look at Venture Capital Industry," *Venture Capital Journal*, May 1984, p. 1.
7. Kathleen K. Wiegner, "The Anatomy of a Failure," *Forbes*, November 5, 1984, p. 42.
8. "Two Lessons in Failure from Silicon Valley," *Business Week*, September 10, 1984, p. 78.

14

AMERICAN RENAISSANCE

The arrival of venture capital as an accepted, even prudent vehicle of investment is a new and significant phenomenon on the American financial scene. It is a development with a profoundly important corollary: Entrepreneurship has become an accepted, even commonplace activity and a vital fuel of our new innovation-driven economy. While economists and other social scientists are intensifying their study of the entrepreneurial process, they seldom agree on the forces that generate it or even the characteristics that define it. There is no doubt, however, that adequate funding is a prerequisite for launching a successful new enterprise.[1] And clearly the ability to mobilize capital for entrepreneurial ventures is a crucial advantage in today's competitive world economy. New companies, and especially new companies in those industries that are most innovative, have become indispensable to U.S. employment, growth, and international status. For the most part, it is the startups financed by venture capitalists that have the resources to create and drive the industries important to enhancing productivity and creating opportunities throughout the economy.

At the same time, venture capitalists and entrepreneurs are providing the financial, organizational, and cultural models needed to transform a formerly risk-averse society to one in which risk-taking is rewarded, individual enterprise is admired, success is applauded, and even failure is respected. And all of this is forcing an important policy debate at local and national levels in the United States and abroad: What is the role of venture capital and entrepreneurship in economic development, job creation, and technological progress? What, if anything, should government do to nurture it? What can established businesses learn from the examples being set by the venture process? Why has the supply of venture capital increased so rapidly in the United States and how can it be encouraged in nations where it has not flourished? Does entrepreneurship offer an alternative to centralized planning and direction as an instrument of public policy in a competitive world?

RETURN OF THE ENTREPRENEUR

The extravagant rewards our society has showered on venture investors can be explained in part by the unique role they play, along with entrepreneurs, in creating wealth—in conjuring something from nothing, in other words. As William Wetzel of the University of New Hampshire explains, venture capital should be thought of as "creative" capital that performs a quite different economic function than other investment vehicles, which primarily serve as "expansion" capital. Investments that help existing firms expand are tightly linked to the book values of the underlying assets and are rewarded primarily out of the income produced by those assets. Risk capital, Wetzel argues, creates new wealth: "It is the cutting edge that, together with entrepreneurs, exploits opportunities to put together apparently neutral or sterile resources to create firms with capitalized earning power, or market value, well in excess of the cost of invested funds."[2] Looked at in this way, the venture capitalist becomes a specialized form of entrepreneur, sharing the risks and also the rewards of entrepreneurship with the founders and managers of the firm.

Although no one doubts the importance of entrepreneurs, efforts to describe them and their role have not produced a definitive portrait. One scholar even tried to express the elusive nature of the beasts by comparing them to the mysterious Heffalump that intrigued Winnie-the-Pooh.[3] Social scientists have been attempting to describe entrepreneurs in terms of sociology and psychology at least since Max Weber's theory of the "Protestant ethic" began to gain currency as an explanation for economic growth in the 1930s. Thirty years later David McClelland shifted the argument from religion to child psychology. By examining the literature, especially children's stories, of several societies, McClelland detected a strong correlation between early training that stressed personal achievement and economic development. It was the achievement-oriented children, given the right conditions, who became the entrepreneurs of the Italian Renaissance and of nineteenth century America, McClelland suggested.[4] McClelland later amended his theory to emphasize the importance of broader societal influences on the achievement drive, and others have added to a now-extensive list of social and psychological factors that may or may not explain the emergence of entrepreneurship. Trying to analyze the entrepreneur, comments business historian Harold Livesay, is no easier than analyzing Monet or Warhol. "Successful entrepreneurship," he remarks, "is an art form as much as or perhaps more than it is an economic activity."[5]

What is important is that it has emerged again. Economists generally dislike theories that emphasize the role of individuals instead of the conditions that enable them to act, but the resurgence of new-venture activities since the bleak 1970s has stimulated renewed interest in entrepreneurship as a cause or at least a conduit for economic growth. It was Joseph Schumpeter, the great Austrian-born Harvard economist, who first made the case for the entrepreneur's seminal role in the economy more than fifty years ago. Where classical economics studied the workings of a closed system, Schumpeter saw that the essential thing to understand about capitalism is that it is an evolutionary process with old industries continually being replaced by new ones in a series of upheavals he called "creative destruction." It is the entrepreneur, in Schumpeter's view, who plays the pivotal role in this process and is responsible for recurring booms and recessions that he argued were due to the upsetting impact of innovations. Schumpeter went on to describe the entrepreneurial function in terms that sound like a job description for a venture capitalist: "This function does not essentially consist in either inventing anything or otherwise creating the conditions which the enterprise exploits. It consists in getting things done."[6]

Schumpeter worried that modern societies, dominated by government, would ultimately destroy capitalism by shifting resources away from the private sector, and he prophesied that entrepreneurship would lose its social function as innovation became increasingly bureaucratized. He may yet prove right, but the great renewal of entrepreneurial activity in the last few years demonstrates not only the durability of the genus—the Heffalump lives!—but the continuing importance of the entrepreneur's role. Indeed, few eras in history can equal our own for the magnitude of social, economic, and technical change that is rippling through society. Entire industries have been transformed or swept away and new ones erected in their place as one economy, based essentially on nineteenth century technology and on limitless supplies of cheap energy, is replaced by another with its roots in twentieth century computer science, solid-state physics, and molecular biology. The transition to a postindustrial or information-based society is accelerating. And true to Schumpeter's model, the driving force behind this change has been the entrepreneur—aided and abetted by the venture capitalist.

As a footnote, it would be well to emphasize that entrepreneurship does not operate in a vacuum. There is a good deal of debate about the exact role and importance of entrepreneurs, but it seems clear that there must be preconditions for their emergence. At a minimum, there should be market incentives to reward their activities and a system for mobilizing the capital they need, as well as an infrastructure of technology, labor, and materials with which to work. One student of the question examined the development of Britain, France, Germany, Russia, Japan, and the United States and concluded that in most cases infrastructure—transportation, energy and raw materials, the cost and quality of labor—played a more important role than entrepreneurship in the process by which these societies industrialized.[7] Even conceding that the entrepreneur's role is primarily that of an intermediary for larger forces in society, it is difficult to imagine economic growth and development occurring without his participation. Someone, after all, must discover the opportunities that allow new industries to flourish and act on them.

MEASURING THE IMPACT

No one could miss the supreme importance of the entrepreneur in the American industrial transformation that has been under way for the last several years. Calvin A. Kent could be exaggerating when he writes that the new entrepreneurial revolution "may have as great an impact on the lives of people in the twenty-first century as the Industrial Revolution had on the lives of those in the nineteenth."[8] But entrepreneurs—and especially the high-technology pioneers of Silicon Valley and Route 128—have already become new American folk heroes, honored as providers of jobs, bulwarks against foreign competition, innovators on the frontiers of science, and role models for small children and corporate executives. William Miller of SRI International cites changes in values, the emergence of new technologies, and the revival of entrepreneurship as factors that could usher in a new "golden economic era." Peter F. Drucker sees the burst of entrepreneurship as evidence that the nation has entered a new Kondratieff expansion which is likely to be "a period of great opportunity, of fast-growing employment in certain areas, and of rapid overall growth."[9] (Russian economist Nikolai Kondratieff theorized that the most important business cycles were those caused by the rise and eventual decline of industries due to basic changes in technologies and markets. The first Industrial Revolution, which began in the 1780s and ended in the 1840s, is the best-known example of a Kondratieff "long wave.")

There have been various attempts to measure the economic impact—in terms of jobs, sales, exports, taxes, research spending, and the like—of new companies. Unfortunately, notes one student of the field, "the data upon which studies of the relationships among jobs, innovation, and company age and size are based do not bear close scrutiny."[10] But some of the evidence is at least impressive. An important effort to prove statistically that startups are beneficial was a survey carried out in 1978 by the American Electronics Association, a trade group of high-tech firms, in the effort to gain support in Congress for legislation—notably cutting the capital gains tax—supported by the industry and its venture capital backers. Because of its self-serving nature, the AEA survey must be suspect, but it makes a strong case. In one year alone, the study showed, every dollar of venture capital invested in seventy-seven electronics startups generated 20¢ in federal, state, and local corporate tax receipts; $7 in export sales; and $3.30 in spending on R&D. The companies in that sample, remarkably, were an average of only four years old. Yet they created an average of eighty-nine new jobs in that year versus only sixty-nine new jobs per company in a sample of companies more than twenty years old.[11]

While most of the companies in the AEA survey presumably were thriving, the survey did not attempt to account for the losing investments and thus may have overstated the payoff. A report prepared in 1982 by the General Accounting Office appeared to correct that bias by tracking 1,332 companies started with venture capital backing between 1970 and 1979. That study again was incomplete because it was limited to data provided by Venture Economics and contained detailed information on only seventy-two firms. Furthermore, the companies studied accounted for investments of only $1.4 billion. According to Venture Economics' figures, a total of $4.5 billion was disbursed to portfolio companies by organized venture capital firms during that period. But again, even allowing for large uncertainties in the data, the results seem impressive. The investment in those 1,332 companies alone, an average of slightly more than $1 million per company, was projected to produce cumulative sales of over $500 billion and exports of $100 billion during the 1980s and to create 1.9 million jobs by 1989.[12]

A number of studies have shown that new companies are the major source of new jobs in the United States. One of these, conducted by David Birch and Susan MacCracken of MIT, used Dun & Bradstreet figures on millions of "establishments" to show that enterprises four years old or younger created more than 60 percent of all new jobs from 1977 to 1981.[13] Interestingly, however, the role of entrepreneurship is not nearly so exaggerated in the high-technology sector, which under the most narrow definition put forth by the Bureau of Labor Statistics includes the drug, computer, communication equipment, electronic components, and aerospace industries and thus takes in most companies backed by venture capital. In high tech, Birch and MacCracken found, average growth rates of new companies were far higher than the average for the group (80 percent versus 17 percent) but 70 percent of the new jobs came from companies in business twelve years or more.[14] Their conclusion: "The greater the degree of innovation in a sector, the greater the tendency for rapidly growing smaller companies to keep right on growing as they become larger."

No one is under the illusion, however, that high-tech companies themselves will create enough new jobs to offset the massive declines taking place in old industries. High technology, again using the most narrow definition, accounted for 2.5 million jobs in 1982 according to BLS statistics. That represented a gain of 40 percent in ten years but increased the share of high-tech jobs by only a tiny fraction—from 2.4 to 2.8 percent of all U.S. employment. High-tech industries, concludes the Congressional Office of Technology Assessment, "will probably provide approximately the same proportion of jobs in the future."[15] Furthermore, high-technology employment can be quite volatile. As onetime growth champions, Atari and Osborne Computer, demonstrated vividly, high-tech jobs can vanish overnight when markets shift or management falters. Growing competition from Asia means that high-tech companies must be prepared to shift production quickly to low-labor-cost areas, and the strength of the dollar has made offshore moves attractive for savings in materials as well. There is a huge ripple effect, of course, as suppliers of everything from insurance to hamburgers spring up around centers of high-tech activity. But if such jobs alone were the payoff from venture investing, the returns would look unimpressive.

One way to look at the entrepreneurial companies in such emerging industries as electronics, information processing, and biotechnology is as engines of new-product experimentation and development. Almost all spending by a startup company goes for product development, and rates of return, both for companies and for society as a whole, are exceptionally high on R&D expenditures. Barry P. Bosworth of the Brookings Institution cites two studies that put the private return on R&D at 20 to 25 percent,[16] which perhaps not coincidentally corresponds to the average returns on venture investing reported in Chapter 2. The social return on such spending is higher still, Bosworth says, "because of the ability of competitors to imitate the innovations." New firms are highly effective at the task of translating new technologies from lab to marketplace because of their narrow focus and because of the incentives of ownership. By one estimate, a startup company can bring a product to market three to five times more efficiently than a large company doing the same job.[17] Karl Vesper of the University of Washington views the process as a kind of Darwinian selection: "A startup has to be efficient and productive to prevail. It must overcome established competitors possessing the advantages of established working and business habits, built-up facilities, and known brands. It must offer something as good or better for as little or less."[18]

Michael L. Tushman of Columbia University has studied the dynamics of entrepreneurial companies and concludes that a basic benefit of the small firm is its ability to experiment with a new product or a new class of products in a way that dominant companies cannot do. "Whether it is in cars or airplanes or semiconductors or consumer electronics," Tushman points out, "there are always uncertainties early on about the technological course to follow. The only way you can really deal with that uncertainty is through experimentation, and so you see a lot of small companies competing with different technologies." Taken as a whole, the proliferation of startups when a new product class is emerging may look inefficient—a waste of talent and resources—since very few will find a combination of technologies and market strategy that will break through the barriers Vesper mentions.

Fewer still will survive the organizational transitions they must make to thrive as large companies. Out of 100 companies experimenting in a new product class, Tushman estimates, perhaps fifty will turn out to be playing in the right ballgame and of those as few as ten can be expected to manage the first transition to operating as a professionally run company. "But you've got to have that experimenting," he argues. "You can't legislate these fundamental technological shifts because the chances of your being right are small." The crucial role of venture capital, as Tushman sees it, is to fund the host of "experiments" it takes to make this product transition.

THE RESTRUCTURED SOCIETY

The entrepreneurial impulse, unleashed by the amazing successes of Fairchild, DEC, Intel, ROLM, Tandem, Apple, Data General, and the other high-tech wunderkinder, is spreading far beyond the boundaries of Silicon Valley and Route 128. It is changing our society in innumerable and probably unguessable ways. The aversion to risk that was ingrained during the Depression and war years seems to have vanished. The regimentation and loyalty to big institutions that marked the 1950s and 1960s seem as dated as Bill Haley and the Comets. New values, new cultural role models, new ways of operating established organizations as well as young ones are reshaping America, and particularly American business, in the image of the entrepreneur. John Naisbitt counted ten major ways in which our society is being restructured, and virtually every one of his "megatrends" had as a cause or an effect the revolution of entrepreneurship.[19]

The success of venture-financed entrepreneurship has certainly dealt a heavy blow to the panoply of organizational and managerial theories with which businessmen have armored themselves through most of the twentieth century. Bill Miller of SRI International, which advises giant corporations throughout the world, sees the pendulum swinging inexorably away from the management styles and theories that were appropriate for centralized decision making. A growing emphasis on new products and fast reaction to market conditions puts a premium on entrepreneurial approaches. Today's best managers, even in giants such as General Electric, are entrepreneurs in the sense that they know the company down to the production floor and feel they are running a business instead of juggling numbers. Miller himself, an expert on computer science, management systems, and other esoterica of the consultant's trade, is an example of this phenomenon. "There isn't a group here that I couldn't work in without making some kind of contribution," he says matter-of-factly. "I don't get down and micromanage, but I can turn people loose more, hear what's going on, and understand it quickly."

The very structure of the corporation itself may be ready for drastic change as entrepreneurs demonstrate the importance of enlisting teams of highly motivated specialists to attack markets quickly and efficiently. Raymond Miles, dean of the school of business administration at the University of California at Berkeley and a student of organization theory, sees something stirring in Silicon Valley that could presage the next stage in the evolution of business organization. As Harvard's Alfred D. Chandler Jr. traces the development of American business, the first companies were family affairs in which a few individuals could administer all activities. Modern corporations emerged in the 1850s as the railroads created divisional structures to manage their far-flung activities, and by the turn of the century huge, vertically integrated enterprises dominated the scene. Then in the early years of the twentieth century new technologies and the opportunity to diversify called for yet another structure, typified by DuPont, General Motors, and Sears, Roebuck, in which multiple divisions operated autonomously while remaining under central supervision.[20]

There are a number of candidates for the next stage in the evolution of corporate structure, including the matrix style that came into vogue in the 1960s and 1970s as aerospace companies grappled with the problem of moving engineers from one project to another. But Ray Miles believes we are on the edge of an even bigger change, one that might discard the whole notion of a large, permanent organization engaging in a variety of tasks. In the "quasi-organizations" slapped up by engineering and construction companies and then disbanded when their task is completed, in the global networks of independent suppliers that have appeared in some consumer goods industries, and most importantly in the instant companies pulled together by Silicon Valley venture capitalists, Miles sees the genesis of a new organizational model. Very probably, the multinational organization of the future will center on an entrepreneurial design-oriented enterprise based in the United States with links to manufacturing groups abroad. "I don't think we will see in the United States large-scale organizations producing standard goods and services except in the highest-tech areas," Miles predicts. As America increasingly focuses on leading-edge products, it will become more crucial than ever to fund the seemingly-redundant multiple explorations of possible approaches. "When things are moving very rapidly and the next model could be a true new generation," Miles points out, "you'd be willing to bet it will occur out of various explorations rather than a concentrated effort. Real breakthroughs come from a lot of people looking for the same thing."

The Silicon Valley model, if that is what it is to be called, already is being adopted in various versions at major companies looking for new ways to encourage entrepreneurial behavior. The business of advising corporations on how to create "intrapreneurship," as some consultants call it, is booming. And such giants as Allied Corp., Xerox, IBM, Air Products & Chemicals, and Tektronix have consciously set out to duplicate the energy and motivation of startups with internal changes.[21] The biggest payoff achieved by this strategy was racked up by IBM's Entry Systems Div., the highly autonomous business unit in Boca Raton, Fla., which designed and launched the enormously successful Personal Computer. "IBM acted as a venture capitalist," commented Don Estridge, who led the development effort for the PC. "It gave us management guidance, money, and allowed us to operate on our own."[22]

It is a little dangerous, of course, for most corporations to think of themselves as venture capitalists. Certainly entrepreneurship cannot substitute for sound planning and analysis in today's global business competition. And Mel Perel, who consults on corporate venturing for SRI International, has run across any number of cases where the company's culture simply was not able to tolerate entrepreneurial activities. Yet some managers feel so strongly about the need to become more innovative that they are willing to force changes in hidebound organizations and are able to create passable replicas of the startup environment.

A good example is Air Products, the Pennsylvania company known mostly as a supplier of industrial gases and chemicals. Hoping to diversify, Air Products called in SRI for help in setting up entrepreneurial units to go after new markets and eventually succeeded, in Perel's opinion, in adapting to the concept. But the change was far from easy. "When we first got involved," Perel recalls, "the notion of treating venture leadership any different from the rest of the company was anathema to them. The company is very egalitarian in style and it is a style that has served them well. Secondly, the notion of establishing a different set of policies and procedures was very foreign. It took six to nine months of repeatedly meeting with the executives of the company to educate them as to the ramifications of a corporate entrepreneurial activity. But it worked, and it changed the culture of the company dramatically." Air Products instituted an experimental compensation plan for its venture people as well as procedures that insulate the ventures from having to meet quarterly or even annual forecasts. Explained the venture unit's general manager: "We are trying to find a way of approaching the speed, the fleetness, the decision-making ability that the small entrepreneurial companies have."[23]

For Tektronix, the venture capital model is at least in part a defense mechanism against painful losses of talent to the crop of startups that has flourished in the Pacific Northwest in the last few years. Tek, as its employees and alumni call it, grew up in splendid isolation. Pastoral Beaverton, Oregon, after all, was about as far from the job-hopping madness of Silicon Valley, geographically and psychologically, as it was possible to get. Tek's engineers were loyal and content and very talented, and the company became a world leader in electronic test instruments. But the isolation came to an end in the late 1970s as California companies spilled into Oregon, and when the venture capital boom of the 1980s began, Beaverton and other Portland suburbs held enough high-tech activity to allow new companies to take root. Tek, the most obvious source of local talent, experienced a massive brain drain. Hoping to create internal alternatives to the lure of outside ventures, and also to revive a flagging growth rate, Tek started creating entrepreneurial organizations called strategic program units to market products that otherwise might get short shrift. And it went into the venture capital business itself with the idea of helping restless employees launch their own businesses.[24]

Tek is not venturing to diversify, the major reason large companies have tried to play the game. Rather, Tek seems mainly to be attempting to change its culture. It is limiting investments to its own people and ideas and half-expecting eventually to pull them back inside. Whether this approach will be any more successful than that of the corporate venture pioneers of the 1960s is uncertain. And the brain drain, while muted, continues. Even William D. Walker, the executive who lobbied hardest for the entrepreneurial approach, left in mid-1984 to join a small company. Some of Tek's managers argue that the venture operation might set employees to thinking more about spinout possibilities than corporate projects. To which Richard J. Reisinger, Tek's top corporate planner, replies: "It puts the burden on you to have really exciting projects going on in your division, so all your key people will be turned on by what they are working on and won't have enough energy to think about starting their own business."

As the managers of companies such as Air Products and Tektronix are learning, corporate cultures are not easily changed. But these companies are only responding to changes in values and motivation that have already infected their workers and much of the American population. Americans have always thought themselves more enterprising than people of other cultures, although there are ethnic and religious subgroups in almost every country that are highly entrepreneurial. The Jews in Europe, the Lebanese in the Middle East, the Ibos in Nigeria, and the Bataks in Indonesia, all are known as compulsive innovators.[25] And, in fact, the American entrepreneurial impulse that conquered the West and created the giants of transportation, electrical equipment, and heavy industry was much less evident during the middle years of this century. Depression and war and the ensuing era of rebuilding sent Americans to big government, big unions and big business for security, for safety, and eventually for prosperity. Self-interest was sublimated or guided into institutional channels, and entrepreneurship, in the language of sociology, lost its cultural legitimacy.

Robert Schroeder, the highly skilled entrepreneur who steered Qume to leadership in electronic printers, recalls the shocked reaction with which his friends and family in the Midwest greeted the news that he was planning to give up an important job in a large company to take a flier on running a California startup. "People told me I was crazy," Schroeder says. "My father had spent thirty years working for Allstate and he couldn't understand how I could give up a job as one of the youngest officers of a Fortune 500 company." But that was in 1973, and a deep cultural change was already stirring. SRI International, which has been studying changes in values and lifestyles, detects an important change in the last decade toward "inner-directedness" and away from reliance on the guidance and opinion of others. While less than 20 percent of the population reflects these characteristics now, the number is growing and will be 25 percent by the end of the century, SRI predicts. "There is a subtle shift in values going on at the pressure points of society," Miller says.

Perhaps more important than such cultural and psychological factors is a phenomenon that might be called the professionalization of entrepreneurship. Howard Stevenson, who teaches entrepreneurial management at the Harvard Business School, sees no particular personality characteristics that identify successful entrepreneurs. "They can be wallflowers at the accounting convention or bombastic, dynamic types," Stevenson says. It is certainly true, he concedes, that those who grew up in the 1960s lack the need for security that characterized their fathers' generation. But that is mainly because prosperity has assured them, especially if they hold an MBA or a technical degree, that they can always find a job. With venture capitalists willing to provide enough backing to fund competitive salaries and benefits, the decision to join a startup is an easy one. "All the person is doing is taking a good upside without any real downside," Stevenson remarks. "You don't have to be irrational to say that might be a good deal."

Responding to the new opportunities or to their innermost drives, MBA students by the thousands are flocking to classes in entrepreneurship. By 1984 at least 150 graduate schools were offering courses or setting up research centers in the science of starting a company. And increasingly, the graduates are choosing to launch their careers at small companies rather than at the corporate giants that have always had the pick of the crop at the top business schools. "We're seeing more and more students who are concerned with starting their own companies," Alfred E. Osborne Jr. of UCLA told *Venture*. "But it's not the family business, or a small business, which they want to run. It's their own growing corporation."[26] The motivation, in part, is money. Someone suggested that the title of this book should be "In Search of Opulence." But very few of the entrepreneurs or venturers I have met talk about their rewards in terms of wealth, although some are not above flaunting it when they get it. What they are after is much more like Jack Melchor's goal: "freedom of action." Trip Hawkins, who left an important job at Apple Computer to start Electronic Arts, recalls a tremendous feeling of relief when he walked out of Apple. "Gee," he thought, "I don't have to report to anybody anymore." And running his own company, pitting his ideas and management skills against a fiercely competitive world, is sheer fun, says Hawkins. "It's like getting to have your hobby be your job."

THE PAYOFF

Freedom was an important motivator for Bill Schroeder and Alonzo Wilson, and how they used it illustrates the power of the venture capital process to drive technology. Schroeder (he pronounces the name to rhyme with raider) is a lanky midwesterner with a sleepy-eyed, bemused smile. In the mid-1970s he was a product planner at Memorex in the heart of Silicon Valley. Wilson, an unflappable engineer, was program manager, head of the engineering team, for the Memorex equivalent of an IBM disk drive called the 3350. Both were itching to leave. Memorex was too big, too splintered, too political for Wilson. "Bureaucratic," Schroeder called it. Schroeder had some contacts in the venture capital community, and late in 1977 he approached Wilson: "Al, if you've got a product idea, I think I could get us the money."

Wilson did have an idea. He could see a discontinuity in the market approaching as disk drive makers shifted from the old-style removable cartridges to the new Winchester technology exemplified by the 3350 and its lookalikes. In the 3350, eight whirling storage disks and their magnetic read-write heads were permanently locked into a sealed enclosure to eliminate contamination. That allowed the heads to "fly" only 20 millionths of an inch above the surface of the disks, a feat equivalent to piloting a 747 four inches off the ground. The 3350 was the size of a dishwasher, held 635 megabytes—635 million characters—of information, and at a price of around $40,000 was strictly for users of big systems. Wilson's idea was simple enough: Shrink the 3350 to one or two disks in a box the size of a phonograph while keeping the price per megabyte roughly constant. He and Schroeder proposed to push Winchester technology, in other words, from the world of multimillion-dollar mainframes to the world of minicomputers and office automation.

That is exactly what they did. With $1.5 million in startup financing from Sutter Hill Ventures, Greylock Partners, and BankAmerica Capital, Schroeder and Wilson set up shop as Priam Corp. in the summer of 1978. At IBM, say engineers who have worked there, development work on a disk drive in the 1970s could take as long as five years. Even at Memorex, which lives by responding quickly to IBM's product moves, the development time was eighteen months to two years. Priam had to move faster. The task eventually consumed $15 million in venture financing, but by June 1979 the engineers had produced the first prototype of a scaled-down Winchester and by August had shipped the first evaluation unit. It stored 34 megabytes and sold to the computer companies who were Priam's customers for about $1,900, or slightly less than the $60 for 1 million characters of storage that users of the IBM 3350 were paying. Since then, new generations of Priam drives and fierce competition from dozens of competitors have brought the price of small-computer memory units down to $20 per megabyte. It will probably be under $10 by the time this appears. For users of word processing systems, telephone equipment, engineering workstations, and small-business computers, this has meant a rapidly increasing capacity to capture and recall information at rapidly decreasing prices.

Priam provides just one small example of the role that entrepreneurship has played in the incredible U.S. leap forward in electronics. Shipments of American-made computers, components, telephone equipment, consumer electronics, and test and medical equipment grew from less than $8 billion in 1958 to almost $100 billion in 1980 and headed toward $150 billion by the mid-1980s.[27] By 1984, the electronics industry was the largest employer among U.S. manufacturing industries, and the products it turned out were revolutionizing every aspect of society, from education to entertainment, health care to warfare. American companies led the world in computer equipment, accounting for 81 percent of world shipments that hit $109 billion in 1984, according to InfoCorp. And despite growing competition from Japan, U.S. producers held 45 percent of the $26 billion world market for semiconductor components, the all-important "crude oil" of electronics.[28] A panel chosen by the National Research Council to study this remarkable performance offered a compelling explanation:

This innovative behavior is linked to a unique industry structure that has supported both basic research and subsequent development efforts. The industry's strength in basic research has been sustained by large, progressive firms that possess the resources and incentives to undertake long-term commitments to risky projects with uncertain commercial outcomes. At the same time, smaller, entrepreneurial firms have played a central role, both in introducing new products and in accelerating the pace of innovation by existing firms.[29]

Progress in semiconductor technology has been the most important force behind the electronics revolution, and it is in the semiconductor industry that the entrepreneurial process, powered by venture capital, has had probably its greatest impact. It was AT&T's Bell Laboratories, of course, that provided the fundamental research breakthroughs that led to the transistor and its progeny of ever-more-complex silicon chips. But it was not AT&T or the established giants of the pretransistor components business which commercialized the new devices. That task fell to new entrants such as Texas Instruments and Fairchild Semiconductor, which between them contributed the innovations that made possible the integrated circuit, and to the later crop of start-ups that accelerated the pace of change in product design, price, and performance. Concluded one recent study: "Entrepreneurial activity by gifted inventors and engineers was the key factor in building the U.S. semiconductor industry."[30]

The progress has indeed been astounding. In terms of physical dimensions alone, the semiconductor industry has moved from making devices with lines and spacings of 25 microns (a micron is a millionth of a meter) in 1960 to less than 2 microns today and will plunge well into the submicron range before it runs up against the laws of physics toward the end of the century. Along with advances in design and increases in chip size, the ever-finer geometries have enabled the industry to put ever-more power into its products and stay close to the curve first described in 1964 by Gordon Moore, then with Fairchild: a doubling every year of the individual circuit elements on a single chip. The capacity of one chip has increased from a single logic function in the early 1960s to hundreds of thousands of functions, enough to make up the central processor of the largest commercial computer, in the mid-1980s. Because the cost of making that chip increases only briefly from one generation to another and then invariably declines rapidly as production volumes increase, the cost per function has dropped steadily. E. David Crockett, president of Dataquest, cites the example of the random access memory, used in every piece of computer equipment to store temporarily the control programs and work-in-progress information used by the central processor. Between 1979 and 1983, Crockett estimates, the cost of one "bit" of semiconductor memory declined from 40 millicents to less than 5 millicents—and a new round of price-cutting late in 1984 put it below 3 millicents.

U.S. computer technology is not only the beneficiary of the advances stimulated by the semiconductor entrepreneurs but is itself driven in part by the venture process. IBM, of course, has dominated the industry at home and abroad for three decades and has been the wellspring of basic research in the field. But most observers of the giant of Armonk credit persistent competition, especially from entrepreneurial companies exploiting price or product chinks in IBM's armor, with forcing the pace of the technology application. "I think it's clear," says Richard Matlack of InfoCorp, "that it was the entrepreneurial startups that put the pressure on IBM to get back in line when it was failing to push the technology." Peter Cunningham of Input, another industry consultant, agrees: "The benefits have been immeasurable. Virtually in any area you look—software, memory systems, processors, communications, office products—where you really start to see tremendous growth is when you have competitive companies starting up and pushing things forward."

A good example is that of the so-called plug-compatible manufacturers or PCMs, whose competition, aimed at providing less expensive or more powerful copycat versions of IBM peripheral equipment, and ultimately of its central processors as well, produced an immediate reaction. As Katharine Davis Fishman points out in *The Computer Establishment*, IBM was goaded into action even though the PCMs, including Telex, Memorex, and California Computer Products, had displaced only 14 percent of its tape systems and 5 percent of its disks by 1970. This was because "the computer business had always been a *systems* business, and IBM believed it was entitled to a 100 percent share of the tape and disk systems attached to IBM mainframes."[31] IBM fought back with new technology and cuts in long-term lease prices that inflicted serious pain on the small fry and led to the historic antitrust suit by Telex Corp., eventually won by IBM on appeal. In the mid-1970s Amdahl Corp., backed by Chicago venture capitalist Ned Heizer, successfully improved on IBM's central processors and triggered stiff price and performance competition at the very heart of its product line. For the users of this equipment, the payoff of all the skirmishing was a rapid decrease in the cost of computing. According to industry consultant Tim Tyler, the cost of storing a bit of data has been cut in half every four years for two decades. PCM suppliers had only a marginal impact on that curve, Tyler feels. But the influence of Amdahl's inroads is clear, he adds, in a sudden acceleration of price/performance trends in large central processors. Between 1954 and 1972, the performance computer users could buy for a dollar tripled every six years, according to Tyler's calculations. Then in the next six years it quadrupled and in the last six years, 1978 to 1984, it rose by a factor of six or seven. "We are getting new hardware announcements at the high end much faster than in the past," Tyler says.

It seems likely to many experts that entrepreneurial activity in the semiconductor and computer industries has been the crucial edge over

Japanese and European competitors. Where competition from startups
has been limited, as in consumer electronics, Japan has been able to
use its strengths—a protected domestic market, low capital costs, a
skilled and disciplined workforce—to decimate American producers.
Lately, the Japanese have made large inroads into U.S. dominance of
the semiconductor field, and smaller but not insignificant gains in
computers. Trade statistics in electronics are showing an ominous shift
from America's historically healthy surplus to an almost exact balance
in 1983 and a sizable deficit in 1984. Many forces are driving this
trend, including the strong U.S. dollar, booming sales for (Japanese-
made) video tape recorders, and nontariff barriers that block efforts of
American companies to sell high-technology products abroad. Perhaps most worrisome of all, Europe and Japan finally have awakened
to the power of entrepreneurship and are taking serious steps to make
it work for them.

NOTES

1. Karl H. Vesper, "Entrepreneurship and National Policy," Heller Institute
   for Small Business Policy Papers, 1983, p. 49.
2. William E. Wetzel Jr., "Risk Capital Research," in Calvin A. Kent, Donald L. Sexton, and Karl H. Vesper, eds., *Encyclopedia of Entrepreneurship.*
   Prentice-Hall, Englewood Cliffs, 1982, p. 148.
3. Peter Kilby, "Hunting the Heffalump," in Peter Kilby, ed., *Entrepreneurship and Economic Development.* Free Press, New York, 1971.
4. David C. McClelland, *The Achieving Society.* D. Van Nostrand Co.,
   Princeton, 1961, p. 127.
5. Harold C. Livesay, "Entrepreneurial History," *Encyclopedia of Entrepreneurship*, p. 13.
6. Joseph A. Schumpeter, *Capitalism, Socialism, and Democracy.* Harper &
   Bros., New York, 1949, p. 132.
7. Paul H. Wilken, *Entrepreneurship: A Comparative and Historical Study.*
   Ablex Publishing, Norwood, N.J., 1979.
8. Calvin A. Kent, "The Rediscovery of the Entrepreneur" in Calvin A.
   Kent, ed., *The Environment for Entrepreneurship.* D.C. Heath & Co., Lex-
   ington, Mass., 1984, p. 1.
9. Peter F. Drucker, "Our Entrepreneurial Economy," *Harvard Business Review*, January-February 1984, p. 64.
10. Albert Shapero, "The Entrepreneurial Event," in Kent, *Entrepreneurship.*
    p. 21.
11. Statement of Edwin V. W. Zschau, American Electronics Association,
    before the Senate Select Committee on Small Business, February 8,
    1978.
12. "Government-Industry Cooperation Can Enhance the Venture Capital
    Process," General Accounting Office, Washington, D.C., 1982.

13. David L. Birch and Susan J. MacCracken, *The Role Played by High Technology Firms in Job Creation.* MIT Program on Neighborhood and Regional Change, Cambridge, Mass., 1984, p. 30.
14. Ibid., p. 36.
15. *Technology, Innovation, and Regional Economic Development,* Office of Technology Assessment, Washington, D.C., 1984, p. 23.
16. Barry P. Bosworth, "Capital Formation, Technology, and Economic Policy," in *Industrial and Public Policy,* Symposium sponsored by the Federal Reserve Bank of Kansas City, August 24–26, 1983.
17. "The New Entrepreneurs," *Business Week,* April 18, 1983, p. 78.
18. Vesper, "Entrepreneurship," p. 29.
19. John Naisbitt, *Megatrends.* Warner Books, New York, 1982.
20. Alfred D. Chandler Jr., *Strategy and Structure: Chapters in the History of the Industrial Enterprise.* MIT Press, Cambridge, 1962, pp. 19–42.
21. "Here Comes the 'Intrapreneur,'" *Business Week,* July 18, 1983, p. 188.
22. "How the PC Project Changed the Way IBM Thinks," *Business Week,* October 3, 1983, p. 86.
23. "Air Products: Trying to Break Out of Its Mold," *Business Week,* October 24, 1983, p. 180C.
24. "Why Tektronix Stopped Hoarding Its Technology," *Business Week,* December 12, 1983, p. 126B.
25. Albert Shapero and Lisa Sokol, "The Social Dimensions of Entrepreneurship," *Encyclopedia of Entrepreneurship,* p. 72.
26. Kevin Farrell, "Why B-Schools Embrace Entrepreneurs," *Venture,* February 1984, p. 60.
27. National Research Council, *The Competitive Status of the U.S. Electronics Industry,* National Academy Press, Washington, D.C., 1984, p. 1.
28. Forecast of the Semiconductor Industry Association, San Jose, Calif.
29. National Research Council, *Electronics Industry,* p. 8.
30. Daniel I. Okimoto, Takuo Sugano, and Franklin B. Weinstein, eds., *Competitive Edge: The Semiconductor Industry in the U.S. and Japan.* Stanford University Press, Stanford, 1984, p. 9.
31. Katharine Davis Fishman, *The Computer Establishment.* Harper & Row, New York, 1981, p. 234.

15

KEEPING OUR COMPETITIVE EDGE

While Americans argue over the advantages and disadvantages of venture capital, the rest of the world is eagerly trying to emulate the process. To Europe and Japan, it is painfully clear that the ability of the United States to harness the power of entrepreneurship is the key to its leadership of world markets in crucially important industries. Early attempts to reproduce the venture phenomenon abroad were embarrassingly unsuccessful. But early in the decade of the 1980s new efforts to start the entrepreneurial engine rolling along by breaking down old cultural and institutional barriers seemed to be working. The process is likely to be long and painful, but it seems possible that America's most important export will turn out to be this potent tool for unleashing individual creativity and motivation.

Although details differ from country to country, the problems that have confronted would-be venture capitalists in Tokyo, London, Paris, and Frankfurt show a common thread. Nowhere has there been a community of bold financiers willing to supply the capital required. There has been no active market for new public issues, nor any tradition of mergers and acquisitions, to provide a reliable exit vehicle for the investors and rewards for the entrepreneurs. Few managers or scientists have been willing to leave the safety of their corporate or academic havens for the uncertainties of independence. Traditions of secrecy and formality have hindered the due diligence process of investigating personal backgrounds and market opportunities that must precede intelligent investments. Domestic markets have been too small, and the power of entrenched and often cartelized competition too great, to allow new ventures to grow rapidly and profitably. Bankers, if not tied directly to the industrial giants by investment or tradition, have at least been loath to offer credit to upstarts with no history and uncertain prospects. Governments have poured massive assistance into established companies and neglected programs that might help new ones. In short, most societies have been structured to favor the status quo in business. As a German executive complained to me in discussing the latest government bailout proposal for a huge competitor: "We make it impossible for companies to die—or to be born."

But the raw material for successful venturing is in plentiful supply almost everywhere. Entrepreneurship is a quality that wells up in virtually every society no matter how severely it is repressed. Europe and

Japan have achieved an infrastructure of technically advanced industry and research that often surpasses our own. Even countries recently considered "underdeveloped" now have the capacity to develop and manufacture highly sophisticated products. Risk-oriented investors are emerging, if only to sink their yen and deutschemarks into American stocks and American venture capital funds. (According to Venture Economics, foreign commitments to U.S. venture funds increased tenfold from $55 million in 1980 to $531 million in 1983.) Most important, cultural biases against individual action and self-expression are crumbling as a baby-boom generation finds traditional opportunities severely limited by industrial stagnation and at the same time sees the impressive results achieved by American entrepreneurs. Add to this mix strong government support for the structural changes needed to modernize capital markets and encourage small business, and the stage is set for the kind of entrepreneurial takeoff that began in America two decades ago.

THE NEW EUROPEANS

It is happening first in Europe, where the bankruptcy of old ideas has been revealed by painfully high levels of chronic unemployment. Europe lags behind both the United States and Japan, not in the fundamentals of science and technology but in the timely application of technical knowhow to new markets. Enormous amounts of government money have been poured into programs aimed at promoting European research, but these have often become what a West German legislator calls "dinosaur projects," huge nuclear or aerospace undertakings with little commercial relevance. Giant European companies—Siemens and Philips in electronics, ICI and Hoechst in chemicals—often spend more on research and development than their American competitors. Yet they lag in such important fields as integrated circuits, computers, and biotechnology in part because they lack the incentives and the mechanisms to translate their technology quickly into new products. As a result, Europe has been unable to build market share, profits, and employment in the new growth industries fast enough to offset declines in heavy industry.

Venture capital will not cure Europe's ills. Far more important, at least in the short run, would be a renewed effort to knock down the vestiges of nationalism, both official and private, that make it difficult for German companies, for example, to operate in France and vice versa. Until European companies truly address a common market for high-technology products, they will find it difficult to achieve the world-scale efficiencies required to compete effectively in the United States, Japan, and the fast-developing markets of the Third World. Managers of Europe's industrial giants recognize that they must also move to replace autocratic central control with flexible, decentralized organizations that can move quickly to respond to new opportunities.[1] But governments finally have recognized that entrepreneurship is another essential factor in the equation for innovation and economic growth, and programs to stimulate the flow of venture capital are appearing all across the continent.

The history of attempts to promote venture capital in Europe is not encouraging. As early as 1960 Laurance Rockefeller's organization opened an office in Brussels and set out to find venture investment candidates. A short time later, after all but one of his foreign portfolio companies turned sour, Rockefeller closed the operation and retreated to America. By selling his stake in a successful Israeli company, Rockefeller was able to keep his losses to a minimum. But it was a painful experience. Venrock's Peter Crisp offers several explanations for the failure: "The European entrepreneurs couldn't divorce the name Rockefeller from philanthropy. They felt they had the right to spend money on research rather than generating sales, collecting receivables, and making profits. A second reason was that entrepreneurship was new to them and they never hoisted aboard the value of equity and what it could mean. The third thing was, we found in several instances there was a third set of books that was kept at home in the controller's kitchen with figures that showed what cash flow really was. A final reason was, in the absence of a public market, there was no genuine route to liquidity."

Even the legendary Georges Doriot was unable to create a successful European venture capital organization. In 1964 Doriot persuaded European banks to put up most of the capital for European Enterprises Development Co., and by 1974 EED had invested $24 million in thirty-five companies in nine countries. But much of the investment was concentrated on a few troubled ventures that sucked up increasing amounts of capital and time. EED ended up owning and operating four companies and by 1976 was in the Luxembourg equivalent of Chapter 11 bankruptcy. As one student of the situation analyzed it at the time: "Overinvolvement in the day-to-day management of its investees is probably the main reason why EED will not survive as an active venture capitalist."[2]

Despite these cautionary tales, European governments of every stripe have placed a high priority on stimulating venture capital in the 1980s. Even socialist France, which started by nationalizing the banques d'affaires—merchant banks—that were responsible for much of the country's risk investment, turned around and rushed through legislation to allow individuals to set up venture capital partnerships.[3] The primary focus in Europe has been on creating local equivalents of the U.S. over-the-counter (OTC) stock market, with the hope of making it easier for new companies to go public and generate the rewards that drive America's venture process. Obtaining capital from private investors and the public market is so difficult for entrepreneurs in West Germany that Volker Dolch, who makes sophisticated instruments for analyzing microprocessors, had to use his Silicon Valley subsidiary as a vehicle to attract venture capital. Dolch did get backing at first from Deutsche Wagnis-finanzierungs-Gesellschaft (WFG), a venture fund that is a joint venture of twenty-eight banks. But WFG provided "participation financing," which Dolch had to repay within five years, and he could see no German source for the kind of long-term capital he needed. "The growth we saw had to be funded by equity that just wasn't available in Germany," he explained.[4] Now West Germany, the Netherlands, France, Britain and Sweden have all taken steps to create or improve OTC markets of their own, and venture capitalists are beginning to respond to the new opportunities.

London's Unlisted Securities Market, launched in 1981, is the most active of the European OTCs. Britain has a long tradition of entrepreneurship, but it was stifled by years of government support for tottering industrial behemoths. Until recently British venture capital was provided largely by merchant banks, subsidiaries of other financial institutions, and government agencies, which rely heavily on debt and look for security rather than growth. But the advent of a strong new-issues market has attracted American-style venture partnerships, many of them backed or advised by American firms, that are putting together equity deals which in turn are attracting a stronger flow of entrepreneurs into startup businesses. In addition, an infrastructure of accountants, lawyers, advertising agencies, and other support services for new companies is developing. "We are starting to see people who want to get involved in the process," says Bryan Wood, an American partner in London-based Alta Berkeley Associates.

Britain has several advantages as a center of venture capital activity, Wood finds. "The talent in software, for example, is as good as it is in the United States," he says, "but it is available at about half the price. I can put together a startup with a much lower investment than I would need in the United States, and we are getting people out of big companies. They are just as motivated as entrepreneurs in the United States and they work hours that are just as long." In the past, startup companies in Britain have been restricted by the relatively small size of the domestic market. But the new venture capitalists use their connections abroad to push their portfolio companies into international markets early in the game. "We spend a lot of time helping our portfolio companies move into the United States," Wood says. Alta Berkeley is tied to Burr, Egan, Deleage & Co., and other important American firms, including TA Associates, Citicorp, and Alan Patricof Associates, also have London affiliates. There is some question whether British entrepreneurs—typically scientists and technical types—can develop the marketing and management skills required to push their companies beyond the startup stage. But as more and more British entrepreneurs plug into the multinational venture network, they should soon be producing their own crop of Apples.

The outlook for venture capital is less sanguine elsewhere in Europe, where traditional patterns of business life have been slow to change. An exception is Scandinavia, which boasts a small but aggressive stock of risk investors and a fast-growing group of startups. Norway's traditionally adventurous shipowners, for example, have started sinking some of their capital into high-technology ventures such as Norsk Data, a leading maker of scientific minicomputers. Norsk Data was able to tap the London and New York securities market for serious growth capital, but most Scandinavian startups must make do with cumbersome local markets. Scandinavian entrepreneurs also must deal with red tape and high taxes that make launching a company a thankless ordeal. If Sweden's new OTC market works well, however, Scandinavia may see the development of several "silicon fjords."

Entrepreneurship still has not really awakened in France, despite various government efforts to promote the concept and despite considerable success in foreign investing. Sofinnova, the pioneering venture firm that sent Jean Deleage to America to such good effect, made only a modest profit in twelve years of operation at home. Paribas, the nationalized merchant bank, is becoming a major venture investor, mainly outside France, as part of a government strategy to transfer technology from the United States, Japan and elsewhere.[5] Individuals now find it possible to manage risk funds in France, and an OTC market, called the Second Marche, has been functioning since early 1983. Furthermore, the French government has set up generous lending programs for new companies. Venture capitalists in France still have not seen a strong flow of deals, probably because the entrepreneurial culture has not yet taken hold. The French tradition of strong state control, and a value system that pushes the brightest young people into the bureaucracy rather than into business, will not change overnight. But some observers claim to detect a significant shift in public opinion. Said an official of the National Council of French Employers: "To become your own boss, that's now the royal road to success."[6]

The Federal Republic of Germany seems, if anything, to be moving more slowly even than France to improve the climate for venture capital. That is ironic, because entrepreneurs played a supremely important role in the industrialization of Germany in the nineteenth century and a strong new-issues stock market flourished both before and after World War I. The Nazis destroyed the mainly Jewish-owned private banks that played a venture capital role, and post-World War II investors have been cautious in the extreme. As late as 1983, an OTC equivalent was still in the planning stage in West Germany and the cautious WFG remained the major source of venture investment.

Like the French, Germans are said to prefer the status and security of a big organization to the uncertainties of independence. But my impression, based on two years as a business and technology correspondent in Frankfurt during the early 1980s, is that a new generation of would-be entrepreneurs is waiting impatiently in low-level jobs at big German companies and at local subsidiaries of the multinationals for a chance to launch their own ventures. Furthermore, the West German government, having little to show in the way of jobs or growth for its massive investments in basic research at the industrial giants, is eager to provide help to small companies seeking to commercialize some of this technology. Companies such as Siemens, Nixdorf, and Bosch have long been investors in fast-growing American ventures, and Siemens recently agreed to join with TA Associates in creating a $50 million venture capital fund for Germany. Even WFG is becoming more aggressive and finally, in mid-1983, was able to take one of its portfolio companies public for the first time.[7] These are signs that entrepreneurship is only dormant, not extinct, in West Germany.

ANOTHER JAPANESE CHALLENGE

Japan might understandably be seen as the world's most hostile environment for venture capital. Not only do close ties between big banks and big companies create a kind of "banking-industrial complex" that excludes or ignores startups, not only is the OTC market virtually moribund, but the whole cultural deck seems to be stacked against the entrepreneur. Traditions of lifelong loyalty to one's employer make it virtually impossible to attract workers to any other company, let alone a new one. One survey of the situation added this observation: "Low labor mobility, at least among top-flight engineers, meant that an entrepreneur had a very small chance of returning to any established or well-regarded firm if he failed in a spinoff attempt."[8] Yoriko Kishimoto, a young Japanese woman who studied at the Stanford Business School and does consulting from a base in California for small companies on both sides of the Pacific, sums up the problems confronting Japanese entrepreneurs: "The entrepreneur by definition does not depend on the opinions of others for support, but at some level of development he must win the acceptance of the larger society, at least from the people he wishes to hire and the companies he wishes to sell to. The entrepreneur in Japan has faced obstacles on almost all levels . . . Even successful entrepreneurs cannot win the same respect in society at large as a high-level executive in a major corporation."[9]

Despite these formidable barriers, a consensus is forming in Japan that American-style entrepreneurship represents the new frontier of industrial development. Japan built its impressive modern economy largely through a coordinated effort of large companies, directed by government agencies into industries thought to offer the most opportunity for an export-based society. Now the growth of these industries, because of energy costs, protectionism, and competition from third-world countries, is fading. "Coordination is all right if you're building a steel and car industry on the model of other people," a leading Japanese educator told *The Washington Post*. "But now we're in an era of rapid change and I don't think our large organizations can move quickly enough to make the changes."[10] Even an industrialist as prominent as Tadahiro Sekimoto, president of NEC Corp. and past chairman of the Electronics Industry Association of Japan, calls venture-financed companies "a great force aiding the advancement of U.S. technology industries." Sekimoto notes that many Japanese engineers and managers are becoming interested in starting new businesses and that increasing numbers of financiers are willing to support them. "We already see the signs of change," he declares.

Japan has now taken a few tentative steps to encourage the venture capital process: Regulations restricting listings on the Japanese OTC market have been loosened, and a Venture Business Promotion Center was created to guarantee loans to new companies. Perhaps most important, officials of the powerful Ministry of International Trade and Industry now openly advocate entrepreneurship. As a result, venture capital organizations are making a comeback after a disastrous attempt to make the process work in the early 1970s. This time around, experienced U.S. firms are adding their expertise to the system, which is dominated by subsidiaries of banks and securities firms and tends to take a short-range view of the business. But a number of constraints prevent venture capitalists from playing the participatory role they play in building companies in the United States. For one thing, they are not allowed to place representatives on a portfolio company's board of directors; they can only advise when problems crop up. Their ability to structure investments with instruments such as warrants and convertible debt is limited. Only since 1982 have warrants been authorized. And they find it difficult or uncomfortable to do American-style investigations of entrepreneurs, because the Japanese are accustomed to doing business on a handshake.

Despite the difficulties, the process is beginning to work. Lore Harp, the founder of Vector Graphics, now is president of Pacific Technology Ventures, which is based in San Francisco and Tokyo and specializes in Pacific Basin investing. She cites the example of Yoshifumi Amano, a top researcher for Sony who was involved in work on a sophisticated new gas plasma display. Frustrated by lack of progress on the technology, Amano began negotiating with Sony's board of directors for approval to spin out with some of his staff to form a separate company that could accelerate the work. "They were initially quite upset about it," Harp says. "They thought he was crazy. But he left and Sony ultimately invested in his company." Pacific Technology structured a U.S.-style equity investment for the new venture, called Dixy, and helped Amano put together a management team. Dixy, says Harp, "is a company with real potential." Pacific Technology has also had its share of problems in Japan. In one case, the entrepreneur died and his key-man insurance turned out to have been assigned to a friend instead of to the company. "The Japanese are very secretive," Harp says, "and sometimes you get a real surprise."

The real question is whether the Japanese disinclination toward independent action is changing. *Fortune* surveyed fifty-five Japanese entrepreneurs in 1983 and concluded that it is. "The world's second largest industrial power may be breaking out of its oligopolistic postwar mode," the magazine opined.[11] But the change is barely beginning. Kishimoto points out that most university graduates still prefer the safety of jobs with big companies. "The cultural bias against entrepreneurship is still strong," she reports. "In terms of social status, income, and career, everybody thinks you would be crazy to leave a large company." Nevertheless, youngsters like Kishimoto, trained in U.S. business schools and steeped in Silicon Valley lore, are beginning to make an impact. It may take decades, but Japan has shown over and over that it is capable of adopting, adapting, and often improving on concepts that originate in the West. Japan's own version of venture capital is likely to be at least as effective as our own.

AMERICA'S SECRET WEAPON

The American response to the growing economic challenge from abroad must be the right one. To make the mistake of attempting to imitate the strategies and cultures that Japan and Europe now are rejecting would be disastrous. "Industrial policy," if it means reducing government support of failing companies and industries or increasing government support of research and technical education, may be quite beneficial. Efforts to work toward a social consensus on wages and prices, like that which normally prevails in Japan and West Germany, are probably harmless and might help prevent a recurrence of the stagflation that paralyzed U.S. capital markets in the 1970s. But proposals for adopting a Japanese-style or French-style targeting policy, in which industries would be selected for favored treatment, are dangerous. So, too, are well-meaning suggestions that American companies mimic the managerial and organizational peculiarities of their Asian and European competitors. In its institutions of venture capital and entrepreneurship America has far more effective tools for targeting new areas for investment than any bureaucrat's computer. And in its free-wheeling, fast-moving startups, as well as in the venture units springing up inside giant corporations, America has a style of business organization that is ideally suited both to a competitive world economy and to the drive for personal achievement and reward that is our national heritage.

Arguments in favor of a targeting industrial policy gained much support in the early 1980s, when the American economy was bogged down in recurring recession and its basic industries appeared to be on the ropes. But economist Paul R. Krugman of MIT argues convincingly that even Japanese targeting of steel—often held up as the prime example of successful industrial policy—had little to do with Japan's growth and America's decline in steelmaking. Rather, it was Japan's relative advantage in labor and capital costs that allowed Japanese steelmakers to build, and then overbuild, new capacity while the Americans lagged farther and farther behind. Not only did targeting have little impact on this scenario, Krugman suggests, but it probably encouraged an excess of investment that inevitably led to overcapacity and low rates of return in the 1970s.[12] There are a number of theoretical and practical reasons for rejecting targeting as a national policy. But the most persuasive is this simple question: Who decides? It is inconceivable that an industrial targeting program in this country would not be directed more by political influence than by economic analysis. Almost certainly it would be inefficient, unfair, and unnecessary.

It is unnecessary because the real function of a targeting policy, to shift resources from played-out or inefficient sectors into more promising industries and technologies, is already being performed by the institution of venture capital. True, the institution does not work perfectly. It overcrowds some markets and ignores others, raids universities and established companies, backs losers as well as winners. But for all its failings, it passes the one crucial test of an economic institution. It works. It does provide the capital and the incentives to accelerate innovation in vital industries, and it targets the candidates for major investment by other sources of capital through a process that has not been improved on since Darwin named it: natural selection. It seems almost intuitively obvious that the winner in the race to develop the next generation of computers, for example, will be a system that encourages multiple experiments by highly motivated individuals rather than a system that attempts to coordinate one huge experiment carried out by institutions.

There is much to recommend the Japanese style, and to some extent the European style, of organizing a business. As William G. Ouchi explains in *Theory Z*, the concept of lifetime employment is basic to all of the attributes of a good Japanese company: concern for people, slow evaluation and promotion, wide-ranging career paths, collective decision making, and collective responsibility for the results. Large European companies display many similar traits, although there is more direction from the top. Ouchi found many of these characteristics in a few outstanding American companies, among them, Hewlett-Packard, IBM, and Dayton-Hudson, and called them Type Z organizations to distinguish them from the typical American (Type A) style of operation.[13] Later, Thomas J. Peters and Robert H. Waterman Jr. discovered many similar themes—"hands-on, value driven," "productivity through people"—in the forty-three "excellent" companies they portrayed in their best seller, but they added several important characteristics that appear to boil down to one commandment: be entrepreneurial.[14]

To be successful in rapidly changing industries, and that means almost every industry these days, a company must have what Peters and Waterman called a "bias for action," an ability to respond quickly to opportunities and dangers with innovative and forceful measures. Whether a Type Z organization can also be entrepreneurial is at least open to question. The difficulty of combining these two cultures in one large organization is well illustrated at Hewlett-Packard, which has stumbled badly in attempting to enter several new markets. To better coordinate its highly autonomous divisions, HP has been forced to centralize many functions and to try to persuade entrepreneurs to cooperate instead of compete. Arguably, HP's struggle to combine the best features of American and Japanese management styles with an entrepreneurial culture is the most important management experiment of the 1980s. It is also worth noting that Japan is undergoing a corporate culture shift of its own. Many companies, including Nippon Steel and Toshiba, stung by competition and rapidly changing markets, are moving away from management by consensus and centralizing their planning and decision making.[15]

WHAT WE ARE LEFT WITH, as we move into the second half of a turbulent decade, is the inescapable need to play to our strong suit. Only by supporting and strengthening the entrepreneurial process and spirit are we likely to keep our precarious position at the top of the economic heap. From the fallible but indispensable brokering of risk carried on by the groups and individuals who call themselves venture capitalists, we can continue to winnow the new ideas and products and processes that will give us a narrow edge. That does not mean there is no role for large companies. On the contrary it is the IBMs and Hewlett-Packards and Intels that will take on Japan Inc. and Europe Ltd., not the Sequents and Priams, at least not right away. But it is the venture capitalists and their brood of entrepreneurs who will keep the giants in fighting trim and ensure that their ranks are constantly refreshed.

Increasingly, the big companies will form alliances with the small ones to tap their unique skills at applying technology to shifting market demands. And they will look to the venture capital community for early warnings of opportunity and competition long before foreign sails appear on the horizon. Furthermore, there is an important role for the venture process in promoting minority business and in local and regional economic development, a role just beginning to be recognized but one that offers the only real hope that minority communities can become self-reliant and that regions such as the Midwest and the Pacific Northwest can break away from dependence on declining industries and begin to rebuild their base of jobs.

Government's task in all this is not nearly so onerous as it would be in trying to carry out a targeted industrial policy. It needs only to ensure that the infrastructure is in place to allow this incredible process to operate and that small investors and entrepreneurs are treated fairly. The requirements are simple and straightforward:

Allow capital markets to operate undistorted by rampant inflation, unchecked federal deficits, and confiscatory taxation;

Place a high priority on capital formation in efforts to reform or revise the tax code;

Promote broad support for and understanding of the role of risk taking and entrepreneurship in society;

Encourage a plentiful supply of well-trained scientists, engineers, managers, and technicians;

Support basic research that pushes the frontiers of knowledge in many fields and does not inhibit the transfer of results to industry;

Enforce the laws against restraint of trade to ensure that established companies do not unfairly use their wealth and power to bar entry to their markets;

Strengthen federal programs for assisting small business by removing them from the heat of politics and the vagaries of the annual appropriations battle.

There are more detailed policy prescriptions that could be written, and indeed many states and cities have set in motion elaborate schemes for promoting the venture capital process. An excellent guide to the national policies required can be found in the report of the President's Commission on Industrial Competitiveness, chaired by Hewlett-Packard's president, John Young.[16] But the beauty of entrepreneurship as a strategy for growth and innovation is that it requires a minimum of intervention and in fact flourishes best when left to its own devices. Its excesses and its failings are ultimately, and usually

quickly, self-correcting. Even the modest and fairly obvious suggestions presented here have been woefully neglected during four years of
an administration that supposedly espouses a free enterprise solution
to most problems. But that has not prevented the greatest outpouring
of risk investment and entrepreneurial activity the country has ever
seen. One wonders what might be accomplished if America's government policies and institutions truly supported the initiative, creativity, and commitment of her people.

NOTES

1. "Europe's New Managers," *Business Week*, May 24, 1982, p. 78.
2. Spiro A. Coutarelli, *Venture Capital in Europe*. Praeger Publishers, New
   York, 1977, p. 110.
3. Maile Hulihan, "French Venture-Capital Industry Lags Despite New Policies by the Government," *The Wall Street Journal*, November 30, 1983,
   p. 36.
4. "A Quest for Risk Capital Ends in Silicon Valley," *Business Week*, November 1, 1982, p. 48.
5. "The Big Money Paribas Is Betting on Overseas Ventures," *Business
   Week*, December 12, 1983, p. 45.
6. Daniel Cohen, "For the French, a New Cultural Hero," *Venture*, September 1984, p. 52.
7. "High Tech Tries an End Run Around Germany's Banks," *Business Week*,
   July 18, 1983, p. 74.
8. M. Therese Flaherty and Hiroyuki Itami, "Finance," in Okimoto et al.,
   eds., *Competitive Edge*. p. 153.
9. Yoriko Kishimoto, "Innovation in Japan," paper prepared for Japan Pacific Associates, Palo Alto, 1984.
10. Joel Kotkin, "Industrial Policy? Japan and Europe are Trying to Copy
    Us", *The Washington Post National Weekly Edition*, May 14, 1984, p. 21.
11. Edward Boyer, "Startup Ventures Blossom in Japan," *Fortune*, September
    1983, p. 113.
12. Paul R. Krugman, "Targeted Industrial Policies: Theory and Evidence"
    in *Industrial and Public Policy*, Symposium sponsored by the Federal Re-
    serve Bank of Kansas City, August 24–26, 1983.
13. William G. Ouchi, *Theory Z*. Addison-Wesley Publishing, Reading,
    Mass., 1981.
14. Thomas J. Peters and Robert H. Waterman Jr., *In Search of Excellence*.
    Harper & Row, New York, 1982.
15. "A Power Shift in Japanese Industry," *Business Week*, October 1, 1984,
    p. 71.
16. "Global Competition: The New Reality," report of the President's Com-
    mission on Industrial Competitiveness, Washington, D.C., 1985.

INDEX